CW00867189

RECOVERY ECOSYSTEM PRESENTS

Pain, Failure, and Misery are the Stepping Stones to Success

Eric McCoy, CATC II

Archway Publishing books may be ordered through booksellers or by contacting:

Archway Publishing
1663 Liberty Drive
Bloomington, IN 47403
www.archwaypublishing.com
1 (888) 242-5904

ISBN: 978-1-4808-8084-9 (sc)
ISBN: 978-1-4808-8085-6 (hc)
ISBN: 978-1-4808-8083-2 (e)

Library of Congress Control Number: 2019912655

Print information available on the last page.

Archway Publishing rev. date: 09/26/2019

CONTENTS

INTRODUCTION

For many years, I walked aimlessly with no goals, no dreams, no passion, and no excitement for anything, while trying to connect with a world that I didn't understand. It was impressed upon me that financial success was what was most important, which required good grades in school and a college degree to serve as the proof that I was educated to fulfill the responsibilities for the career that I desired. What I wanted and what others wanted were two different things because I wanted to be happy and live a life that felt good instead of the material world that I felt that I lived in. I felt different from most of the people I interacted with, and I couldn't understand why pleasure seemed to be forbidden, which was my greatest pursuit. Success to me wasn't money but instead to eliminate all the horrible anxiety and depression that seemed to consume my existence.

I have a story that I want to tell that may give hope to those who feel lost and shunned by a society that fails to teach you some of the most important lessons that you need to learn, which are self-control, self-respect, self-worth, and self-confidence. "Just say no" has been the mantra that was expected to slow down or stop drug abuse but hasn't fully worked because it fails to consider the mind's desire to understand and make choices to solve problems that drugs temporarily fix. All those lessons identified above that we should teach can be found in a drug-induced state temporarily, and by the time the drugs stop working, dependency has taken hold, and lives are lost.

My story in this book is designed to offer an example of someone who has walked through the depths of hell while on drugs but was able to emerge with my head held high. Many times, horrible things happen to us that can either destroy us or lift us. I decided many years ago to allow my weaknesses in life to become my greatest strengths and advocate. Drugs and alcohol no longer control me, and through everything that I went through, I can now share this story with you and hopefully help people save their own lives.

There are many ways to finding success in recovery and a black-and-white approach can be a disservice to people because everyone is different, and my way may not work for you. It's possible to find that happy, serene, and joyful life that's free from chemical abuse. I've remained vague in certain areas of this book to allow you to draw upon your own conclusions without any influence on my opinions, values, and standards that could potentially sway you.

This book was designed for families, those struggling with addiction, individuals currently in recovery, anyone interested in learning about the difficulties of drug dependence, and clinicians. The dialogue that's included in the stories is as accurate as I can recall, but my memory isn't completely intact, as many of the examples I use were heard or occurred while under the influence of chemicals. Names have been changed, and it's designed specifically for substance-abuse disorders instead of co-occurring psychiatric disorders, even though some are mentioned.

Much of this book is based on my opinion through years of research, studies, personal experience, and lessons that

I've learned from the clients that I've worked with, as I'll always remain a student. I believe that we're all teachers, and we're all students, which is an attitude that allows me to keep an open mind to new possibilities. I've defined abstinence as the way to success for myself, but that's my solution based on years of experimenting with different tactics. Everything failed, and trust me when I say that I attempted every option I could think of because I really enjoyed drugs until they nearly killed me.

Most chapters begin with a poem because, for me, poetry is an expression of beauty, creativity, and inspiration that I feel that connects me with hope. If you're newly clean or sober, you've caused brain damage, and I understand how horrible that sounds, so our brains need a good workout and creative thought can do that. I encourage everybody to grab a piece of paper and pen so you can take notes, identify how this applies to you, and then make it personal. I've included questions at the end of some chapters so you can make your recovery your own.

There are sensitive topics in this book that I've included, such as politics, religion, youth violence, suicide, criminal activity, and other ideas that are very controversial. Substance abuse is killing people in record numbers, and it's time we talk about everything that's happening in this country. There's no better time than now to bring these topics to the forefront. It's time that you allow your pain to be your teacher and review your understanding of failure and misery so you can start looking at the world differently.

PART 1

Pain, Failure, and Misery

CHAPTER I

Heartless Dying Vulture

Evil was the face, and I was hateful at best.
Love had deflated, the anger enmeshed.
The high superseded and no longer cared.
I failed to see the signs, and my head was unaware.

Laughter had eluded, as I sought for a hole.
Pleasure became a ghost, and surviving was the goal.
Picasso was a painter, and Michelangelo was a sculptor.
Sadly, I was nothing, but a heartless, dying vulture.

Living day to day, with a scale and empty baggies,
Living off of dope, and selling lies of nothing happy,
Crime became my constant, as I'd steal for nothing more,
Than to live in a world of shadows, as life was easy to ignore.

Hope became a dream, and life was fading fast.
Nothing was often pure, unlike whiskey to William Taft.
I didn't want to live this life I chose for me.
How can I get out and create a life that is so free?

How ironic is this story that shows a man at sail?
It was freedom that I found as I was locked up in a jail.
Think with me this moment and open up your mind.
Nothing can be taken away that is solely found inside.

Your story is a map that shows your life in time.
Let it be your guide, and lessons you will find.
Embrace your pain and guilt, for gladness will remain.
Your pain can be a teacher as your suffering was not in vain.

Let me give you some advice that may not be that clear.
Love will be your answer, and let joy be your souvenir.
Commit to a new beginning, and let power be your stance.
A purpose has a place, and without, you live with chance.

I'm proud that I overcame, and I sit on solid ground.
The glimpse of faith I saw, pulled me to the mound.
Let me share my story since we are much the same.
The first step toward your future is to stop and take the blame.

I killed that motherfucker was the first thought that came to me when I awoke from my slumber that early morning in 2002. The lifeless body that I saw in front of me was a person whom I'd killed many years ago. The beginning was the same, as it is for most, but my story evolved each day where the difference between life, which was so fragile, and death stood side by side. Dying physically that day would not have been a tragic tale since emotionally and spiritually I was already dead, and I didn't feel that anybody would miss me, nor did I care anymore about anything.

With all the hatred and abhorrence that I had for the world, I decided to fulfill the most selfless act that I could give to the world and commit suicide. The cure for my condition was a sacrifice of losing my life to gain that peace, serenity, and comfort that I had so longed for. What kind of bullshit is that? "To lose is to gain." My father always told me that suicide was a sin and would result in an eternity in hell. I believed that when I was ten, but I no longer held onto those ridiculous views of a supreme, all-powerful, all-knowing God of love. I wasn't stupid, and I had a hard time praying or talking to something or someone who I couldn't see or shake hands with. I had an ability to think, and I wasn't going to base my decisions and choices off a faith in an idea that I didn't believe existed. As Nietzsche said, "God is dead." Where was this loving God that everybody spoke so highly about?

It was all lies! I didn't know what was real anymore, as everything that I felt, or thought, was manipulated by something that had full control over me, and it wasn't me. The sad truth about drug use is that, no matter the reason we start, we reach a point where we maintain that course to either numb or avoid our physical or emotional pain. I didn't think that I could ever get clean, and if I was able to, I'd never be happy or able to function in any normal capacity.

I was broken, alone, and living day to day by sticking a needle in my arm just to stay awake. Friends don't exist because we don't care about each other, and we've pushed family away since they usually don't support our lifestyles. I had nobody that I trusted, and I was stuck making decisions with a mind that seemed broken and unable to make rationale choices. I didn't know what I was doing anymore, and everybody was either dead, in rehab, or in prison.

I pulled out my dwindling bag of meth and loaded my syringe so I could catch a little buzz and clear my head for the morning. After drawing the perfect combination of water and dope through some cotton, I found a vein, and without hesitation, I forced down the plunger and almost immediately felt the relief. My mind began to focus, some energy crept my way, and a small feeling of pleasure gave me that little push to get started in the day.

I sat there in that motel room, looking at the mess that I knew I had to clean up, and I made a decision to move to another location because I didn't want to stay at any particular spot too long since I knew they were looking for me. When they found me, and it was only a matter of time, my life would end as I knew it, and time would become my sentence as a prison would become my new home. I needed to move, and I needed to move quickly, but the mess I had in that motel room wasn't going to be something I'd be able to clean quickly.

I had syringes and baggies of meth scattered around the room along with all the stolen items I'd accumulated over the last six months. My clothes were in piles and boxes of paperwork, stolen mail, and electronic equipment lay throughout the dirty motel room that I'd been staying in for the last week. Things would accumulate quickly when I was running around at all hours of the night and stealing property from residential houses, businesses, and cars. I hated to move, which is why I sat at that little table, staring at the room and trying to get the motivation to start. I loaded another rig, and this time I used more meth than the first that morning and blasted it into my vein. Doing more than I normally did at one time, a powerful shiver ran up my body, and I went cross-eyed for a moment. I couldn't think straight at first, but once my head began to clear, I heard a key being inserted into the door to the room and the knob began to shake. It happened too quick for me to move, and once the door flew open, I had a gun pointed at my head, which wasn't a new experience, but this time, it was the beginning of the end, or maybe it was the end for a new beginning. It was January 3, 2002.

Let's Go Back Three Months

It was about 6:30 p.m. on a Sunday afternoon when I'd run out of dope. I was frantically trying to connect with my dealer. After speaking with him on the phone and learning of his location, I drove to the apartment complex he'd instructed me to. I called him as I was pulling into the parking lot, and he told me he'd walk out to my car in a few minutes to exchange the money for that thing that my body was craving and keeping me alive, or at least that's what I felt that meth did for me. As I was sitting and waiting, I noticed some strange activity, and I saw a police car drive toward the back of the building.

"There's a cop on the property and something strange is going on here," I told him as I phoned him back once I saw my dealer walking toward my car.

"Where are you headed? I'll call you and head your direction once these cops leave," he told me.

"I'll be in south county somewhere," I responded. I was worried. I was worried that he was about to get busted because he was my only connection with good dope. I've been up for three days, and I knew that I wasn't going to last much longer without my body shutting down. I was tired, and even though falling asleep sounded good, I couldn't because I had things to do the next morning, and I was afraid that I wouldn't wake up.

My life was a mess, and nothing about it was fun anymore. Sure, the adrenaline of living on the edge, participating in activities that will be explained in a moment, and smoking speed with the anticipation of the high you're about to get can be exciting, but then you're let down when the pleasure doesn't meet your expectations. Pleasure was my demon growing up; it's what started me down this path that I couldn't see me getting out of. I hated myself and wished that I'd never started doing this shit. It's kind of funny how we refer to it as "shit," because that's what it is. No matter what you call it—*shit, meth,* or *dope*—it's all the same, but it's closer to the meeting of Beelzebub or maybe the devil. *Evil, seductive, temptation,* and *hateful* are terms we could use interchangeably with meth. I was a puppet controlled by a substance that was holding the strings.

I drove south on the freeway and went to the town I was staying in to wait for my drug dealer. I didn't think I was going to be able to stay awake much longer, but I couldn't fall asleep. I went into Denny's to get a cup of coffee, hoping this would help, and then I decided to drive around with the window down, as the night air was getting cooler, and it could help keep me awake. It was about 11:15 p.m. when I received a call from him. He told me that he should be in the area around midnight. I only had about forty-five minutes to waste, and it seemed that the night breeze was working to keep me alert. I turned in to a residential neighborhood, just wasting time while listening to music and smoking cigarettes.

It was unbelievably unnerving as I awoke to the sound of my car slamming into the side of a parked van and the cigarette I was smoking fell into my lap and began burning my crotch. I was confused at first, but I quickly realized what had happened. Fight-or-flight kicked in motion as I instantly resorted to flight. I turned the wheel to drive off, and a loud noise followed that sounded as though I'd blown a tire, leaving me the only option of a getaway on my rim.

Running from an accident doesn't feel right when you're creating enough commotion to wake neighbors who are blocks away. I was able to drive the car to another area so I could assess the damage and hopefully fix the problem.

The tire was the only damaged part that I cared about, and luckily, I had a spare in the trunk that would get me back on the road. I pulled everything out of my trunk to gain access to the spare tire. I knew I didn't have much time before my medicine man was supposed to be in the area, so I raised the car, changed the tire, and put everything back in the trunk quickly. I checked my phone and saw that the battery had died. It was about 12:30 a.m., so I drove to 7-Eleven and purchased a precharged Nokia battery, so I could instantly turn on my phone, hoping that he had been running late. I had a message.

"Hey, it's me. I'm in town, but your phone is off. I'm going to be back up north at a hotel. Call me and we can meet up there."

Shit, I thought. I called him, and he told me that he was at a Best Western in north county, so I immediately started driving. It wasn't but ten minutes into the drive that I awoke to the sound of a car, my car, grinding against a guardrail. "Fuck."

I pulled off the freeway to look at the car, and thankfully, I hadn't blown a tire, because I had no more to spare. I arrived at the hotel he'd instructed me to, but he'd never given me the room number, so I called him. He didn't answer. I called again and no answer. After about five attempts, I realized that he had probably fallen asleep, which was what I should have been doing. After a final attempt, I knew that this was going to be a problem and that I was in trouble. I didn't know what to do, so I decided to drive back south and see if I could locate some dope through a different source. I knew it wouldn't be the same quality my body had been used to. This was my life. It was a life of chasing something that had no real value except to keep me awake. Once I fell asleep, I could easily lose three to four days and miss out on something important.

I got back on the freeway and returned to the same area I'd left an hour ago. I shouldn't have done it, but I decided to blink and awoke to my car leaping in the air after it bottomed out on a curb. The prognosis wasn't good. I noticed oil pouring out from underneath the car, and it wouldn't start. I was stranded, and I had three hours until my first court appearance for charges that are all too common for a meth user. I was in bad shape and unsure on how I was going to get to court, let alone stay awake in court. I called a friend of mine who was a tow truck driver I sold meth to. He towed my car back to the townhome I was living at and then to court after I put on my new suit. I didn't feel human at this point. The closest term I could describe me as was a *zombie*. Yes. Zombies do exist.

It Might Have Been Four Months Previously

If "three months earlier" into "maybe four months earlier" is confusing, then you're in the story and wondering the same question as I, and all meth users, as time is inconsequential. One day can equal four days of earth time if you define a day from when you wake up until you go to sleep. We're now at what seemed like a month prior to the time at the motel but was closer to seven months when I had a gun pointed at my head, and it was at the time I'd returned to California from Maryland.

Drugs created my existence, as every decision I made was based on chemicals that I abused, and those decisions were usually to get off a substance. I decided to move to Maryland in 1995 to get off meth, and I returned to California in 1998 to get off the substances I was abusing there. I returned to Maryland in 2000 after discharging from a treatment program as a protective measure so I wouldn't return to that demon. And then I decided in 2001 after smoking crack that I wanted to return to California because that was becoming a problem. Insanity has always been my way of thinking because I didn't believe that I was the problem. Instead, I thought the problem was the location.

The potion or elixir that I acquired after returning from Maryland would separate good from evil into two separate entities. This potion, which I took at will, brought forth my evil counterpart who took full control over the good. Hold on a second, because I may have switched to another story of Dr. Jekyll and Mr. Hyde. It doesn't matter because it's the same story. My elixir was methamphetamine, and I became something of your worst nightmare, but while sober I was your greatest ally and best friend.

I always wondered why I was incapable of using moderately and being able to put it down at will. Many would say that it's impossible for someone to use meth sociably, but I've seen it. If anybody is thinking that he or she may be the exception, beware, because I've only seen it once. When I'm clean and sober, I'm honest, respectful, caring, and loving, and I'd give anybody the shirt off my back if they truly needed it. I'd never steal or purposely harm anybody, even my worst enemy, in a clear state of mind. One hit off a meth pipe will bring out Mr. Hyde, and there's no turning back. I leap into a world that's difficult to describe in words because it doesn't even seem real. Supply is the only thing that matters because I must survive.

Deep in the midpart of our brains, which is classified as the old part of our brain, sits the nucleus accumbens, where methamphetamine stimulates the release of and blocks the reuptake of dopamine, which is a neurotransmitter that gives us pleasure. The midbrain is the part that's designed to help us survive by reinforcing activities that must be done to keep you alive. Eating, drinking water, and using the restroom are examples of things that release dopamine, and when something feels good, we naturally want to continue doing it. Methamphetamine, along with all drugs of abuse and addictive behaviors, will encourage continued use because it feels good. Since we're playing with a part of the brain that's designed to keep us alive, the brain will tell me, "I'll die if I run out of this shit." Maintaining my supply is top priority, and I'll do anything except for murder or rape. But everything else is game. It's on.

Once I returned to California in 2001, I connected with some old friends and got high. It felt good at first since I hadn't done it for over a year, and my tolerance was back to normal. That switch turned on, and "supply" was now my focus, with survival being all that mattered. All those positive qualities I carried while clean were gone, and Mr. Hyde could now take the stage. What does an unemployed person with no money do to get the funds to purchase drugs? Get a job? Hell, no. It wouldn't bring the money quick enough to supply my habit. That door that I step through with meth is a place of adrenaline, fear, anxiety, and uncertainty all rolled up into one. Methamphetamine had been a problem for me in the past, but once I used, it became the solution to all my problems for the present.

It was never difficult, and it always seemed easy, for me to meet the right people to purchase the drug from, at the right price for me to sell it and to make profit. The problem, as using drug dealers understand, is that when we're digging into the supply, we lose profit and usually break even. This was helpful for being able to live in motel rooms, purchase food (although I rarely ate), pump gas for my car, and buy any other amenities I required. More had to be done. Methamphetamine made me creative and helped me to seek out ways to make quick money since I was living day to day.

The Scam in 1999 That Opened My Eyes to Money in 2001

In 1999, I was living in an apartment, and I formulated a scam that opened my eyes to a venture that I carried onward in 2001. I enjoyed acting, even though I'd never done it professionally, and I created characters with full names, professions, and companies that didn't really exist. Creativity, ingenuity, and imagination has always been a skill set that I carried. Using Photoshop, I created driver's licenses for my identities to make purchases in stores, using corporate checks that I made. I started small by calling companies to order merchandise that I, or an associate, would pick up at the store once they were ready. I printed a check with the exact amount of the purchase, and I presented my driver's license to confirm my identification.

Many might think that creating a name, address, and company was enough information, but not I. I created background stories with a vacation that I'd just taken with my wife or a medical condition that I had just been released from the hospital for to make things more entertaining. How did I make money on this? I bought items that I knew I could sell to my acquaintances for half the purchase price, with a checking account that sometimes didn't even exist.

After I returned from Maryland in 2001, I decided to

take up that job again, but this time, I went big. I called ten companies and purchasing, on average, ten items per store with different characters, companies, and accounts, which required some serious organization. After acquiring the merchandise and selling the items to various people, I made $7,500 minus gas and supplies for printing checks and making IDs, for one day of work. It was profitable, and I decided that I didn't want to stop there.

Arrest Number One

Methamphetamine has a powerful influence on repetition as it induces pleasure and amplifies adrenaline, but it does this in a way that almost feels unreal. It can appear that you're seeing the world through a tunnel, a dream, or a fantasy that causes no real harm to others. The operation I created in hotel rooms was like something that may have only appeared in movies and imagined through the vision of a storyteller. Computers, although less technologically advanced than today, were the tools that allowed my creativity to flow by mastering a template for driver's licenses that had much fewer security features than we see on today's identification cards. With the ability to focus meticulously on small details, I could manifest an almost identical replica with the help of Photoshop 6. 0. Alongside the computer, I had a color printer for the photo IDs and a laser printer with magnetic ink that produced checks for purchases that I could sell at 50 percent off. Aside from the laminators I used for the cards, my room contained boxes of paperwork that allowed for consistency in information. We're talking about social security numbers that match names, birthdates, addresses, phone numbers, driver's license numbers, and account numbers.

Collecting information was a high that seemed, at times, to be more powerful than the drug, although the combination was unlike anything you could imagine. Where do we gather personal information identified above? You go to where people keep it. At their houses. Night after night, I broke into cars, garages, and houses, looking for this sort of information or anything that seemed interesting or of value. This was a world that wasn't real, and I wasn't harming anybody. Or was I? Days turned into weeks and weeks into months, as it all blended together into long days. I was comfortable, confident, and very sure that I'd not get caught.

I came across a goldmine one night as I was breaking into businesses for a change of scenery. I was driving through town, and I came across a store that had a garden area, like you find at a Home Depot. I always carried bolt cutters, and I entered through the back fence to see what was there. I noticed a small shack that sat in the center, with its door ajar. After looking inside, I noticed boxes of paperwork that contained all the information that I was looking for in one place. Identification numbers, social security numbers, birthdates, addresses, credit card numbers, and checking account numbers. I couldn't believe my eyes. I took a box of files, and with this information, I was able to make checks and identification cards that matched. A goldmine isn't something you give up easy, so I frequented this location monthly so I could remain current, as continued use of a person's information will eventually be flagged, making it no longer useful.

This business had a policy that allowed you to return merchandise for cash or store credit without a receipt. I gathered items and took them to another location and returned things with the story that I had been given this item as a gift, and I really hadn't needed it, so I'd wondered if I could return it. If the store only gave me store credit instead of cash, I was then able to acquire items from within the store since I never broke into the building during the night.

On June 30, 2001, I returned to this store at around 3:00 a.m. and started my usual process of cutting the lock, getting high, and looking at merchandise. I walked up to the shack, opened the door, and noticed a police car slowly pass on the other side of the fence. I sat very quietly and waited for this officer to leave. About thirty seconds had passed, and I heard a scream from the roof of the retail store.

"This is the sheriffs, freeze."

I was startled, and freezing didn't seem to sit right with me. I looked on the roof, and I could see a flashlight and the faint shadow of an individual, but I couldn't make out anything else. A rush of adrenaline overcame me, and I ran as fast as my legs could move toward the gate that I'd entered from. Many would assume that if a police officer was on the roof, other officers were nearby, making it impossible to get away. A rush of adrenaline mixed with methamphetamine shuts down your rational thinking, and survival is all that matters. Fight-or-flight doesn't think clearly, nor does it care about how you get away—just *that* you get away. Did I get away? No. The assumption I stated earlier was correct, and once I exited the gate that I'd entered, I had multiple officers pointing guns at me.

Realizing that I was caught and there was no possibility of getting away, I followed directions and laid on the ground. One officer approached me and jammed his knee hard enough into my back to knock all the air out of my lungs. The officer's knee slid up toward the back of my neck. I couldn't breathe, and I was attempting to speak, but nothing was coming out. Feeling faint and weak, I forced out,

"Can't breathe," as I attempted to move to take a breath, making it appear that I was resisting the officer.

"Stop resisting, or things will get worse," an officer yelled.

"I can't breathe," I forced out again.

This back-and-forth scenario went on for what seemed like a long time as they held me down and I fought back to get some air. It seems unfair to have officers cutting off your ability to breath, forcing you to fight for oxygen and then accusing you of resisting arrest.

Handcuffed, they lifted me up to my feet and patted me down, finding methamphetamine in my pocket and my bolt cutters next to the fence. I was driven to the sheriff's sub-station and questioned about the evening and the various other days the property had been broken into. I'd learned many years ago not to say anything to the police and to let them do all the work to prove my guilt. I denied any knowledge of prior incidences at that location and spoke very little about my intentions, actions, or desires that evening. I was transported to the county jail for booking. I was booked on second-degree burglary, possession of a controlled substance and possession of burglary tools with a bail set for $10,000.

The processing, known as "the loop," can take anywhere from twelve to twenty-four hours and is a painful experience when you're detoxing from substances. Methamphetamine doesn't have physical pain like heroin withdrawal, but instead the fatigue and depression creates a strong desire to fade into a dream and never wake up. The holding cells are uncomfortable, dirty, and noisy at times, making it difficult to sleep but sometimes you can get lucky by snagging a roll of toilet paper for a pillow and finding a "less-dirty" spot on the floor. After moving from cell to cell over a ten-hour period, I was finally brought into the room where we would change out of our clothes, take a shower, and don the infamous orange jumpsuits. I was relieved to know that "the loop" was coming to an end as we would soon be walked in a single-file lineup into the jail to be housed and given a bed for me to sleep in for hours, days, and months. It didn't matter to me either way. Sleep was the only thing that was important.

Once I was suited up, I was put back in another holding cell for about an hour and then lined up for the long walk down the halls of the facility. I was excited, relieved, and ready to find that one-inch mattress, lay on it, close my eyes, and drift away.

"Stay in a straight line, no talking, and follow me," the deputy told us.

We reached a second hallway. They stopped the line and announced something that seemed good but disappointing.

An officer told me, "Step out of line and follow that deputy. Your bail has been posted, and you're being released."

"Ugh. I want to sleep. Can I leave tomorrow?" I asked the deputy.

"Someone has posted your bail," the deputy stated. "You can ask the bail company to refund the money."

If I was having to postpone my sleep for speaking with the bail company after being released, I was going to lay in a real bed somewhere. The process of being released took additional hours as I switched back into my street clothes, signed release documents, and gathered my property. It almost felt like torture as I'd be woken up every time I fell asleep to do more fingerprinting, switching cells, or asked questions.

"You're free to go," the deputy informed me as the door clanged open.

Finally, I was able to leave and contact my girlfriend,

Mary, to pick me up. It turned out that Mary had posted my bail, which I would have realized if I'd had the ability to think, since she would have been the only person to know that I hadn't made it back to the room by sunup. I walked outside into the sunlight, and Mary arrived to pick me up. What a life. I didn't go to sleep. Once we drove off, Mary filled a pipe, and I felt better.

This Has Nothing to Do with Love

Not long after I'd returned from Maryland, I met Mary in a hotel room where I was getting high with a friend. Two females knocked on the door, and in walked Mary, whom I instantly felt an attraction to. I was intrigued, curious, and horny. We smoked speed for a while, and she shared with me the story of what had brought her to California close to a year prior to us meeting. Her move had been the result of a traumatic experience with her husband, who had struggled with major depression for most of his life and had committed suicide. Mary was beautiful, but it appeared the dope was taking a toll on her body as she was thin, had mild sores on her skin, and was seven months pregnant. Seven months pregnant! The sad part was that none of us had any problem with her drug use while pregnant nor did we attempt to help her get prenatal care.

She had been pregnant for months before she learned of her developing baby, and she claimed that she had no emotional connection with the child who was inside her. The father of her child had been arrested not long after she'd become pregnant, and he was eventually sent off to prison. Many who have never struggled with drug abuse will argue how horrible of a person she is, since there's no more powerful love than the love of a child. Addiction has nothing to do with love. How does anybody offer something that they don't have? Emotions are something that addicts have very little of or don't have at all. I was emotionally numb to everything and everyone.

Unsure on why I decided to get involved with a girl who was pregnant, other than thinking with the wrong head, I decided to help her through this as best as I could. We had discussed the concern with a hospital delivery because of the possibility of the hospital drug testing her and how this could affect things if social services got involved. The time was nearing, and I reached out to a woman I knew who worked at a local hospital for help. She was a nurse whom I sold meth to. I needed her assistance in walking us through this to avoid detection. When Mary went into labor, I gathered her belongings, loaded her into my car, and drove her to the hospital the nurse had recommended.

"Ask for Helen once you arrive at the hospital, and she will take care of everything. Don't worry. She gets high, so it won't be a problem," she told me.

I felt good about the plan until I learned something that would have been very helpful to know earlier, and that was that Tiffany was angry with me and appeared to want revenge. Tiffany, for me, was nothing more than a girl I'd had sex with prior to Mary. Her desire, even though I was unaware of her wants, was an emotional relationship that was far from anything I'd have been able to give her, even if I'd had knowledge of this. My only real emotional connection was to methamphetamine, as I wasn't able to offer much to Mary as well.

Helen, who I asked for, didn't exist. She was made up, or at least nobody knew of a Helen at the hospital, but we were stuck with this location and our hopes that things would go smoothly. Honestly, I had no interest in taking care of a baby, and how would it even be possible to raise a child, jumping from hotel to hotel every few days? I was confused about a solution to this dilemma, and I decided to ride it out, or I was at least curious about the outcome. That girl lied to me. Oh, did I mention that meth users lie?

Mary gave birth to a healthy boy who was slightly underweight and tested positive for methamphetamine. Social services was introduced into our world, and Mary had to make a decision about what she wanted to do. After her son was released from the hospital, he went into the care of the county and resided in a foster home with a reunification program that would allow Mary the chance of getting custody back. Something interesting happened at the time of the delivery that altered her perception of this child. The birth process, and maybe it was because she hadn't used for about fifteen hours, created feelings for this child, and she wanted to keep him. It was going to be a hard road filled with many potholes, and she was with a man who was going to take her down a path that was the wrong way, at the wrong time, and force her to make a choice that was almost impossible to make for someone physically and emotionally addicted to a drug like methamphetamine. Does something like childbirth for a woman cause a love that can be more powerful than meth? Which love will prevail?

Even though Mary wanted to get her child back, I wasn't willing to stop using drugs or to give up selling and the lifestyle that I was living. I hated everything about my life, but it was all I felt I could do to survive. Her reunification program required that she drug test twice, and sometimes three times, a week, which wasn't going to be easy if she was unable to stop and offer samples of her own urine. We had a plan that required a bit of practice to master as she gained skills for a new art form. How do you test clean while using a drug that they're testing for? The answer is simple. Give somebody else's pee, which is an easier task for females than for males. Take a small bottle and fill it with another person's urine, preferably one not using drugs, cover the top with aluminum foil, hold it in place with a rubber band, and insert it into the vagina. When she sits down on the toilet to urinate in the cup, she pops a hole in the aluminum foil and voila, you have a clean drug test. Keeping the bottle inside of her for the trip to the lab will keep it warm to pass the temperature gauge. She passed every test, giving the impression that she wasn't using, allowing her to visit her son in the foster home. She was passing every requirement needed, and she was moving forward to getting custody of her son. Or was she? Which love would prevail?

A mother's love for her child may be the most powerful love that exists and may be so strong that it can destroy an evil like drug addiction.

CHAPTER 2

Cat and Mouse

A Free Man

When bail is posted, a court date is set that's approximately thirty days after your release from custody. I appeared in court on August 1, 2001, in a suit and ready to face my accusers. Nothing had been filed by the district attorney's office, and I received a document stating that I was present, so by law, they had to drop my charges and exonerate my bail. I was a free man with no charges pending, although I was informed that my charges could be refiled as they had three years to refile on felonies and one year to refile on misdemeanors. Once I walked out of court, I pretended as if none of it had happened, and any worries of future problems related to that arrest were gone.

Mary and I traveled out of the county for the night and returned the next day. We stopped at Denny's and purchased breakfast that we decided to take with us on the travel back to our hotel room. Eating was very infrequent, and I usually ate once every few days as my stomach couldn't handle food well, and everything tasted like chalk. I always purchased more food then I ate, because I knew I needed to eat, and I attempted it, but I gave up as I felt nauseas. I received a phone call from a girl who purchased from me. She was requesting to buy a few grams, and she wanted to know if I could meet her. I was headed that direction, so we agreed to meet in the parking lot of a restaurant right off the freeway.

Arrest Number Two

When we arrived at the meeting location, I pulled up next to her vehicle, walked up to her car, gave her the bag, collected the money, and immediately walked back to my car to leave. It was a quick transaction, and we were back on the road. I left the parking lot and stopped at a red light before making a left turn onto the freeway. A police officer pulled up behind me, making me nervous as I had about an ounce of meth sitting next to my gear shift. I was sloppy, and I wasn't careful much of the time. Paranoia didn't exist within me like some people that I knew. The signal turned green, and the police officer's lights immediately turned on before I could get onto the freeway. I decided to keep driving to give me a moment to hide the drugs, so I carefully popped the cover that surrounded my gear shifter, tucked the drugs inside, and snapped the lid back on. It was a decent hiding spot, but it had never been tested by the police department.

"Pull off at the next exit," I heard the officer inform me over his speaker.

I wasn't sure why I was getting pulled over, but I felt a little more comfortable after hiding the drugs. My car was a mess, with clothes in my backseat and paraphernalia scattered throughout the piles, including scales, baggies, pipes, and a good chance some pockets contained small vials of dope. I pulled over once I exited the freeway and waited for the police officer to come to the window.

"Good morning," the officer stated. "I pulled you over because you swerved slightly and crossed over the line at the stoplight. How much have you had to drink?"

"I don't drink, sir. The last time I had any alcohol was probably about nine months ago," I told him. This was a true statement because I never consumed anything that would bring me down, especially alcohol.

"Well, I'm going to need you to step out of the car, and we're going to do a sobriety test."

I looked over at Mary, and I could tell that she was nervous and worried about getting caught with what was in our car. I stepped out of the vehicle and followed the officer to the back of the car where he had requested.

"Can I search you?" he asked.

I wasn't sure if I had anything on me, so I told him no. "I'd prefer we just do the sobriety test." I wasn't worried about this test because I had good balance, and I knew I'd pass the test. He informed me that he did need to pat me down to make sure I had no weapons on me, which I obliged. I pulled my wallet, lighter, and room key out of my pocket and raised my arms as he felt my waist, chest, and legs for anything that I was hiding. He was standing behind me as he reached into my jacket pocket and pulled out my cigarette pack, which confused me about the difference between patting someone down and searching them. A cigarette pack doesn't seem to be in the shape of a weapon, nor did I understand how the following statement came about.

"Now I have a reason to search your vehicle," he arrogantly stated.

"What the fuck are you talking about!" I abruptly yelled in anger.

"You have marijuana in your cigarette pack," he reported.

"No, I don't. I don't smoke weed."

He set a large bud on my trunk with the cigarette pack and told Mary to exit the vehicle. He said for us to have a seat on the curb. I was dumbfounded, confused by what had just transpired, and disappointed that I was going back to jail, and this time with Mary. The officer radioed for a canine that was probably going to be my downfall with this arrest, and it arrived within minutes of the request. Let me repeat that: minutes after the request. Does this town have canine units posted on every corner? Does anybody feel that something out of the ordinary has just happened? I was suspicious, feeling set up and angry as the officer informed me, "If you have drugs in your underwear, the dog may rip off your balls."

"Fuck you. This is bullshit, and you know it!" I yelled at the cop.

The canine was pulled from the police car and stood about five feet from me as the officer began pulling things out of my back seat. He set the scales, baggies, and vials onto the trunk, stolen checks, and other paperwork that was very incriminating. I had hope that the large bag of meth I'd stashed in the gear shift wasn't going to be found, but I worried about the dog sniffing it out. After everything had been found in the car except the drugs, the dog jumped in the front seat and turned around to jump back out. He was pushed in the car and immediately forced himself away from the car. I wasn't sure the reason for this, but I snickered as the canine wasn't very productive. I thought that maybe our food, which was still in the car, made it difficult to smell the drugs.

The dog was put back into the police car while the soon-to-be-arresting officer continued to search the vehicle, pulling side panels off and attempting to open my trunk. I'd lost the key to the trunk a long time ago, and I informed the officer of this. The trunk was full of my equipment as this was something I was hoping they were not able to open. He identified the button in the car that opened the trunk, but it failed to work, and I realized that when I'd opened that panel, it must have disconnected because the button sits on it. Unfortunately, as the officer looked closely at the gear shifter, he noticed that the cigarette lighter, also on that panel, fell in, cluing him in to the space underneath. He found the bag that was inside, which I knew just tacked on more jail or prison time in the future. They never were able to open the trunk after all the attempts, including the use of a "lock buster," which destroyed the keyhole. Arrested again, this was literally one day after I'd appeared in court and my charges had been dropped from that first case.

We were transported to the police station and separately questioned about the items found in the car. I took full responsibility for everything, except a small bag of meth and a scale in her purse they'd found, which I wasn't able to take responsibility for. We were taken to the county jail, and this time, I had nobody who was going to post my bail. We were each charged with possession for sales, transportation, and a slew of other charges with bails set for $25,000 each. "The loop" was horrible, but after fifteen hours, I reached a mod and slept for a few days, with intermittent wakefulness to eat. The arrest was on a Thursday, and by Sunday, I was awake enough to get my brain working and identify some tactics to get out of jail. The cravings were painful, and all

I wanted to do was to get high. I kept thinking about Mary and how this arrest was going to affect her custody battle.

I Am Invincible

I phoned a friend of mine, collect, from the day room and asked him to pull some money together to post Mary's bail. I was unaware if he accomplished the task, but I felt that he was going to pull it off. On Tuesday morning, I was transported to the courthouse for my arraignment, which was a very unpleasant experience. Normally, court consists of spending most of the day in a holding cell to see the judge for about ten minutes, but this time was different. Instead of waiting all day in a holding cell to see the judge for ten minutes, I waited in the holding cell all day long, never saw the judge, and was taken back to the jail that evening. I wasn't sure what had happened, but I got a surprise that night that would change things again.

"Pack your belongings. You're being released," I heard over the loudspeaker at about 11:00 p.m. that Tuesday night.

Wow, I thought. Maybe Mary posted my bail? It didn't happen that way, and since I wasn't arraigned within seventy-two hours, they had to release me from custody, and once again, I had no charges pending because the district attorney hadn't filed any. This didn't make any sense to me since they'd had plenty of evidence to convict me on some very serious charges. Either way, I was very excited to get out of jail, reconnect with Mary if she had been released, and get high again so I could feel normal. Once I was released, I called her, and she did answer the phone, confirming that my friend had posted her bail and she'd been picked up a couple hours later. Since she had posted bail, a court date had been set for around September 3, and the same thing happened to her, with charges being dropped and her bail being exonerated. I felt invincible having been arrested twice in thirty days and both cases being dropped, able to walk free with nothing pending.

The Third Time Is a Charm

On September 4, 2001, Mary and I checked into a hotel and paid for a week stay. I set up my operation. I needed to make money quickly for all the costs that had been accumulating, as getting arrested can become expensive especially when posting bails. I had to keep up my habit, and I was still in the process of paying back the money my friend paid to get Mary's bail posted. On September 10, 2001, Mary decided to visit her son at the foster home. I informed her that I'd meet her there because I had a few things I needed to do. Social services hadn't learned of her arrests, so visiting was still allowed, at least for the time being. At around 1:00 p.m. that day after purchasing some needed supplies, I drove to the foster home to visit the child. We spent a few hours at the house and around 4:30 p.m. decided to go back to the room. We each jumped in separate cars, drove to the freeway, and arrived at the hotel around 5:00 p.m.

After I parked, I observed a lady through my rearview mirror mouth the words, "Holy shit." I'm not a lip-reader, but I saw this very clearly, and before I knew it, I had a gun pointed at my head by a man who I'd never seen before, and he quickly opened my car door.

"Put your hands up and step out of the car. We're with the sheriff's department, and we have a search warrant to search your vehicle."

I stepped out of the car, noticed there was about six or

seven of them and was quickly handcuffed. Mary had a similar experience at her car, as I observed her being removed from the vehicle and handcuffed. This wasn't the average group you would think of with a sheriff's department as they were all in plain clothes and blocked our vehicles with nothing that would resemble a government vehicle. I requested to see the search warrant. He denied me being able to see one, showed me his badge, and reiterated that he was with the sheriff's department. I should have paid closer attention to something I noticed earlier, but I was losing my attention to detail or caring about things. While using, I dismiss events that don't matter at that moment in time. My observational abilities were beginning to diminish as I thought back to something that had happened but I'd seen it as unimportant. When I had been driving to the house where Mary was visiting her son earlier, I'd parked the car, and when I stepped out of my vehicle, I noticed a black car that had quickly stopped not too far from where I'd parked. The black car had backed up and turned its headlights off, and the driver had stayed in his vehicle. Besides the fact that I was losing attention to detail and not caring, I wasn't thinking clearly anymore.

Prior Experience

I knew of this task force and had experience with them back in 1999 at my apartment. Unfortunately, with all my encounters with law enforcement, I knew many things that many of us shouldn't have to learn from personal experience. I was working graveyard at a store, which is a great job for a meth user, staying up all night and working by yourself. I came home one morning and spent a little time with my roommates, smoking meth, before they left to do some errands. About ten minutes after they left, someone banged very loudly on my door, and a voice echoed through the walls.

"Sheriffs, you need to open the door now!"

It startled me, and I scrambled to figure out where my dope was. I realized I had very little, which I was able to tuck away in my wallet.

"Open the door now, or we're going to break the door down."

"I'm coming," I yelled back.

I opened the door and was greeted by four undercover sheriffs and a city police officer, who handcuffed me and sat me down at our kitchen table. The police officer placed the search warrant in front of me allowing me to read the contents.

"Where are the guns? Where is the dope?" one of the sheriffs asked me.

"Guns? I don't have any guns, and I don't have any dope," I told him.

"Don't bullshit me. I'll start cutting holes in your walls if you don't tell me where your dope is," he told me. "We know you sell it."

"What the fuck are you talking about? I don't have any shit. As you can see with the glass pipe in your hand, I get high, but I don't have guns, and I don't sell dope," I responded.

I started reading the search warrant and realized very quickly where this was coming from and why they were there. As I started reading, things started making sense, even though they black out names. It clearly painted a picture of who, what, when, and why. I was seeing a female who helped me relieve my sexual tensions who was on probation, which I was unaware of until I read this paperwork.

She frequented our apartment regularly, getting high with my roommates and me. She spent time with me at my work periodically when I was alone. I didn't like spending too much time with her as she was highly erratic and talked way too much. I enjoyed our private encounters, but I was very content when she left afterward.

She was home one evening and was surprised by her probation officer, who conducted an apartment search. Methamphetamine and paraphernalia were found, which violated her probation, and she decided to work with the police and probation department to turn on someone and hopefully get out of trouble, or at least reduce her violation time. She informed the police that we were dealers and sold dope to her regularly. From what I could gain from the report, she fabricated a story to include an arsenal that we maintained and large quantities of meth, which is why they'd upgraded to a task force. This explained the number of officers, as three more arrived with my roommates, who were stopped at the gate as they were leaving the complex. I learned a few things from this experience, including the evidence needed to get a search warrant.

The United States have laws that keep us from unreasonable search and seizures, defined by the Fourth Amendment of the Constitution. It requires governmental searches and seizures to be conducted with a search warrant that was issued, sanctioned by a probable cause that's very questionable (as I'll describe), and supported by an oath describing the place to be searched and the persons or things to be seized, which it did. The search warrant described the determination of issuance based on facts identified by this drug user that were confirmed but had no probable cause related to drugs or guns. She informed them that I drove a 1994 Chevy Corsica, which I did, where I worked, that

I arrived home around 8:00 a.m., which I did, and that I lived at the apartment complex they raided, which I did. This information was validated by the police and used to confirm, based on her oath, that she was truthful. This, to me, wasn't probable cause, and we were experiencing an unreasonable search and seizure. The police were very angry, as they didn't find what was described to them as being in our apartment. Whether they were angry at us for not getting the bust that they were hoping for or with the girl who'd lied about what they would find, we were treated with disrespect, which was evident as one of the detectives spit sunflower seeds all over my clothes, room, and floor, which I felt was uncalled for.

Let's Get Back to the Story

I'd learned that a search warrant must be issued at the time of their search, which didn't happen on that day in 2001. I asked the person who I felt was in charge three times for the search warrant, and the same answer was given every time. "Ok, but not now." He showed me his badge and confirmed he was with the sheriffs. I gave up asking, and since I was handcuffed and they had the guns, there wasn't much I could do about this.

They found methamphetamine in my car and in Mary's car, immediately giving us another charge of possession and another visit to jail. I had in my possession in my wallet three fake driver's licenses with my personal one as the only one without the hologram. Following the search of our cars, the detective informed me that he had a warrant to search our room but also failed to provide evidence of that mysterious document. Despite the questionable legality of the actions for the task force, I felt that my life was over, and not only was I going to state prison, but federal charges could easily be filed once they searched our room. I was a little unclear on how that worked, but I did know that having bags of stolen mail is a federal crime.

We were escorted to our room and watched as they began gathering property that included my computer that contained all the credit card numbers, checking account numbers, and templates of my fake IDs. As they were collecting all this evidence, I looked over at Mary, who was in tears as each item she saw taken away was one more nail in the coffin of getting custody of her son back. When I hadn't gotten high in a few hours, I started to feel emotions, and I felt guilty and sad for her predicament. Besides all the property they gathered of my criminal activities, the police seized my scales, baggies, and meth that once again confirmed that Mary was using drugs and not following the rules of her reunification program.

What do detectives do when they find drugs in your possession? This isn't a secret for anybody who has been arrested for that offense or experienced yourself as being the target. Wait for it. They want you to roll over on your dealer to get the bigger guy. I wasn't a "rat," and in fact, I firmly stood strong on the saying "If you do the crime, you do the time." I'd been given the same proposition at the prior arrest, and I'd refused that opportunity as well.

"You're in a lot of trouble, and you can help yourself by helping us. We'll let you go free tonight and talk to the district attorney about how you were of assistance to reduce your sentencing," he told Mary and me.

It made me wonder if this was taught and memorized by all law enforcement as each department states something very similar. I refused the offer, but Mary was much more willing to give someone up because of the situation with social services and her desire to get out of this lifestyle and be a mother to her child. She asked me if I'd call our supplier and do a controlled buy to help her save her world. I told her I would, but I didn't call our dealer, nor did I attempt to set anybody up. Instead, I created an illusion that I was working with the police, not being able to locate drugs, but hoping this attempt would do something for Mary.

The handcuffs were removed, and I was handed my phone to make the call. I called a guy that got high with us but who wasn't a supplier or involved in anything that would come back on me.

"Hey. I was wondering if you had an ounce of shit I could buy from you." I knew he wouldn't have anything close to this, but my attempt was all that mattered.

"I only have a little, and I wanted to know if I could come by? Why do you think that—" he began asking as I cut him off.

"All right man, let me know if you get anything. Don't worry about coming by," I responded and hung up the phone.

"Shit, he said he ran out and won't see his guy until tomorrow," I told the detective. "I'd love to help you because I want out of this lifestyle, but unfortunately, I don't have any other connections. What if you let us go tonight and tomorrow we can set something up?" I had no plans of helping these detectives, and I was still angry over the illegal seizure of my property.

Well, it didn't work. I was put in the front seat of a Porsche while Mary was loaded into a jeep, and we were transported back to the jail in Santa Ana. This was getting very repetitive, but we had developed a relationship with a company that became my worst enemy from these situations that I put myself in—a bail company. When you're released on bail, you visit the company's office to sign papers that you promise to appear in court, and they explain the reason it can be revoked. The same bail company had been used for our other arrests, which helped me to memorize his phone number, and my previous visits allowed for no confusion on who I was, if I called.

"John, I was arrested again with Mary, and we need you to post our bail. We have $25,000 bails each," I reported to him with my free phone call.

"You're kidding me. OK. Don't worry. I got your back. I'll have you guys out in a few hours," he stated, giving me the impression he was going to post our bail requiring no down payment. When you're faithful to a company and making them money, they sometimes help you out when you're in a bad situation. That's true with many companies, but when it's a company such as the one we were dealing with, it's a bad sign that things were not going as planned for me.

"The loop" was once again the journey ahead of us, and "tired" was the normalcy because it had been hours since we got high. The only good thing, and you can decide if that's true, was that we had a bail company processing our release prior to starting our intake nightmare. It took about four hours in "the loop" before we were processed out the door, and I called the guy who I'd asked to purchase an ounce for with the detectives who'd driven down and picked us up. He was furious, as he thought I'd wanted him to bring drugs as my fall guy, but I informed him that this wasn't what was happening. I explained how everything had gone down and the conversation we'd had. I don't think he believed my story, but it didn't matter to me either way. He drove us back to the hotel we'd been arrested at, and I had to ask the front desk for a key, which I'd left in the room when we'd been arrested. I was informed we had to move out by the end of the day because of the commotion that had been caused by the arrest.

Mary was about to change in a scary way, and it all started on that morning, a day that none of us would ever forget. It was a day that "poor me" still seemed to exist, but I wasn't able to get the pity I desired as thousands of people lost their lives in a selfish act by a few individuals.

The World Is Coming to an End

I'd fallen asleep not long after getting to the hotel, and I awoke to Mary screaming that the world was coming to an end. I didn't have a clear head, and I was confused about what was happening, when I realized that she was watching the news. The day was September 11, 2001. She was panicking and pacing the floor as we watched the Twin Towers collapse in New York. It almost seemed surreal. I needed to get high, which always seemed to be my answer to every problem I had, so I contacted our guy to score meth, especially since I needed energy to pack up our room and move to another location. Once I was able to get the dope that would allow me some energy, I gathered our belongings, or at least what the detectives hadn't taken, and began packing my car.

This time, instead of moving to another hotel, we moved into the loft of a friend's townhome. We wanted to hide away somewhere so we wouldn't be easy targets, and I was able to slow down on drug sales because we didn't have to pay the daily or weekly rates of a hotel. Mary was more comfortable with this location, but she started becoming convinced that police were everywhere, making this uncomfortable for everyone.

We now knew the game of posting bail and the approximate time frame for the next court date, which we appeared for, and we weren't surprised when the district attorney's office hadn't filed our cases. I had now been arrested three times in less than three months with very serious charges, but nothing had been filed.

"If nothing changes, nothing changes." My arrests had no effect on my decision to keep using, and it probably increased my desire to use more to forget about the real world and continue to live in an idea, a fantasy, and a lie that I was invincible and unreachable. That lie would keep me stuck until I was shown otherwise. Reality was about to hit us, and my lies were about to fall apart as it seemed that the world I was living in was about to come to an end.

Somehow someone, and it may have been the bail company, notified me that the commercial burglary case had been filed and a court date had been set for September 17, 2001. I purchased a suit and hired an attorney because I knew that this case was only a small piece of the puzzle that I needed to solve. It was the morning of September 17 that I crashed my car three times while falling asleep, and I knew that I wasn't going to make a great impression in court.

Court Date Number One

My attorney arrived as I was sitting in the courtroom watching the judge call case after case, not feeling positive as he appeared to have an attitude and angry reactions to defendants as they stepped in front of him one by one. I briefly spoke to my counsel and then waited as he spoke with the district attorney about my case. Numerous times, I fell asleep and was awakened by my attorney, slapping me on the shoulder and telling me to wake up. He told me that because I wasn't out on active bail, the judge would have me taken into custody, and I'd have to repost my freedom. I asked him if I could step out of the courtroom, so I could call the bail company. I quickly made the phone call, and I was told that he'd be on his way to the courthouse to secure the paperwork and keep me out of custody. My case was called, and I stepped forward.

After reading the charges, the judge informed me, "You're a danger to society. I have paperwork that says you've been arrested twice after you posted bail on this case. Your bail had been exonerated, and you'll need to post bail again. I'm going to increase your $10,000 bail to $35,000." My attorney informed the court that I was pleading innocent and set a court date for my pretrial. The bailiff walked up behind me, handcuffed me, searched me, and then walked me out the back door and down to the holding cells to wait for the bus to return to that place that I was getting to know too well. I was so tired, and it wasn't just physically as this life was wearing on me. I didn't want to do this anymore, but I felt trapped and imprisoned in my head. I sat in that cell most of the day, and I was released before the bus picked us up. "If not much changes, not much will change."

Let's Fix My Car

As meth gives us energy and offers more focus and concentration, many meth users like to take things apart to either learn how something works or break something to fix it. I wasn't that type of tweaker. My car was broken, so I pushed it into the garage of the townhome and purchased an oil pan and engine mount. The engine mount was easy, but the oil pan wasn't something I knew how to repair. I had no idea what I was doing, but I unscrewed the oil pan. I was unable to remove it because things were in the way. I started taking out bolts, screws, and parts that were blocking the oil pan until I was able to twist the passenger-side tire sideways and remove the oil pan. It was a lot more than I'd expected, but I was able to install the new one with a few problems that I discovered later. After the pan was secure, I began to put everything back, and once complete, I had numerous bolts and a couple of brackets that I could not locate placement for. What do you do when you have items left over and unable to find where they belong? Exactly. You throw them in your trunk, which is what I did. I fixed the car, as it drove perfectly except for an oil leak that may have been because of parts I'd left out or I'd cracked the oil pan by screwing a bolt in too tightly. It worked, and I drove it, but I needed to put an ounce of oil in daily to not blow up the engine. Ironically, this car would run for a few years after this incident.

The Scary Consequence for Some Meth Users

This was wearing on me, and things were slightly beginning to change in my thoughts. I knew what the right thing to do was, but I wasn't willing to give up yet, and I needed to continue to make payments for the bail that had been accumulating. I was unhappy with my attorney's lack of effort, so I wanted time to find a new one. Money was running thin, and sitting in jail would make it impossible to secure funds for the debt I had been accumulating. I was up to $110,000 in bail, and I was faithfully making payments to keep Mary and me out of custody.

Ten days after that court hearing, my second arrest, which was Mary's first arrest, was filed in a different courthouse and started a wave of new problems, as Mary became very uncomfortable to be around. Meth-induced psychosis began to set in, and it was looking very similar to schizophrenia. "The police are listening to our conversation, and they're outside our townhome," I heard regularly from her. At one point, she made comments about me being with the FBI or something of that sort. She became difficult to deal with, but what seems to be a problem can sometimes be an asset.

We had visited her son again at the foster home one day, and upon returning to the townhome, she began shouting about a car that had been following us for some time. I was getting irritated with her paranoia, and I decided to prove to her that this wasn't real. As I was approaching an off-ramp, I turned into the exit lane with my signal on as if I was going to exit the freeway, and the car she'd identified was right behind me, appearing to be going in the same direction. Just before getting off, I quickly moved left to remain on the freeway, and we observed the car do the same thing. Two exits down, I decided to get off the freeway, and I remained in the right turn lane and stopped at the light. Once the light turned green, I made an illegal left turn and realized that Mary was right, as the tailing car did the same thing. With the car behind me as I drove under the freeway overpass, I stayed slow and waited for cars to come from the other direction so I could make my move. Once I had an opportunity, I made an illegal U-turn right in front of the oncoming cars, keeping that driver from having the opportunity to follow. I quickly drove up through the hills and never saw that car again. Does paranoia exist if it's real?

A Needle in My Vein

Mary decided that she wanted to enter a treatment program, which I drove her to and dropped her off. She was
done using, and maybe the love for her son would prevail.
Love was gone within me, and it was this day that I took
my addiction to a new level and started something that I'd
always been opposed to. I drove back to the townhome and
told the couple we had been living with that I wanted to
"shoot up." They showed me how to load a rig and stick it
in my veins. Snorting and smoking meth can get you high,
but using it intravenously creates a high that sits well above
the rest. It was on, and life was about to get crazier, if that's
even possible.

I needed a new attorney and started looking around.
This was when I met Paul, who I felt good about as he was
easy to talk to and nonjudgmental. He could see that I was
in trouble both criminally and physically. He asked if I'd be
willing to return to jail and remain in custody until my case
had been resolved. I refused and told him not to worry. I had
this under control, and I would appear at court as directed.

Since I'd now been charged with two separate cases
and only out on active bail with the first case, I had a warrant out on the second case, which I didn't address, but I
appeared at all my hearings on that first case. I knew that
if the court learned of my warrant, I'd be taken back into
custody and required to post a new bail for that case since
it had been exonerated for the district attorney failing to file
the case in the time frame required. Every time I appeared
with Paul in court, I notified my bail guy, informed him
about my hearing, and said that he might receive a phone
call from someone I was bringing to court with me to post
my bail. I appeared five times before the judge learned

of my warrant in the other courthouse, and I was taken back into custody with another $25,000 bail. The female I brought to court called my bail bondsmen as she had been instructed, and I walked out once again before the bus took me to the county jail. Does anybody see the absurdity behind this?

I appeared one more time in South Court before I decided that I was done with court, so I decided to run. I knew that getting caught was inevitable, but I wanted to keep using, and I thought I'd decide to stop once they caught me. My drug use was beyond any control that I had, as I was slamming an eight ball a day and whittling away to nothing. My dealer had been arrested as he had absconded from his parole. He was charged with possession for sales and felon in possession of a firearm. Most of the people I associated with were either in jail, in treatment, or dead, and I was the lone soldier holding onto the motto that "I'm not a quitter."

The End That Brought About a New Beginning

On that day of January 3, 2002, they tracked me down, but it seemed unfair as they used Mary, who was doing well, to give up my location. They arrived at her work and used fear as a motive, threatening her with incarceration. She informed them where I was, and one stayed behind to make sure that she was unable to notify me.

They searched my room and found the meth, bags of syringes, and plenty of other items that were illegal to possess. I was driven back to the jail and processed for a final time. I was determined to remain in custody with the encouragement of my attorney, but it wasn't easy, and I had some weak moments. After about ten days in custody, with my cravings beyond painful, I called my bail company, but he informed me that he needed at least a $1,000 to get me out. I reluctantly called my father and asked him to borrow the money, but his reply wasn't exactly what I had been hoping for, and today, I agree with his response.

"I'm glad you're there because I know that you're safe."

What Was My Future Going to Look Like?

I was very lucky to have hired that attorney who assured me that I wouldn't get the maximum sentence that had been presented to me. Fifteen years is a long time to sit in prison, even though I'd have only done two-thirds of that time. I was anxious, and I felt uneasy every time I went to court because I had to do this clean. My attorney was convinced that I was eligible for a three-year term, which I was OK with, and I felt it was a good opportunity for me to get away from my influences and clean up my act. Court appearances became painful as I was shuffled around to different court-houses within days of each before my attorney brought the cases together in one courthouse. I was tired of court, still dealing with post-acute withdrawal symptoms from coming off methamphetamine and the cravings for a cigarette pushed me to want to sign on any prison term.

On February 5, 2002, I was ready to sign on a three-year term, encouraged by my attorney because of the deal he'd made with the district attorney. What did I deserve? After hearing this story again today, fifteen years is long, but I probably deserved even longer, as I was caught for only a fraction of the things I'd done. Dyke Huish, my attorney, decided to speak with the judge and district attorney one more time about a lesser sentence than the three years he had worked out with the DA. I was unsure of how he'd pull this off, but he did. The arrest at the hotel with Mary was never filed because they didn't have a search warrant, so it was an illegal search and seizure. The last arrest was a legal search because I did have a warrant for my arrest, but no additional charges were ever filed. The lead detective from that task force arrived at the jail requesting my help in offering up dealers.

"I'm done, and I'm sorry, but I won't help you," I told him, and I never saw him again.

I was sure that my lack of assistance was going to stack on more charges, but it never happened, and I always thought that maybe they felt sorry for me. My attorney walked out of the judge's chambers with a huge smile on his face, and I knew something good had happened. He walked over to the cage I was in and informed me that I was going to be sentenced to 270 days on each of the two cases, six months in a residential treatment program after I finished my custody time, DUI school for driving under the influence of methamphetamine, three years' probation, and some fees and fines. I opted for a little more jail time in lieu of some of those fines. All of this was to run concurrently, which meant I had only about seven months left to serve in jail. To get the district attorney to agree to such a minimal sentence, he was going to require that I sign on a seven-year prison term that would be suspended *if* I remained out of trouble, and that was a strong *if*.

My record of success wasn't strong, and I felt victimized by people and circumstances. The last six months of my use in 2001, I'd been set up, illegally searched by the task force, had marijuana planted in my cigarette pack, and lied to many times by law enforcement. "Fuck the world and fuck the system." I signed on those terms, but I knew that I had a hard road ahead of me and that this wasn't going to be easy. Everybody knows that getting drugs in jails or prisons isn't a difficult task, and in fact, I turned down plenty of opportunities to get high. It was my release that I was afraid of. What was I going to do once I walked out? Would I stay strong like I felt inside, or would I weaken as those doors opened? People talked about a life of normalcy or stability that I knew nothing about.

That concept of living "one day at a time" was all I knew. It was a principle that kept me stuck with no direction in life. What did I want to do as a career, or who would hire me with my record? Nothing was clear, but I knew that I wanted something different, something new, and something that meant more to me than methamphetamine or that adrenaline-filled lifestyle. As I studied myself and the events leading to my incarceration, I realized that my chemical of abuse wasn't the methamphetamine but was instead the adrenaline involved in the lifestyle. Sure, my body didn't function appropriately without the methamphetamine, as things changed within me because of the drug, but it was much bigger than that. The behaviors mixed with the manipulation of my own chemicals by the meth was a battle that I was going to need to overcome. It was loading a rig, sticking a needle in my arm, breaking into houses, running from the police, stealing from companies as they shook my hand and thanked me for the business, selling drugs, and never knowing what today was going to bring was more addictive than the meth itself. I was addicted to that rush of adrenaline and pleasure that kicked in.

For me to only *hope* that I'd succeed, or that I would just *try*, was never going to be enough to make it, and I knew it. Every time that I said I would try, I never succeeded because they were words that I used to get someone to think I'd do it, so they'd stop bothering me. Hope without action isn't a path to succeed, but instead a dream that will be lost as a "what might have been." Did failure exist, or did my pain and misery keep me stuck as a victim? I had seven months to figure this out, or I was going to prison for seven years. I hated to think about my childhood because I never felt like I fit in with anything or anybody. What happened to me? How did I end up in this situation? Was I destined for failure because of how I was raised or maybe God failed to include the part of my DNA that included love, sympathy, or care?

Regret will never solve your problems; it will only inhibit your ability for success. Turn your regrets into the power that you need to identify your values and morals, so you can live with integrity even though you violated a standard that you believe in.

CHAPTER 3

Pain Was the Reason

Death was slow and methodical, as a thousand cuts would kill.
Lingchi's process of torture severed any other chance to heal.
The thousands of people who died from the town of Saint Pierre
Had warnings of a dirty thunderstorm, but nobody seemed to care.

The death that was an awakening was a life that I held dear.
Staph was among our community, as a few knew exactly where.
Health became a burden, as weight was fading fast.
Do I die for this illusion, or are my values to burn and crash?

The pain of medieval torture could never change my mind.
It was nothing less or nothing more for me to win the fight.
You can threaten me with death or a dagger through the heart.
To stop this execution, emotional pain will be the start.

The bars inside the prison, the ones we know so well
Will never hold you back, and keep you running for the hills.
It's the dream that kept me wanting, the care I gave myself.
Nothing was going to stop me, as I was craving for the help.

Control became an asset that the judge could not ignore.
To live with goals of pastures as life became a sport.
Sitting on an apex, no knife within my side,
I saw a beautiful architecture that blinded me with light.

The castle has a bridge, a moat that has faded green.
I can offer her a position to be an almighty queen.
Nothing is ever perfect; rejection empowers your station.
Pain will never last as we seek out a new motivation.

Reaching for the stars, as we strive for something better,
Don't settle for comfort, or anything as light as a feather.
Happiness is not a feeling, but instead a search to find.
Loving you is easy, but fear has changed your mind.

Listen to me carefully, as I describe your greatest out.
Change your greatest desires and lose that horrible doubt.
It is not about the pain, and focusing on what you don't want,
But instead to find love, and hold on to what you do want.

Pain Was the Reason

"You're a stick! I'll break you like a twig. Be careful: the wind may blow you over." The mean things that kids will say about you can be daunting. The hate I had for myself didn't begin from my drug use but instead started as a child. I was socially awkward, quiet, and very withdrawn from everyone. Growing up was a very uncomfortable and a difficult experience, and it was hard for me. Unlike the stigma that drug users grow up in very unhealthy environments with abusive parents, live in a gang infested neighborhood or even struggled to have enough money to eat, growing up was actually the complete opposite of that for me, as I had good parents who worked very hard to provide a good upbringing and environment for all of their kids. I have two brothers. I'm the middle son in my family. We lived in very nice neighborhoods, went to good schools, and had all the things we needed and even many of the things that we wanted.

There were a few things that made growing up hard for me. To start with, I was very thin, and this gave many kids an opportunity to make fun of me. This may sound a little strange, especially for those who struggle with weight problems, but I was the target for name-calling. Physically, I was very healthy growing up, but emotionally I was a disaster because of the hurtful things that were said about me. I really wanted to have people like me, and the things that kids would say really did hurt.

The laughter of others and the hurtful things that were said caused me to lose any positive image I may have had of myself. During junior high and high school, I was in a few fights over weight jokes that had been said about me, and they were from what I'd considered to be friends of mine. I wasn't a good fighter and usually was the one who got hurt both emotionally and physically.

A second reason that growing up was difficult was that we moved a lot. I learned at a young age to never get too close to friends because our relationship was going to be temporary. Around the age of eight, our family moved from Southern California to Northern California. After my fourth-grade year in school, we moved to Pennsylvania for about a year and a half and then moved back to Northern California. This moving made things difficult for me because I was always leaving friends and needing to connect with new people.

The third reason that growing up was hard for me was the conflict between what I was taught as right and wrong (morals) and how I felt about things that went against those morals. From an early age, I questioned things more than many because I didn't trust people, including my parents and teachers, which put me in some very awkward positions that exacerbated my discomfort with the world. I had a curiosity about everything, and when I was told that drugs were bad and sex before marriage was wrong, I wasn't sold on it—I felt that adults just didn't want me to have fun. From the moment I had my first orgasm and understood how my body worked, I became compulsive with masturbation, and I sought out opportunities for sexual encounters that included many partners over the years. I couldn't understand the taboo, and I enjoyed many avenues of sexual pleasure—females, groups, and individual exploration, getting caught in some very awkward scenarios. When I was fifteen, I videotaped myself masturbating and left the tape in my parents VHS player, ending up having to discuss how inappropriate this was with my parents.

There's a very fine line between pleasure and pain. They are two sides of the same coin, one not existing without the other.

—E. L. James, *Fifty Shades of Grey*

"A fine line between pain and pleasure" can mean different things to different people, and aside from the physiological impact of endorphins (neurotransmitter released to alleviate pain) and their effect on dopamine (neurotransmitter that causes pleasure), I relate that statement to how powerful an effect my drug use had on the experience of pleasure as I had a debilitating level of emotional pain. I was more emotionally charged than most people I knew, and I had a harder time resolving emotional pain. I was an emotional being who was controlled by discomfort.

Failure Was My Destiny

I was destined for failure, as I felt unsuccessful in every area of my life because I was taught that success meant financial stability, college degrees, and a house with a white picket fence. I didn't fit in with societal norms, and I decided at an early age that I wanted to be happy and I cared very little for materialistic things.

As a child, I was convinced that I was going to fail in high school because no matter how hard I tried, I could not find any motivation or interest to work hard and get good grades. In 1988, I was a sophomore in high school, and as an awkward kid who wanted to be popular, I never felt like I fit in with my classmates. I didn't like myself, and I tried hard to find some way to avoid having to feel and preferred being able to disappear as I didn't think people would care including my family. I had very loving parents who I know love me today, but I never felt that I could relate to them or that they could relate to me. I had no goals or vision for myself, and I was very superficial with people, as I didn't want anybody to know me, my weaknesses, or the insecurities I had. I had very few friends, and I somehow latched onto people who were like me, with no direction or any desire to succeed in school but outwardly strong, because that was the image I attempted to portray even though I was far from that.

Edward was one of those people who I looked up to. I was envious of his father, who allowed him to get away with things I was punished for. If there's such a thing as a gateway drug, it was cigarettes that interested me the most and for similar reasons that the majority define marijuana as the gateway for many. I enjoyed smoking because of the effects it gave me as I puffed heavy, strong, and deep, causing a strong head rush. Smoking introduced me to the ability to use a substance and enjoy a change, even though it was minor compared to what would come, but it paved the way for an interest in trying alcohol.

Edward encouraged me to grab a bottle of alcohol from my parent's liquor cabinet and arrive at his house about an hour before class, which I did because I wanted to be cool and experience something stronger. I wasn't sure which bottle to grab, so I took a large bottle of vodka for the occasion. After arriving at his house, I took a twenty-ounce glass, filled it halfway full, toasted our friendship, and gulped the entire cup. It tasted horrible, but I decided to drink more as I didn't get the feeling I was hoping for. After the two rounds of vodka, I walked to class, feeling good. I was calm and cool, and I experienced drunkenness as I entered our first-period class. I quickly sat down as I was feeling sloppy. I was in a private high school, and we opened our first period of class with a prayer, but my prayer was very different than the teacher presented. It was something like this:

"Oh God, I feel like I'm about to die. If you would help me get through this, I'll never drink again."

I didn't really believe in God, but at that moment, I was really hoping that I was wrong. Immediately following the prayer, the teacher asked if I was all right because I turned as white as a ghost and ran out of the room, throwing up in the dirt outside. That was my first and last drink of vodka as the odor continues to make me nauseous to this day. Every substance I abused from that point on was very similar in my attempt to consume as much as possible without concern for the consequences. I realized later in life that if anyone was born with an innate desire to consume any substance that would change your consciousness compulsively and without care for any negative consequences, it was me.

My Criminal Story Begins

That same year, my parents were going out of town for my father's business trip. This was the first time that my older brother and I'd be left alone, and I knew that things were going to get ugly because of the relationship that we had. My older brother was about a year and a half older than I am, and we didn't have a close relationship. It was a mutual dislike that we had for each other. He was going to invite his girlfriend over, and he'd already informed me that I needed to leave after our parents left. While my mother was in the restroom, I acquired the keys to her van, which they were leaving behind, so I had transportation to get away, or a fight would have ensued.

My parents left town, and I drove, unlicensed, to purchase a case of malt liquor from Dirty Red, who I believe was a pimp, and then drank throughout the night while driving around. It was about 3:00 a.m. when two other kids joined me for the rest of the night. They claimed to have broken out of juvenile hall in Oregon. As the drinking continued, I was presented with a master key to the school by Edward, and I entered the classrooms, with alcohol taking the lead, and as you can probably guess, things were about to get ugly. Completely drunk, we stole money, smashed computers, and took everything that had value and wasn't tied down. We broke into a liquor store down the street and stole a car before going to my house to divvy up the loot.

My parents returned home on Sunday, and after spending hours cleaning the van and hiding all the items I'd taken, I was convinced that I was free and clear. As a sixteen-year-old who was invincible and knew everything, I knew that there was no way that I'd get caught. I was wrong, and I'll admit that this wasn't the first or last time that I'd been wrong. When I returned to school on Monday, the police were investigating the incident, but I was still convinced that they wouldn't be able to identify me as the culprit. Tuesday morning, our principal asked me to come into his office. He informed me that they knew I'd committed the offense and that the police were on the way. Sometime earlier, a student had taken a key, duplicated it, and sold it to someone who duplicated it and sold it to someone else. This was how I was able to acquire a key, and somehow the school was able to trace this back to my source, who told them that I was involved. I was arrested, expelled, and sent to a public school for the remainder of that semester. My parents were upset, but I learned how to manipulate them by promising drastic changes in my behaviors.

I was alone, going to school in a new town, and I isolated myself further as my self-esteem plummeted to a new low. It wasn't easy finding new friends, and school was far from important to me. The summer following my sophomore year, I rode my bicycle into town and decided to hot-wire a tractor on a construction site with an acquaintance of mine. Not thinking things through as I acted solely on impulse, we drove this equipment up ramps, jumped dirt piles, and crashed into walls. It wasn't long before the police were called, and I was arrested for grand theft auto, later reduced to joyriding. The prior arrest for the school incident was still pending, and I was facing some serious consequences that included two years at California Youth Authority (CYA), a juvenile prison.

Sixteen and Off to Rehab

My father hired an attorney who was able to get a thirty-day residential treatment program because alcohol was a factor in both of my arrests. After spending a few days in juvenile hall, I was released to the custody of my parents to immediately enroll in a program.

I left juvenile hall and flew to Southern California for my treatment, as my family was relocating again with a change in my father's employment. I had to leave my girlfriend and move away to never see her again, and since I'd learned to not get too close to people, it made it easier and a new person would take her place

After my thirty-day episode in treatment, I started seeing a girl who became pregnant within a couple of months of us meeting, and I became a father at the age of sixteen. Since lack of responsibility was the theme of my story, I failed drastically and evaded responsibility as a father. I landed at a public high school for six months and then ran away to Oregon for a few weeks, which set the stage for a new and exciting venture that would come in the future, but not before getting arrested in Northern California for violation of probation. I was transported to Southern California to serve thirty days in juvenile hall. I was released on house arrest and fitted with an ankle bracelet to confirm that I was home during all hours except for the time I was in a new private school, which was for a very short period of time. I cut the bracelet off, headed to Fullerton to see my girlfriend, and was arrested the following morning to complete another thirty-day incarceration stay. Graduating high school was seeming impossible because of the choices I was making.

Once I was released from juvenile hall, I enrolled in

independent studies to attempt to acquire that fleeting diploma that seemed to be disappearing. This was my fifth high school I'd attended, aside from the school that was in custody, and I really had no interest in education because my desires were women, drugs, and independence. What I wanted and what others wanted were two different things, but because of my people-pleasing quality, designed strictly to get people off my back, I graduated high school, which became my first and only real success in life at that point.

A Change in Direction

That trip to Oregon that I mentioned earlier introduced me to a counterculture that had begun some years before I was born and that gave me an interest in a new set of drugs that were really known to alter your state of consciousness. It was a world that most see as irresponsible, but I saw as freedom, and it taught me many lessons on survival, as I learned to panhandle money, sleep in homeless shelters, bathe in bathrooms at gas stations, and go to churches where I was able to get free food. Cougar Hot Springs, Oregon, offered clothing-optional pools that are set in the forests near Eugene, and was frequented by hippies who seemed to be the type of individuals I'd been unknowingly seeking because of the comfort I felt around them.

In 1992, a friend of mine and I went to a Grateful Dead concert in Las Vegas, which turned out to be a pivotal moment and probably saved my life, as ironic as that sounds. It gave me a break from the drugs that were killing me by switching to something that was less lethal. Pushing aside alcohol, meth, and other drugs, we explored the world through a new pair of eyes fueled by LSD and mushrooms. From 1991 until the death of Jerry Garcia, the lead guitarist and vocalist for the Grateful Dead, in 1995, I'd leave or quit anything I was doing once the Grateful Dead returned to the West Coast. Nothing mattered more to me than having fun, being comfortable, and being around people who I felt had my back.

Is College the Answer?

In 1993, with the push of my parents, I moved to Chico, California, and moved in with my older brother. I was going to attend community college while my brother attended Chico State University. I learned quickly, and with great enjoyment, that Chico had been awarded the honor of being the number two party school in the nation at that point in time. I began frequenting different apartment complexes each night and joining in keg parties, negatively affecting my ability to succeed in college. And, in fact, I was dropped from all my classes except one, which took place at 6:00 p.m. in the evening. I had no ability to drink moderately, even though stimulants were what I preferred, but alcohol made me comfortable, more outgoing, and happier.

After being there for a couple of months with my parents financially supporting me, I needed additional money since my drinking, partying, and the concerts I was attending cost more than I was getting. I applied for different jobs before becoming employed delivering newspapers in the middle of the night. I'd like to say that I was sober while driving around tossing newspapers out my car window, but that was rarely the case. It was a miracle I didn't kill anybody or myself, as I'd return home covering one eye just so I could see straight.

Brain Damage

It was during this time in Chico that I caused a situation that would nearly kill me in the future. My brother, two girls, and I were drinking at our apartment when we decided to drive to Taco Bell for a late dinner. We were unsure who was sober enough to drive, but one of the girls volunteered, and I didn't disagree or volunteer myself because I was barely able to walk, let alone drive. Upon arriving at the Taco Bell, which was only a few miles away, our driver pulled toward the window when I heard a loud bang toward the back of my car. I stumbled out of my vehicle and heard someone yell, "This is a walk-through not a drive-through, you idiots."

"Who the fuck hit my car!" I yelled, which was difficult to understand, as my slur was strong because of the amount of beer I'd drunk within the last few hours.

"Who the fuck hit my car?" came out of my mouth again as a crowd began to develop as you might see in high school as a fight was being egged on. I was standing amid a group of people when someone tapped me on my shoulder. I turned around, and the next thing I knew I was attempting to sit-up on the pavement of the parking lot with the worst pain I'd ever felt on the right side of my forehead. I reached for the area that hurt, and I could feel a lump that was hot, scraped up, and growing as the minutes passed. I was confused as the police had already arrived and were threatening to take me into custody from what I later concluded as being drunk in public. I wasn't arrested, but this was a clear sign for me that drinking and college weren't right for me, so I returned to Southern California, and it was just in time for the return of the Grateful Dead tour of 1993.

Maybe the Military Will Work?

After attending some concerts and a rainbow gathering in the Shasta Mountains, I stopped in a small town as I was heading back to Southern California, where I was stopped by some naval recruiters who tried to sell me on joining the military. I wasn't interested at that point, but that meeting got me thinking about how my life was heading nowhere, and unless I decided to do something different, failure would surely be what I'd succeed at.

Upon arriving back in Southern California, I decided to join the navy, but I was informed that I was unable to join active duty because of my failure to live a life of integrity and honesty, which was evident by my arrests as a juvenile. I enrolled in the naval reserves and went to boot camp in Great Lakes, Illinois, and I succeeded. I went to Port Hueneme, California, for my training as a construction mechanic for the Seabees, and I succeeded there also. Success was in my path, but as my story seems to unfold, I decided to self-sabotage my success and remind myself of failure. Once I was released from active duty and stepped down to the reserves, the Grateful Dead returned to the West Coast, and I left for a month, missing my weekend obligation. Each choice I made led to new adventures and new experiences that usually made my life more difficult because of my failure to think and, instead, acting on my impulses.

Maybe My Location Was the Problem

In 1994, while traveling north to see some Dead shows with a friend, I met a girl in Cougar Hot Springs, Oregon, with her boyfriend. They followed us to California and rented an apartment with us where life quickly spiraled out of control due to our meth use. Meth was a drug they'd never tried before. Rebecca returned home by herself after separating from her boyfriend, but we stayed in contact, leading me to flying to the east coast to run away from my demons. This was the first of three times that I landed in Maryland, and each time I failed to learn from my prior experiences. The location was my problem, or at least that's what I thought.

When I arrived in Maryland, we both acquired a job as servers in a diner at a hotel, and I received a complimentary room that we lived in for about six months. During this time, methamphetamine wasn't a problem since it wasn't available, but we did do heroin, alcohol, marijuana, and ecstasy regularly, and it wasn't long before Rebecca was pregnant with my son. Rebecca proposed that we move back to California and get away from the lifestyle that we were living in Maryland, and in early 1995, we moved back to California. Maryland was the problem, we thought, and if we moved away, we would be fine.

California wasn't the ideal location for me, as I reconnected with my dealer and rented a room in his apartment, where Rebecca and I resided. With unlimited supplies of meth at a very low cost, I returned to use with a vengeance. I was very little support and a nuisance to Rebecca as she stayed clean throughout the entire pregnancy. As the delivery date was approaching, she decided to return to Maryland to gain support from her mother and, once again, remove herself from the environment that we were living in. California was the problem, and if we moved away, we would be fine, or at least that was the lie I told myself.

Her mother purchased her a plane ticket, and she returned home while I gathered my belongings and drove my car across the country to meet her. Methamphetamine can have its perks, as it helped me stay awake, with enough energy to drive to Maryland in three days. Once I arrived in Maryland, I'd run out of dope, and I decided that I was going to clean up and avoid all substances except marijuana and alcohol.

With the help of Rebecca's mother, we purchased a mobile home in Woodstock, Maryland, and I held to my commitment to the limited use of substances as we waited for the birth of our child on October 26, 1995. Rebecca's mother was clean and sober and heavily involved in the twelve-step program. A lady she worked with, Carol, owned a painting company, and she hired me, since I was unemployed with very little experience in the job world and I needed an income to support the family financially. I'm a very fast learner, and I improved very quickly, becoming a foreman within a year of starting.

Woodstock, Maryland, was a very rural area, and very different than I was used to, as I'd lived in urban areas with populations of over thirty thousand, compared to six thousand there. I was from Southern California, living in a forest on the east coast with deer hunters as my neighbors. I didn't mind until that first winter, where I was able to experience the Blizzard of 1996 that caused more snow than they had seen in fifty years. From my recollection, it snowed for three days straight without letting up, and to top off the excitement, my heater shut off a day into the storm. Unsure on how to fix a heater, since we rarely used them or even had them in Southern California, I called the gas company and was told to climb onto my roof and clear away the stack as it may be covered with snow.

Are you kidding me? I thought when they told me this. With my newly born son and the risk of us freezing to death, I climbed onto my roof and cleared away the stack.

I relit the fuse after climbing back down, and we had heat for another day until the stack covered again. I once again climbed onto the roof, cleared away the stack, and then learned a very important lesson of physics that I'll never forget. When snow falls from the sky and melts slightly during the day from the sun, it freezes at night and turns into ice. When you put an object on ice and push forward, gravity takes hold, and things fall. After I cleared away the stack and stepped toward the edge of the roof, I slipped on ice and fell through the roof of my shed. Luckily, I had plenty of snow to cushion the fall, but my shed was crushed. It was never usable again.

Living in such a rural area, there wasn't much to do on your free time except to drink and smoke weed. I wasn't a hunter, and I had no interest in shooting animals during hunting season, but I didn't mind eating the meat when our neighbors returned from their murdering escapades. Tom, our neighbor in the last trailer, periodically came to our home and smoked weed with us. We felt sorry for Tom, as his wife had left him. She'd taken their children with her, leaving a man who was in turmoil. He talked about his woes and how angry he was with her and why he'd lost his spark in life, causing him to struggle financially. Before he left one night, he asked if he could borrow a pipe for the night, saying he would return it the next day.

After returning from work the following evening, Rebecca and I were sitting in our family room when we heard a gunshot from nearby.

"I bet Tom shot himself," I said jokingly.

A short time later the police, the fire department, and the paramedics arrived at his trailer, and it was then that we learned that he had shot himself in the head. Our neighbor across the street told me later that he and Tom were both sitting in his kitchen while Tom was cleaning his gun and talking about the hate that he had for his wife, and before the neighbor knew it, Tom put the gun to his head and pulled the trigger. I was sad that he had done this, but I also wanted the pipe back that I'd given him. I went over to his trailer to find the pipe, and I almost regretted going in there, as neither the police nor emergency personnel had cleaned up his brains that had been splattered on the wall behind where he'd been sitting. I didn't find my pipe.

My drinking progressed as I was living in Woodstock, and after about a year, Rebecca and I started having problems, arguing every morning because we had one car to get to work and she struggled to get out of bed. I woke up at five and got my son fed and clothed as I was yelling for her to get up so I wouldn't be late to work. I eventually gave up, moved out, and rented an apartment in Laurel, Maryland, that was close to my employment. Maryland wasn't the place I wanted to be, as the summers were hot and humid, and the winters were cold and freezing. Alcohol and marijuana were not the substances I preferred as they didn't give the effects I preferred, but I was able to manage and control my use to maintain my job, pay my rent, and stay out of trouble, although I did deal with horrific hangovers at times. In 1998 after drinking heavily, I decided that it would be a good idea that I spend one night celebrating, although I didn't have anything to celebrate, by smoking crack.

Cocaine or crack wasn't something that I preferred, but I felt that since it wasn't methamphetamine, I'd be fine. I bought $100 worth of crack from a coworker and smoked it within a few hours, only to need more. After $1,000, I decided that it was time to return to California, so I could get out of the life I was living in Maryland and get clean.

Maryland was the problem, and if I moved away, I thought I'd be fine.

Each choice I made altered my course and, without impulse control, led me to new problems. Every decision I made was led by drugs and not by my own rational mind.

Another Rehab

I had to test many theories out for myself, and I struggled with listening to others' experiences so I could navigate the pain personally, which probably did have more of an impact in gaining the lessons I needed to learn. I was determined to manage a psychoactive substance other than my drug of choice and remain in control. Those charges that led me toward a fifteen-year prison term began with my belief that I could handle another substance without consequences, but I was wrong, and I rarely have seen many be successful with those of us who have had a very serious chemical-dependency issue.

In 1999, I entered a rehabilitation program in Tustin to detox from methamphetamine with no intention of staying clean and sober from marijuana and alcohol. I held a belief that speed was my problem and that marijuana and alcohol would help my anxiety and that they had never caused the damage to me that I'd seen with speed. I was mistaken, but the attempt that I made to switch to another substance taught me some of the greatest lessons about the severity of my chemical-dependency problem, helping me gain what may be a success in the future.

The reason for entering the program in 1999 was in lieu of jail time after being arrested at my apartment. I enrolled in a six-month program that included detox, residential, and aftercare that consisted of sober living with outpatient.

After a week into the residential portion of the program, a mother visited her son David and brought a jacket that contained an ounce of marijuana and some rolling papers that we used to roll a few joints and smoke around the side of the house in between groups. This obviously violated the rules of the program, but I wasn't there to refrain from the substances I mentioned above. It wasn't long before David got caught by himself and was discharged from the facility for using drugs on the property. I evaded any responsibility for this, even though they drug tested the entire facility and I tested positive for marijuana. They failed to complete a urinalysis on me during intake, so they had no levels to compare them to, even though I'd have tested negative for THC during my admission because I wasn't smoking weed. After transitioning from the residential program to a sober-living house, I began drinking beer with my room-mate Jack during the day and calculating the time I needed to stop so I could blow zeros for the breathalyzer every night.

This control that I was able to maintain to not get caught confirmed my belief that I could manage alcohol and be successful in the future without having to refrain from it. Thinking about it today, the notion doesn't hold much validity since I wasn't even able to stay sober during the six months I was in the program. After about two months, Jack arrived late for a house meeting and was clearly drunk, which resulted from him being discharged and flown back to New York where he violated his parole. It appeared that I was invincible, and as a result, I continued my activities until I successfully completed the program and was discharged in 2000. I was in control, or at least that's what I thought, and I returned to Maryland as an extra precaution, since methamphetamine wasn't readily available on the east coast, and that's what I thought my problem was.

It Must Be True if I Believe It

This was to be my third time in using Maryland as my safety zone from methamphetamine. After I left the treatment program, Carol, the owner of the painting company, purchased a plane ticket for me to fly to Maryland and live with her and her girlfriend so I could reenter society and get back on my feet. Carol and I became great friends and took me to these Gay Pride events that were so far out of the norm for me, but I had so much fun. She attempted to get me to attend twelve-step meetings, but I refused as I had no intention of staying completely sober. I was able to drink and smoke weed with control, which I'd proved at the treatment center I was in. It wasn't a problem. Or was it?

After going to a bar one evening, I decided that I was going to smoke crack again, and I reached out to an employee with the painting company. I purchased it, began smoking it, and then once the morning came, I realized I was broke after spending $750. I felt like shit that morning and got into an argument with Carol that resulted in me deciding to leave for California again because I needed to get out of that lifestyle. Maryland was the problem, and if I moved away, I'd be fine.

Wait a minute. I think I wrote that same statement every time I left California for Maryland and vice versa. Do you think it's the place? I didn't anymore. I knew I was the problem, but sadly, with a cracked-out head, I didn't care.

We've now arrived at 2001, and you have a glimpse of the story that led to my arrests that put me in a position where I was facing those consequences. The pain that followed forced me to look at my past experiences and taught me some of the most important lessons of my life, lessons that have brought me to where I am today. I've proved through my actions that I'm unable to use any psychoactive substance if I want to remain in control of my life. Alcohol altered my thinking and allowed me to rationalize the ability to use something else and having the rationalization make sense to me. Using a drug like alcohol or weed had always led me back to methamphetamine without fail. The three attempts in Maryland were not the only examples, as I was able to get off methamphetamine for the Grateful Dead shows, only to return to it, after I returned home.

Life is what you make it, and did I care enough to make a difference? I wanted to change, but was I really being honest with myself? As the day for my release from custody was coming, fear began to consume me, and I didn't want to leave. My determination, desire for change, and commitment to staying clean felt right; but was it real? It felt good being clean and sober, and I didn't want to change that feeling. I didn't think I did. Maybe I didn't. Or did I? Time would tell, and time was what I was facing.

Part 2

A Step into the Unknown:

I Became a Teacher

When you get to the end of all the light you know and it's time to step into the darkness of the unknown, faith is knowing that one of two things shall happen: either you will be given something solid to stand on, or you will be taught how to fly.

—Edward Teller

CHAPTER 4

How Honest Am I?

The mind has a power that is surely unknown,
A rose that we have or a weed that has grown.
I give you my love, the plant you adore.
You reach out and grab it, but are struck by a thorn.

The ocean of vastness that is told through a rhyme,
Creation of majesty, let's put the story aside.
Remembering a time, the sky created the blue.
Time has changed, and nothing was true.

Wander through the trees and search for the chap,
Doubt you will find him because our world is still flat.
Mystery surrounds us with stories before.
Truth is mistaken that I can't take anymore.

I know what is true, and I know what is right.
I saw what is real but flew away like a kite.
I thought for a moment of your beauty outside,
But I realized your beauty was greater inside.

I don't understand why the boat was not there.
I saw it today, and I saw it there.
What's real can be covered with a fog that you make.
Don't be sure that you know it's all a mistake.

I got on the plane as I searched for the land.
We crashed in the desert, and I don't have a fan.
We didn't have a problem, or at least what we thought.
Until the heat of the day as heat stroke we had caught.

We could have saved time by working at night,
But truth wasn't with us as we smoked on the pipe.
Unsure on our future that can't be ignored,
No need for water but my body was sore.

Let me make clear that the answers were coming.
But a fog blocked the way as a wall began forming.
Forever, I ask you if you could tell me a "why,"
But the answer was nothing more than a lie.

From the age of sixteen as I entered the world of recovery up until the age of twenty-eight, I never acquired any clean time longer than six months. The reason for this was that I wasn't willing to give up on doing everything I could to be happy, successful, and stable while still being able to use drugs. There wasn't a single time that I returned to using with the following mind-set: "I'm going to completely fuck up my life today. I can control it. It will be different this time. I'm older and smarter. I can just smoke weed. There's nothing wrong with a beer occasionally." None of that was true.

I attempted every plan I concocted that I was sure would work. Besides my attempts at controlling substances that I believed I could control, I felt that it was the location that was the problem, so I moved to Maryland. I felt that since I really had nothing productive going on in my life, I joined the military, which I eventually gave up on. I tried to find happiness in jobs, relationships, music, and even adrenaline through bungee jumping, while attempting to control my use. It was failure after failure. My ability to control my drug use didn't exist, and I was left hopeless, helpless, and deeply depressed. It was at that point in 2001 that I gave up, unconsciously hell-bent on destroying my life.

I'd been incarcerated for about thirty days at sentencing since my fourth arrest, and something had happened to me just prior to this day. Was it that I had a little time clean, or that I was vigorously working on myself, or was it a spiritual drive that sparked a change within me? Maybe there was a little connection between each of those ideas? Unlike what many may think, it wasn't fear or loneliness of being locked up that did anything to me, and I began to understand and feel that safeness of myself that my father had mentioned. For the first time in many years, I felt free— and I was behind bars, which may sound odd. I was clean, thinking better, reading, writing, and working on myself for the better. Those actions, activities, and altercations saved my life, whether it was legal or not. I realized that if I hadn't been breaking the law and committing all those crimes, none of this would have happened. I deserved to be in prison for the rest of my life if I'd been caught for everything I'd done. The fact that I had choices, took responsibility for my actions, and became humble to the reality behind my current situation set me free. There was nothing that the district attorney, police, or judge could do to me that would take that away. I realized that freedom comes from within and has nothing to do with anything external.

A World of Possibilities

All that pain, failure, and misery brought a possibility of success beyond anything that I'd ever dreamed of. Could the hopes that I had become a reality if I put effort and actions into my goals? I knew I needed to stop hoping and dreaming of a world that didn't exist and instead focus on a world of reality. I didn't have a full understanding of my path when I walked out of jail, but I did have a direction of what I wanted and a humble nature that was willing to ask for help. I decided that I no longer wanted to walk alone and was willing to join society in a manner that was new to me. Jail became a security, safe place, and a life that I feared leaving the day of my release, but I felt that I was as ready as I could be, and I did look forward to better food, a bathroom I could use in private, and a refrigerator I could put my own food into. I made a list of things I was grateful for, with over a hundred different items the day after my release. When you have very little in a cell and you walk out into a world of possibilities, you can appreciate and be grateful for even the smallest little things.

I had almost nine months clean when I walked out of jail, which was the longest I'd ever been clean since starting my drug use, and I was able to stop for a moment and smell the roses. I was able to look around and find an appreciation for something that would have seemed small and inconsequential in the past and not even worth no-ticing. I was grateful for Humphry Davy who invented an incandescent light bulb in 1801 and created the arc lamp in 1809, which paved the way for Thomas Edison to create an effective bulb for commercial use, allowing me the ability to read a book. In some ways, this appreciation for the more conventional life I live today has never left, allowing me the ability to care more about things.

After being released, I entered a residential treatment program for six months, as my court order required, and I decided to remain another six months in a sober-living facility following the completion of the residential program. I was committed, determined, and ready to find a better path while making sure that I was in a safe place. It was very difficult at times because I had cravings so strong that I wanted to give up. That life I described in an earlier chapter was miserable at the end, but I missed the adrenaline rush and the cat-and-mouse games I'd created. Staying busy and distracting myself was helpful, along with spending time with family and supportive friends who cared about me and were looking out for my best interests. Treatment facilities are not always safe places because drugs and alcohol make their way inside from clients who have relapsed or are planning to relapse.

I did something that was a new concept for me as my thinking changed, and again, I was living in the real world. Friends will not destroy your life but instead can help save your life. This is backward thinking from living on the streets. If another client, who is my friend, brought drugs into a facility after relapsing and presented the thing that would risk my life, freedom, or future, my job as the friend was to save that person's life. Allowing this individual to continue the use, lie to the program, and manipulate circumstances wasn't being a friend while using but was instead being an enemy. I became a rat to save my life and my friend's life. This scenario happened on a few occasions, and as hard as it was, I was a friend and did the right thing.

A counselor in the program I was in, Helm, encouraged me to enroll in school and become a drug-and-alcohol-addiction counselor because of my ability to communicate intelligently, or at least that's what he told me. I didn't feel that way, but I decided to follow his direction since my criminal background wasn't as problematic in that industry and was appreciated, because of the experience. After about four weeks into the program, I took a job as a telemarketer, using my manipulative skills to sell things that nobody really wanted, and I enrolled in school after I'd completed six months in the residential treatment program. I stayed very busy, as I was working full-time, going to three-quarter-time school, and participating in outpatient treatment. I was productive, clean, and happy, which was new to me, and it felt good.

I began working in the industry in September of 2003 as a live-in house manager of a residential treatment program. I began interning as a counselor, and by 2005, I'd completed my drug-and-alcohol studies, receiving my certification after taking the exam. From 2005 to 2007, I worked at a residential facility in Newport Beach as a case manager, and I was promoted to program director in 2008. In 2009, I had an opportunity to open, as an owner, Serenity Life Counseling, which had both an outpatient and a residential program. I took my work very seriously and began studying clients, observing results, and realizing that the industry had a lot of problems. Some counselors were inflexible, wanting things done their way and not looking at strengths, abilities, knowledge, and skills of the clients. The therapeutic approaches that were used failed to teach the clients one of the most important ideas, which was that being clean and sober can be fun. Many clinicians will request honesty but then punish real honesty. Programs have been using the same approach for years, and some of it doesn't work. If it doesn't work, we need to change it.

In 2012, I left Serenity Life Counseling because of a conflict I had with my business partner, but at this point, I'd acquired a college degree, and I was speaking at universities to upcoming counselors and therapists and doing things that allowed me to utilize my knowledge and skills. I genuinely started caring about people, and I felt that I had something to offer others.

Many families will wonder if their children will ever make it back from the grips of their drug abuse, or the substance-abusing individual will question if he or she will ever survive and learn how to live drug-free. I want to assure you that they can. My story should help you understand the hold that drugs had on my life, which means that it's possible, no matter how far you've gone, to live a life of happy success while clean and sober. I needed to get honest, so I could look at the real world and not the crazy, delusional world I'd been living in.

What Is Real?

Pain is the greatest motivator. It will help push many to achieve positive things, such as getting a job when they're unable to pay rent, or it could influence a decision to seek out therapy to save their marriages, but with substance abuse, we're dealing with a different animal. For me, the pain that was caused by my drug abuse reinforced the desire to continue doing the substance that had caused the pain in the first place. The reason for this was a dishonest view of what was real. Many of my friends have died as pain motivated them to continue their drug use and hide from the pain that their drug use caused. Insane? Yes.

What is real? Don't ask someone who is currently abusing drugs because his or her perception of reality will not be aligned with anything factual. A friend or family member will become angry when a drug abuser lies as he or she promises to be somewhere when the drug abuser never planned on going, or they feel sorry for the drug abuser and offer gas money so the drug abuser could pick up his or her child, only for the abuser to use the friend or family member's hard-earned money to purchase dope. This dishonesty will surely lose trust, but it's the lies that they tell themselves that will kill them.

There are teachers in this world who can show you things, even though you may not see it at first, such as this example in 2001. It was noon on a Saturday afternoon when I was running out of gas and decided to stop and fill up before returning to my hotel room. It was hot, and the sun was beating down, making it difficult to see as I pulled up to the pump at a gas station.

As I was stepping out of the car, I heard someone yell, "Tweaker!" from a gas pump nearby.

Who was this guy talking to? It only took a second before I realized it must have been directed at me because, even though I hated that word, I was a tweaker. How did he know? I kept such good composure and handled myself well in public.

"Tweaker" echoed through the gas station once again. I looked over and saw this guy laughing at me while I was pumping gas. I don't recall what I said, but I was angry, and I'm sure it was explicitly rude and vulgar. It bothered me most of the day, so I looked at myself in the mirror when I got back to my room, and I realized how disgustingly emaciated I looked. I was a poster child for methamphetamine use, a great example for the public to see the manifestation of the pain, torment, and suffering I was trying to hide. I was six feet, three inches tall, and I weighed 130 pounds.

This man, who I'd never met before, opened my eyes to information that I couldn't see even though it was right in front of me, as I believed, up until that point, that I looked good, was healthy, and was fully in control. This awareness that I developed from that gentleman did nothing to change my interest in using, as I quickly converted the problem away from the drugs and focused on not eating correctly, which I promised myself to do more of.

The drug wasn't the problem—it was actually the solution to every problem that I faced because it eliminated all the pain and discomfort in life, which allowed me to not care. The problem, as I saw it, was when I was forced to see that living life devoid of emotional pain was an unrealistic goal because nothing was ever constant. Physical and emotional pain is real, and once the drugs run out, your connections disappear, money runs thin, and you get arrested. Then there's nothing left to do but feel, and those feelings are exaggerated.

The only way to be numb of emotional pain permanently is to commit suicide, and that solution requires a state of hopelessness that isn't real to most people. A state of hopelessness is usually reached when all avenues have been exhausted and there's nothing else that can be attempted. This perception that all avenues have been exhausted can never be proven, and a state of hope is always possible unless you've tried everything, which is highly unlikely.

Lies Will Kill You

It may be difficult to understand being arrested four times in six months and facing a maximum sentence of fifteen years in prison. A "normal" person would have thought to stop using, stop selling drugs, and possibly to check into a rehabilitation facility for help, but not me. I was far from "normal," and I was not ready to give up on that life of crime and pleasure that I'd once experienced.

We do not describe the world we see.
We see the world we describe.
—Rene Descartes

As I posted bail, which became the norm in those sprees of arrests, each arrest after that began to stack on charges and increase the amount of bail I posted. I believed at that time that I needed to be free on the streets to make money so I could continue to pay for the bail, and hire an attorney to fight my charges and keep me out of prison. "We don't describe the world we see. We see the world we describe." The pessimist sees a situation and twists it into something ugly, keeping himself or herself ill, running for answers that will never be found, while the optimist views an identical situation but uses it as an empowerment to see the world in a positive light. The only reason I'm alive today is because of the immense work I did on myself, which began with an honest look at my life, ideas, thoughts, and perceptions that were killing me. Many lies that we tell ourselves are provoked by an immense, debilitating fear or a hope that something isn't true, and unfortunately, some of those lies will kill you.

When I look at my past and how dishonest my thinking was, I realized that it was a miracle that I made it out alive.

1. "I'll never be happy or feel pleasure clean and sober." The truth behind this statement is that continued drug use will destroy any chance you'll have to eventually find happiness or pleasure while using drugs, let alone sober. Anytime that you use

something, like a drug, for an extended period, your body adapts to it, and you'll no longer get pleasure from it. "Highness isn't a property of drugs but a property of people." If you continue using drugs or alcohol, you're destroying your ability to experience pleasure. If you want to feel good or experience pleasure for the rest of your life, sobriety is the only way you'll find it. There are people who can do just one line, smoke one bowl, or drink one glass of wine, and for them, sobriety may not be the only solution. This has never been a possibility for me.

2. "I don't have a problem and can stop anytime." This is a commonly used argument for many, and most truly believe it, because none of us wants to feel controlled or held captive. This is a lie that has killed many people over the years, including friends of mine.

3. "I can't stay clean." Every person who abuses drugs or alcohol can stay clean and sober, since your use began at some point in your life that predated years of being clean. Statements such as this are used to justify behavior and offer an excuse to someone instead of speaking the truth. "I won't stay clean" is the more honest phrase and is usually known to be the truth.

4. "I'm not ready because I have things to do" If you truly have a drug problem, you're being dishonest because we know that nothing is being done except further drug use. My experience has shown me that while we're high, we're likely to not do anything except get drugs or get high.

How many times have you delayed getting clean because

you're not ready, have things to do, or believe you'll never be successful without drugs? How many of your statements are manipulated by a confused state of mind? Many may think that those are true statements, but I'd challenge you to rethink them.

I didn't feel ready in 2002 to get clean and sober. Many of my friends, family, and colleagues felt that they weren't ready but are clean and sober today with many years under their belt. How could it be that they weren't ready but were able to succeed in this game of recovery?

What will it take for you to be ready? Are we really, truly ready, for anything? This can be a scary concept when we're talking about chemical dependency. Do you need to get fifteen years in prison, get a DUI while killing someone, or die yourself? Common sense says that you'll never be ready if you reach the latter of these. "Yet" says that it hasn't happened now, but it will happen. If you say, "I'm not ready yet, but I will be soon," and you die, then you were wrong. Having my life experience has allowed me the gift of being able to help others and also having the ability to work through people's dishonesty as "you can't bullshit a bullshitter." Much of what I hear from clients, I've said myself at one point in time or another.

The Death of Lies

Individuals who've been in recovery or people who have a high recidivism rate for rehabilitation facilities have an advantage over first-time recipients. We have a life experience that has taught us things and an awareness that reveals many of the lies we may have told ourselves in the past. Awareness can be the death of lies. I entered my first treatment program when I was a juvenile and then four others as an adult, offering me plenty of experience to qualify me as expert.

**Nobody ever did, or ever will, escape
the consequences of his choices.
—Alfred A. Montapert**

I can say today that every program I attended wasn't a waste of time, because of the knowledge I learned. I'm going to describe how I repeatedly lied to myself, but then my awareness made me realize the truth. Those lies that I told myself nearly killed me, and because my addiction progressed to the point it had, my awareness destroyed those lies, but it was almost too late (i.e., crossed the line of no return.)

In 2001, I could no longer dispute that I had a drug problem. Methamphetamine was nearly a part of my DNA and my cognitive abilities to control my drug use were gone, or at least that's what I thought. After being arrested three times in four months, I contacted a counselor from a rehabilitation facility I'd attended in 1999. I knew from personal experience exactly what I needed to do, but I believed I couldn't get clean, which had to be a dishonest statement, because I'd gotten clean in the past, so why would it be different this time?

I wasn't sure exactly what I was looking for in the meeting with this counselor, but it was the best decision I could come up with. I think I was hoping for a miracle answer that I wasn't aware of, but I can tell you that the response I got wasn't what I was looking for. After telling him that I'd been arrested three times, was out on bail, and was intravenously using about an eight ball a day, he responded, "You're fucked."

What? I already knew that. I wanted the miracle answer. He gave me a list of free detox facilities, which I crumpled up and threw away after I left his office because I didn't believe that I could stay clean. My life experience and awareness had destroyed all the lies that I'd told myself where I finally knew that I had a drug problem, I couldn't control it, and I was fucked, which he confirmed.

Since I didn't believe that I could stay clean, which would have been my only saving grace, I was left in a state of true hopelessness, helplessness, and hatred for myself. Hopelessness resulted from my belief that I'd tried everything, including treatment programs, twelve-step meetings (which I'll discuss in the next chapter), having a sponsor, moving to another location, and joining the military. When I went back to meth, I told myself that I could control it, and it wouldn't be a problem. I couldn't control it, and those lies nearly killed me.

Some individuals in their teens and early twenties will suffer for many years before exposing their lies for what they are, if they survive. At that age, drugs are fun, and it's hard to imagine the anguish that will greet them in the future if dependency is in their life script. Some people will not be able to have just one drink or just one experience of drug use without it destroying their lives. I've always wished that I could have the ability to show them their future pain, with the hope that it would impact them enough to alter their courses before stepping down that road. Drugs are fun when you choose to do them, but when you must do them to be functional, the fun dissipates. In 2001, my drug use was no longer fun, as the methamphetamine was required to stay awake, be productive, and produce enough dopamine to eliminate the symptoms of major depression. For any teens and young adults who are reading this book,

I'm going to describe in some future chapters how invincibility doesn't exist, as I once believed, and if you walk this path as I had, it will happen to you. I promise. I'm not a fan of the phrase "I told you so," but consider your choices so I don't have to say, "I told you so."

Getting arrested the fourth and final time in 2002 saved my life. I can honestly say that the law enforcement organizations saved my life, even though I didn't see it that way at the time. The last two arrests were by an organization that was targeting me for sales, transportation, and potentially smuggling methamphetamine across county and even state lines.

Why am I focused so much on lies? I'm hoping to break apart the lies that you tell yourself. We've all heard that lies will kill you. Those aren't the lies we tell others but instead the lies we tell ourselves. I'm sure that we can all agree that honesty and integrity are important qualities that we look for in other people. Every person that you distrust, or have no confidence in, comes back to integrity.

A study was published in the *Journal of Basic and Applied Psychology* that recorded conversations of pairs of individuals over a ten-minute period. They concluded that 60 percent of the pairs lied within ten minutes and the average number of lies was 2.92 per subject. That correlates to over two hundred lies per day for an average human. Many lies people tell could be simple exaggerations, white lies, or even blatant lies to manipulate other people.

Thoughts for Clinicians

Clinicians in the industry are responsible for opening the door of honesty, allowing the client an opportunity to see the truth, and presenting a view of a life that's intriguing, fascinating, and exciting. As a professional in the substance-abuse industry, we must be careful and honest with the people we work with. It's our job to help each person find what's going to work the best for him or her. It may be the twelve-step program, church, school, or sitting and talking to frogs at a lake. It's not my job to force my beliefs or opinions on a client but instead to help them see the answers that they already have.

Sadly, I've worked with many counselors and therapists over the years who make statements about their clients "not being ready yet" or being "in denial." A counselor who uses "denial" to define the position of a client isn't working hard and is being incompetent, in to my opinion. "You're in denial" is said by many counselors to their clients, instead of helping them see the lies they're telling themselves. How can someone believe that something is untrue if I can show them through their own experiential knowledge that their information may be wrong. Counselors diagnose clients according to *The Diagnostic and Statistical Manual of Mental Disorders* (DSM–5), which is a book that an individual who abuses drugs would, most likely, not read. Denial only applies to someone's limited understanding, but breaks apart with an expanded awareness. What truths have you held that you later defined as lies?

Many counselors, therapists, and facilities use commit a great disservice to their clients by telling them that they have a drug problem, expecting them to just believe what they say. The more you tell an individual something that he or she doesn't believe, the more a disconnect will occur because of that person's lack of trust due to the client's perceived dishonesty. The only way to get someone to believe that he or she has a drug problem is to get that person to make that decision for himself or herself. I'd been told I had a drug problem for many years, but it never meant anything until I was able to see it for myself.

Some of the most difficult clients to work with are teenagers and young adults. Many are pushed into treatment because of worried parents who have caught them smoking marijuana, drinking, or even using illicit drugs. Are they dependent on drugs? Most aren't, according to diagnosis codes, and because of this, they're very difficult to get them to see that it may be a problem. From my experience, rarely have I seen a person come into a treatment program by accident, and this was evident by a dependency that developed in the future for these individuals. To tell them they're addicts, or have a drug problem, will many times push them away. The more they're hammered on that concept, the further and further they go away mentally, spiritually, and even physically when they run from the program. It may not be the horrible consequences that they have received up until this point in their lives compared to others, but instead focusing on what may happen to them in the future if they continue using drugs. Don't tell them what will happen but instead help them identify the possibilities of what might happen to them in the future. We then focus on self-esteem so they can learn to care enough about themselves, so they don't desire to experience the information they've developed for what their futures will look like.

From 2005–2009, I worked for a facility whose clients were primarily young adults with very wealthy parents. They were in a very dangerous position because many of them had codependent parents willing to pay as much money as they needed to "fix" their children. These young adults knew this, which created entitlement issues and put a sense of false security within them that allowed them to do whatever they wanted because their parents would always pick up their pieces. In the four years that I worked at that facility, ten people died within six months of them leaving the facility and the majority were in their teens and twenties. I was very new to the industry, having started in 2003, and I felt an enormous amount of guilt after hearing that they'd passed away. "What could I have done differently?"

I learned some very important things throughout that experience, and my lack of effort, even though I was unaware, was a major concern that I was able to see later. "He's in denial. He isn't ready." These are statements that I made when I gave up on the client because I had no answers instead of persevering.

Many in the recovery community believe that staying away from much of the world and avoiding places that may provoke an interest to use is most effective. I disagree with this in most cases because of the support that most have if they're in treatment. It's about learning to live in a world where drugs and alcohol are and not having to use them ourselves. If a client that I'm working with has fears of attending a concert because there are triggers and memories of using, why do we tell them not to go to a concert for a year when they'll no longer have the support of people there to help them? Let's take the client to a concert so he or she can realize that recovery isn't about hiding from the world but, instead, enjoying the world while clean and sober.

The greatest gift that we can offer people early in recovery is when we can target, very specifically, things that will work for each individual person. When I was working at that facility in 2005 I discussed earlier, I had a caseload of twelve to fifteen clients on average. Group sessions were very generalized, and I had very little time to focus on anything in depth with my clients. Many owners of facilities will tell staff that they have forty-five minutes to complete an individual session, allowing staff fifteen minutes for notes. This has never worked for me because of the possibility that the person I'm working with may need more time or less time.

Many years ago, and even in some programs today, the idea was to "tear you down to build you up." This model implied a belief that the client was a horrible person and a detriment to society. An owner of a facility I worked for many years ago lectured clients in group and told them that they were "pieces of shit" and that people hated them. Most people I've worked with over the years are already torn down pretty well, and it should be the counselors' or therapists' tactics to empower them. The pain, failure, and misery that's brought in can be utilized by their counselors to help them succeed. The clinicians can take their greatest enemy and transform them into their most powerful ally.

Speak the Truth

Truth can be the greatest enemy to our addiction, creating unpleasant emotions and feelings that promote our continued use. Communication has always fascinated me as I explored the words that are used that can be very misleading.

- "Everything you do makes me angry."
- "Everybody hates me."
- "Nothing has ever made me happy."
- "My entire life has been nothing but failure."

These are powerful statements that can defeat you. They're dishonest in their nature. Do you know everybody? No person, place, thing, or situation will ever make you happy because that comes from within. Failure doesn't exist, as we'll explore in a future chapter. Nobody can make you feel anything, unless you allow it. Unless you've tried everything, which is highly unlikely, hope can be possible so don't give up and let's give it a chance.

Many want to stay clean and sober, but how many are happy, confident, and optimistic in their recoveries. I realized many years ago that if I can feel good and be happy, staying clean and sober will be much easier. I want to live in a state of "positive paranoia." I had a professor who identified that idea. We're all students, and we're all teachers. Instead of feeling the world is out to get me, maybe the world is out to give to me. Let's keep that "open mind" and learn from each other. Life is a bowl of lessons, and each bite we take, we learn something new. Let's take all the pain, hurt, and sorrow and do something positive with it. Take a moment and think about how honest you're being with yourself.

- "I need to get high."
- "My pain requires I take these pills."
- "Life is boring without drugs."
- "Nothing works."

Statements like these are too black-and-white, with no variables to adjust, while honesty his meticulous by defining statements that understand the possibilities of change, circumstances, perceptions, and beliefs.

I've worked with many clients who feel that optimism is a form of lying because they believe realism is more honest. Optimism and pessimism are only the ways that we decide to view something. We're not changing facts but instead deciding to see things as problems (pessimism) or opportunities (optimism). Lessons or a curse? How will honesty affect your life?

Questions to Consider

1. What have others said to you that is different than what you believe about yourself?
2. What has your life experience taught you about your drug or alcohol problem or other problems in your life?
3. What generalized statements have you made that are inaccurate?
4. What is missing in your life that's stopping you from seeing the truth?
5. Can you define any lies that you're telling yourself or at least question the truth? How are these lies stopping you from seeing success?
6. How is your life out of balance?

Nothing is impossible unless you make it so.

CHAPTER 5

Let's Get Spiritual

Sentient creatures in a world that seems lost.
No meaning or purpose seems a norm that we cross.
The answer we reject, or often seem to lose,
I hate to say that the solution reminds me of you

An overture that set this game that is in motion,
Was from pain or a hurt with a bandage that was rationed.
I am sad when I think that my feelings are irrational.
To heal and to save is found through something spiritual.

You're a queen in my eyes and a staple to my throne,
Deserving of the best, a love you're always shown.
I will always be your rock, a friend that you can trust.
I am sorry that my words have tried to sway and crush.

The love I have for you has offered up a meaning,
I tried so hard to show you, but I know you are fleeing.
I feel stupid when I think that my feelings set me up.
How could I be wrong? It was happiness that set it up.

Control is my foundation and universal rock.
I can't understand how the pain made me stop.
Something hurts inside, as the answer is not right.
The mind plays awful games, and it's weak during the heist.

I wonder why I crumbled and lost my self-control.
Love has offered pain to set emotions to revolt.
I can't promote a blame, but tell me what to do,
To live in a path of righteousness and nothing to do with you.

To heal in this lonely place at a road I've never crossed,
Filled with empty words and crashed on jagged rocks,
I look above for purpose, some meaning to my life.
It dawned on me today that your timing was just right.

I've tried so hard to push you toward me and then away.
What am I to do when I've emptied off my plate?
Today I feel much better as I made a better score.
It's control that's back within me, and my spirit has opened the door.

Starting at the age of sixteen, while attending my first treatment episode, I was introduced to the twelve-step program, which became the only solution that I was offered. As the only solution to a life of being clean and sober, it started working against me, and many people fail to understand the reason for this. It seemed easy for a lot of people to state that if you worked the program as it's outlined, you'll stay clean and sober.

In this chapter, I'm going to discuss the conflict that arose for me, the troubles many find with the spiritual nature of that program, and how it changed for me, where we can find it, and many of the pros and cons to this simple program that I believe has helped millions of people, but the reasons why I'm no longer a participant. There may be

statements that contradict other statements, and this is because I believe that there's nothing wrong with the twelve-
step program as it gave me a foundation that I was able to
build upon. I realized that I needed more than this program
was able to offer me, and it began to inhibit my growth.

When I'm referring to the twelve-step program, I'm not
referring to just Alcoholics Anonymous but also to Narcotics
Anonymous, Cocaine Anonymous, Methamphetamine
Anonymous, and so on. All these programs developed from
Alcoholics Anonymous that was created by Bill W. and Dr.
Bob, who were influenced by the Oxford Group, a religious
organization founded by Frank Buchman. He believed that
selfishness and fear was at the root of everyone's problems
and that looking to God for his plan was where the solution
lied. Alcoholics Anonymous expanded the six steps from the
Oxford Group to the twelve-steps that we see today.

The philosophy of the twelve-step program is to find a
power greater than yourself (God), identify character defects, change those character defects with the help of (God),
make amends to those you've harmed, consistently evaluate
your performance and make amends as needed, improve
your relationship with (God), and help others by teaching
what you had learned. If people have a problem with that
solution-oriented approach, then don't go and maybe treatment facilities shouldn't force those who we know will never
embrace it to go and become statistics for the failure of the
twelve-step program.

The twelve-step program absolutely fits the principles
of problem solving that I've always appreciated about the
program. We identify the problem (step 1), we identify a
solution (step 2), we "make a decision to live in the problem
or the solution" (step 3), we follow through on the action
steps of achieving the solution (steps 4–9), we evaluate our

performance (step 10), we continue to improve our solution (step 11), and we share our newfound knowledge with others (step 12).

From my first introduction to the program up until today, the failure of that organization for me comes with the members, not what is in the text and teachings of the original program. Alcoholics Anonymous was founded in 1935 and things have been changed over the years in the teachings, perceptions, and opinions of members of the organization. I've always been very intuitive and struggled with contradictions I hear, which many times will cause me to lose trust and faith in something once it no longer makes sense to me. The Big Book, which is the main text for Alcoholics Anonymous, states that the steps are "nothing but suggestions." If I'm reading a book that defines somethings as suggestions then why am I being told that I "need to get a sponsor, work the steps, and go to meetings or I'm going to get loaded."

Stop Wasting Time

I'm not going to discourage the twelve-step program for anybody, and I encourage everyone to find your own way. When I was younger and heavy into my addiction, I spent hours and even days trying to argue and dispute things because I wanted everyone to think the way I think. Many of the problems with society today is that so many people tend to focus on debunking, disputing, or discrediting people, organizations, opinions, or ideas rather than identifying solutions. When I began looking at the world differently, I stopped blaming people and disputing opinions or ideas in lieu of identifying solutions to many of the problems I faced and how I could help people. It isn't surprising that our culture is accustomed to this practice because politics and religion seems to waste time identifying the problems instead of offering a solution-oriented approach seeking answers.

Presidential debates, especially what we saw in 2016, are more about discrediting, and in many ways defamation of character, than about solutions. As Donald Trump became president, he realized that he had limited control in certain areas of government and quickly blamed the other party for something he had promised to do during the election. The United States of America was designed with checks and balances to protect us from an individual being able to rule with an iron fist, and because of this, the president has limited control, which should be praised by all Americans. Personal interest seems to blind us from appreciating those checks and balances when you're in favor of the president's decision, but we enjoy the accountability when we're against the decision. We're a country that spends more time arguing and blaming others for things that have passed and less time offering solutions to improve the future.

Religion has always fascinated me because of the wars, murder, and hate it inspires, yet many believe in the same God. Christianity, Catholicism, Judaism, Jehovah's Witnesses, Mormons, and Muslims believe in the same God. All the books of these religions have many of the same characters, such as Abraham and his illegitimate child Ishmael. Rules are different, and interpretations vary, but God or Allah is the same according to those holy books. What I find interesting is that people have been murdered since the forming of these religions, for these religions, while believing in the same God. All these religions tell the story of Adam as the first human, which means we're all from the same family if we go back far enough—brothers killing brothers because of our beliefs. Many religions work to recruit but fail to understand the principle behind appeal. Is God love? Does God hate? Does God want bloodshed or comradery? Maybe, since God created all, He wants us to come together and learn about tolerance, patience, and forgiveness because if you believe in God, that's what God is, if you think about it. Without tolerance, patience, and forgiveness, we would be obliterated, and our world destroyed with a snap of his finger. Look around and imagine that you were the creator of this world—Tolerance, patience, and forgiveness.

I had a disheartening feeling when I came across a book by Lance Dodes, MD, *The Sober Truth: Debunking the Bad Science behind the Twelve-Step Programs and the Rehab Industries.* I've found very little benefit in spending my time with the attempt to debunk something that has worked for many individuals who've had long-term recovery. Many critics of the twelve-step program argue that there's only about a 5–7 percent success rate—therefore, it's a failure. It's estimated that twenty-two million Americans have a substance-abuse problem in the United States. That's 1,100,000 Americans who would succeed in the twelve-step program, according to the 5 percent statistics. The failure rate for the twelve-step program isn't entirely a fault of the organization but maybe a societal issued blamed on twelve-step programs for something that's out of their control.

For anybody to say that it's wrong for two individuals to create something that they believe works and test it on numerous alcoholics with great success is absurd. There's no secret behind the religious or spiritual nature of the program as you may define it, and many people accept it and believe it, as it works for them. Much of the failure that you may define as being the responsibility of the twelve-step program is invalid and an unfair argument. Much of the blame for the statistical failure, even though I'm not a fan of focusing on blame but rather on solutions, should be on facilities, the criminal justice system, and family or friends who force people to attend these meetings when the addicts have no intention of following through or embracing the solution Bill W. and Dr. Bob outlined. Maybe it's possible that only about 5–7 percent of individuals who come into the twelve-step program are interested in following the steps and traditions, which would set a 100 percent success rate for those willing to follow the program. I've yet to see many articles or debunkers of the twelve-step program with solutions to offer. Criticism leaves you stuck in the "box," while constructive criticism that offers new ideas will gain much more support.

The twelve-step program, as I mentioned earlier, offers a solution-oriented approach, with the first step being one of the most important things that all need to accept to remain clean and sober. "We admitted we were powerless over (the substance of abuse) and that our lives had become unmanageable." If you can believe that you're 100 percent powerless, you'll never use again. If you're 100 percent committed to achieving your goal, you'll succeed. Why do many relapse in the program? They believe that they are 80 percent powerless, which leaves them with 20 percent power. The chemically dependent individual will focus on the power. "I can use just once and stop."

Are We Weak?

While using, I had no ability to control my use, but once clean, that lack of control dissipated. An excuse that I've heard from many clients is that "I fell," "I relapsed because

I have a disease," or "relapse is a part of recovery." No, no, and no. As I mentioned before, recovery is when we take control back over our lives. There's no slip. There's no fall. Relapse doesn't have to be part of your recovery. It can if you choose. A relapse is a choice that you make, whether you're aware of it or not. It's your responsibility to manage your cravings. It's your responsibility to expand your awareness. It's your responsibility to direct your life. I've never had a syringe full of methamphetamine that just slipped and fell into my arm. When you're clean and sober, take the power you have and utilize it. Be proud of your recovery and learn to be yourself. I understand that many will disagree with the prior statements because of the harsh stance of the Big Book of Alcoholics Anonymous.

> **The alcoholic at certain times has no effective mental defense against the first drink.**
>
> **—Alcoholics Anonymous (43)**

> **The fact is that most alcoholics, for reasons yet obscure, have lost the power of choice in drink. Our so-called will power becomes practically nonexistent. We are unable, at certain times, to bring into our consciousness with sufficient force the memory of the suffering and humiliation of even a week or a month ago. We are without defense against the first drink.**
>
> **—Alcoholics Anonymous (24)**

As I encourage living with a mind that's energetic, lively, and spry, it's difficult for me to accept the black-and-white reality behind the prior statements. Relapse is defined as a return to use after improvement has been made in recovery efforts. There's a chapter in the Big Book of Alcoholics Anonymous titled "Bill's Story," where Bill W. returns to drinking after periods of sobriety, but did he have improvements because of his recovery? The solution that he found wasn't presented to him prior to him returning to alcohol. Therefore, it's difficult to insinuate that he had "no mental defense against the first drink" while in recovery because he found his story of recovery after his last drink. I've never met an individual who relapsed after recovery efforts who had no ability to decide an alternative, who mindlessly wandered into a bar after years sober, stable by their definition of recovery, who was controlled by the alcohol that they had yet to drink. We're not weak individuals, and those of us who have survived what became a death sentence for many have qualities that shouldn't be downplayed. Never underestimate your skills, strengths, determination, and courage because your life and purpose may be grounded in something great that you haven't seen yet.

Balance Needs to Be Taught

Recovery is about power. We're not weak individuals and, in fact, can utilize the passion we had for drugs and transform that same passion toward our goals. Even the first step of the twelve-step program clearly defines the powerlessness as past tense. "We admitted we were powerless." This is about taking power back over my life, which is only possible by staying clean. What I learned about power is that life requires an appreciation of balance that isn't taught by many in the twelve-step program. "All you need to do is get a sponsor, go to meetings, and work the steps, and you'll be fine" is a common phrase that you'll hear. This is one of the downfalls in treatment today. Does anybody have anything new? Can we think outside the box?

I recall a gentleman I worked with in the past who had been through five treatment programs and could not understand why he continuously failed. He claimed that he had a sponsor, went to meetings, and worked the steps as everybody always directed him to do. After speaking with him for about thirty minutes, it dawned on me to ask him a simple question. "How many meetings did you attend in a week?" As he began counting, needing his toes for additional numbers, I realized a simple step that would move him in the right direction. The answer he was looking for was balance.

Anytime that I feel overwhelmed in life, it's usually a result of my life being out of balance. If I'm going to twenty-eight meetings a week, which is what he claimed, what else am I doing to better myself? Nothing. How could he have any time to get a job, relax, exercise, spend time with family, or even have any fun? I directed him to attend one meeting a day for six days a week. Sunday was the day that he was to not think about recovery and to spend time having fun. He bought into the belief that many people have: "All you need to do is to get a sponsor, work the steps, and go to meetings, and you'll be fine." This is an untrue statement as it backfired on him.

Misperceptions That Can't Be Ignored

The twelve-step program has various teachings of individuals that conflict with each other. What is truth, and what is a belief or a perception? I was taught by members of the twelve-step program, which isn't an actual part of the program, that "we're not to make any major changes during the first year of our recovery." I've been told in the same meeting that "the only thing I need to change is everything." Which is it? I'm not opposed to the twelve-step program, nor do I agree with everything about that organization, which leaves me ambivalent. If we're to require or demand honesty from others, we must teach the same principles in a manner that's clearly understood and doesn't sway with perception.

For those who have attended a twelve-step meeting, you may have seen the following quotes, plaques, or signs. I don't think that we can dispute the sayings, but unfortunately, many of them are misunderstood or taken in a way that can become harmful. "One day at a time." This is a well-known statement that becomes an excuse for many to not look any further than today. It's true that the only moments we'll ever enjoy in life is right here, right now. I remember reading somewhere that the "past is gone, the future is nothing but expectations, and all we have is now." It's true that "all we have is now" to enjoy, but does my life experience give me the opportunities to grow through my mistakes? I don't have to dwell on my past, but my past gives me knowledge. If I don't plan, nothing will be accomplished. We must be able to find the harmony in planning for the future while enjoying the moment.

"Let go and let God." Do we throw our hands in the air and let God do the work? Another excuse is formed from this saying, **"Let go and let God."** Some individuals in the program refuse to make decisions about things because they enjoy saying, "I'll leave it up to God." I'm a firm believer that God doesn't want anybody to stay seated, put no effort into accomplishments, and wish for the miracle. For those who believe in the Bible, Proverbs 12:11 states, "Those who work their land will have abundant food, but those who chase fantasies have no sense." The Quran says, "Indeed Allah will not change the conditions of a population until they change what is in themselves." Aide-toi was a French society that had a motto, "Aide-toi, le cielt'aidera" meaning, "Help yourself, and heaven will help you." We can go on with various religions and cultures that have concluded "God makes those who make themselves."

What Made the Twelve-Step Program Impossible

The twelve-step programs solution is that a "power greater than myself would restore me to sanity." As an atheist at the time and being introduced to this organization at the age of sixteen, I was required to first believe that I was insane, which is almost impossible at that age, because I was invincible, or at least that's what I believed. I was then required to believe in a power greater than me and was told that it could be a doorknob if I chose. If I'm going to believe that a doorknob is more powerful than me, then I'm in real trouble. Post-acute withdrawal is taught in treatment facilities that identify symptoms that are experienced following the acute withdrawal. One of the symptoms is difficulty in abstract thinking, which can also create struggles for individuals in believing in God. It wasn't until I met this priest that everything changed for me.

Atheist versus Priest

I asked the priest, "Why can't I believe in God? I see many people who have this blind faith in something that helps guide them."

"Maybe you're asking the wrong question," the priest said.

"What do you mean by asking the wrong question?"

"Exactly," he stated.

I was very confused with his response, but he intrigued me. After being in custody for about a month, I requested a meeting with a priest, or spiritual advisor, because I was searching for something. I wasn't sure exactly what I was looking for, nor who I'd find those answers from, but I felt that this may be a good place to start. Having been in and out of the twelve-step program for twelve years in 2002, I felt that this spiritual connection was that one detrimental thing that I lacked, or at least that's what I was told. I undeniably felt that I was incapable in believing in God, and it wasn't from lack of effort. My understanding of effort was probably not real as I'd been to church with my parents, prayed when I felt I was going to die from alcohol poisoning, and talked to various pastors about my inability for abstract thinking. If I couldn't touch it, taste it, smell it, or feel it, it didn't exist. Believers would say that they felt God or God spoke to them. Why didn't God speak to me?

The priest told me, "God is everywhere and is everything. God will speak to you if you're watching or listening. God is waiting for you to come to him, but you may be asking the wrong question."

"You already said that and never answered. What do you mean by that?"

"Exactly," he said again.

I started getting irritated, and I asked him, "What is the question?"

He asked me, "How many times have you asked why? Why can't I control my drug use? Why can others manage it and I can't? Why can't I believe in God?"

"Yeah, I've asked those questions many times."

He answered his own question. "When you asked what you mean by asking the wrong question, I responded with exactly. Let's stop asking why and try something different."

"OK, what is a good question I should ask?"

The priest asked me to repeat the following, "God, I don't believe in you, but if you're there, please help me find you. Where are you, and what do I need to do?"

I was impressed with his tactics. He helped me pray such a truthful prayer, asking exactly what I was looking for. He transformed that "Why can't I believe in God?" to "If you're there, please help me find you."

The experience of that day will always be with me, and I'll never forget that. Just for the record, I never saw a blinding light or an angel appear before me, and I never heard a voice that told me what to do. The indescribable miracle I witnessed was nothing more than a desire to seek out this spiritual connection, this new way of life, and an understanding of some sense of purpose that had always eluded me. This new inspiration wasn't something that I'd ever felt before, nor did I think it was solely through my own power. Something happened that day that may have been from a source beyond my understanding.

Hold On before You Run

My father told me once, "You may not believe in God, but maybe God believes in you." This controversial topic in recovery is something you need to prepare for, as it will be thrusted upon you whether you embrace it or reject it. Life is short, and I learned many years ago that I wasted a lot of energy and time attempting to dispute and argue something that I didn't understand. The first, and probably the most important thing I learned from that priest at the age of twenty-eight, was that I know very little. The step I took that day was tremendously important, because for the first time in my life, I asked for help, and it was genuine.

Spirituality is a vague and misunderstood term to many of us in recovery. It has religious connotations that are forced down our throats by some, creating a stigma that pushes many out the door. Most information you hear from people is very subjective and at times wrong because of biases, perceptions, and information taught to them that may be inaccurate. As the analytical thinker that I am, we're going to dissect spirituality based on linguistics. We're going to break down this term in the English language.

I began this practice of breaking down words with clients who struggled with name-calling. I had a client who was a homosexual and was very reluctant to talk about himself and disclose his sexual preference with others because of the taunting he dealt with most of his life. An example we'll use is *faggot*. We explored the linguistics behind this word, and we realized it can be just as misunderstood in the English language as spirituality. It's unclear on the original origin, but *faggot* refers to a bundle of sticks. Slang is rampant in our society, as derogatory terms are used to antagonize, abuse, and taunt individuals. The interesting idea about the use of the word *slang* brings another topic of linguistics as ignorance prevails.

The earliest use of *slang* referred to the vocabulary of individuals that were classified as stupid, ignorant, and not considered to be respectable in character or nature. In many ways, *slang* is very similar today and lacks an intelligent, clear form of communication. I'm not calling anybody stupid who uses slang but instead a desire to get people to think about what you're saying. For those who are called derogatory names, just sit back and watch the ignorance unfold and just know that those individuals lack a well-informed vocabulary. Although spirituality isn't *slang*, we can break the word down to find the meaning according to the English language.

Sentient Beings

According to the Merriam-Webster dictionary, *spirituality* does have definitions relating to the church and religious values. It also identifies spirituality as "the quality or state of being spiritual." *Spiritual* is defined as "of, relating to, consisting of, or affecting the spirit." As we continue breaking down the relatable words, we find something interesting when we reach an understanding of the word *spirit*. *Spirit* has multiple meanings, and we're going to focus on a few that will fit in nicely with our newfound search for freedom, happiness, and meaning.

Spirit is defined as "the immaterial intelligent or sentient part of a person." Nobody can argue that humans are sentient creatures who question our existence. We have an intelligence that we believe sets us above the rest of the animal kingdom by our ability to seek answers to questions that far supersede our understanding. How did the universe come to be? Is there life in another universe? Is everything the Bible says true? Many have answers to these questions according to their belief system, but does that make it true? The human "spirit," according to this definition, is what creates this debacle and rage for many that ends in the murder of millions of people. Whether you're an atheist, agnostic, or religious, we all share a common goal of understanding our existences. Why are we here?

Spirit is defined as "a person having a character or disposition of a specified nature." Our characters, which was discussed earlier, can be a moral strength or a sense of integrity. Our characters will determine how we cope with things in life. Many get caught up with "morals" as being defined by a religion. Define your morals, but be careful because integrity states that what you define as right or wrong must be able to be reciprocated onto you. I believe that murder is wrong, stealing is wrong, and cheating on my wife is wrong. These are all identified in the Ten Commandments of the Bible, but does this make me religious? No. Let's not get too caught up on intellectual debates and use that inner knowing. Good decision makers can combine their intellects with their intuitions. How many times have you rationalized a decision while your gut was telling you the opposite? Our minds can manipulate while that internal feeling doesn't have that ability.

The *spirit*, according to the definitions in the English language, is real. Nobody can argue that humans, through all of history, have attempted to define meanings to our existence. We question many things and want answers. Our "spirit," based on our understanding of our existence, defines a set of morals that tell us how we address things that come our way in life. If spiritual consists of and affects my spirit, can I be spiritual without being religious? Yes, I can. My spirit drives me to find a meaning or purpose to my life and determine that code to live by.

Do You Have a Purpose?

Some never fully pursue or even contemplate this meaning or purpose of their life. Some never appreciate what they have until they lose it. On January 25, 2014, according to *Today.com*, Makenzie Wethington went skydiving for the first time on her sixteenth birthday as a gift from her father. It was a solo jump out of an airplane at 3,500 feet. Her parachute never opened, and she landed in a cow pasture in Chickasha, Oklahoma. Despite suffering multiple fractures, lacerated liver, and broken teeth, Mackenzie Wethington survived the fall and doctors expected her to make a full recovery. Was this a miracle, or could it be explained away with a natural explanation? Does her example violate the laws of physics?

It's estimated that a skydiver jumping out of an airplane will reach a speed of somewhere between one hundred and two hundred miles per hour, depending on many different factors of angle, wind resistance, and so on. What are all the possibilities that could happen, and was there any form of divine intervention? You'll justify an answer that's based on your belief system. The believer in God will state that his hand came down and softened the fall, while the atheist will justify the miracle as soft ground in a pasture softened the fall. The one thing that we can all agree on is that she easily could have died, and it's hard to explain. Too many people spend so much time and effort attempting to prove or disprove ideas, beliefs, and perceptions for things that are unexplainable. Can someone prove to me without a doubt the reason this girl survived?

Makenzie Wethington survived the fall and decided to turn her pain into a triumph, according to *www.DailyMail. co.uk*, and become a trauma surgeon to help others with life-threatening conditions. Spirituality, or that spirit, was a driving force to find some meaning or purpose in her life. Plenty of things in this world are unknown and can't be explained through reasoning.

Shannon Stone was attending a Texas Rangers game with his son and died after falling twenty feet from the left-field stands on July 7, 2011. How did Mackenzie Wethington survive a thirty-five-hundred-foot fall, while Shannon Stone died after falling twenty feet. He was conscious and speaking with paramedics as he was taken off the field on a stretcher but passed away sometime after. Why do some survive while others don't?

"Why did I survive my drug use while I watched many of my friends die?" This is a common question asked by many individuals I've worked with over the years. Maybe this is where spirituality comes into play. The one common theme, as we've discussed in this chapter, is meaning and purpose. No matter what your belief is about God or an afterlife, we all can have a purpose for this life. Spirituality is something we can utilize for the present moment, and it doesn't have to be related to your death. Once I stopped fighting the beliefs of others and focused on what was important to me, my spirit came alive and energized my existence.

I don't have to force my beliefs upon others, nor do I have to accept other beliefs. If science disproves a belief that I hold strong, where does it say that I must change my belief? Spirituality doesn't say that you must believe in God, nor does it require an approval from others. Spirituality is what creates your purpose that's derived from your belief system and molds your character based on your moral and ethical guide. Our society allows you to hold beliefs with free will, which can't be taken away. My pain has driven me to help others because my life experience has shown me the power behind drug dependency but also the ability to walk through it and proudly declare a solution that may be different than we see from others.

Why Did We Survive?

In 1992, I was sucker-punched outside of a Taco Bell, blacked out, and came to after the police had arrived. In 1998, I had the grand mal seizure while driving seventy miles per hour on the freeway. In 2001, I fell asleep while driving down the I-5 after running out of dope and miraculously exited at just the right moment. I broke an engine mount and cracked my oil pan, but I survived. In 2002, while I was in custody, I had a nocturnal seizure while sleeping on the top bunk, rolled off the bed, and landed on my forehead, cracking my skull. These are a few more examples of times I could easily have been killed.

The AVM that I mentioned was a ticking time bomb, according to the doctors. I was informed that over time the blood vessel would weaken, leading to a slow bleeding aneurism that could potentially kill me or cause a lifetime of neurological and physical impairment. Methamphetamine use constricts your arteries and induces a narrowing of your blood vessels that reduces blood flow, increases blood pressure, and possibly causes a stroke. How lucky was I to survive my use with an already-weakened blood vessel that will dilate over time? Do things happen by mistake, or is there something bigger that we're too ignorant to see?

What Is Your Potential

It's time we start looking at things a little bit differently. *Self-actualization* was a term used in numerous theories of psychology, but it became the most prominent with Abraham Maslow's hierarchy of needs. Not everybody reaches this level on the pyramid, according to Maslow, but is it possible for us to? Self-actualizers see the world differently and judge honestly. It's an ability to understand and see your flaws with acceptance and tolerate the mistakes of others. These self-actualizers are independent, true to self, and task oriented. Abraham Maslow believed that everything is miraculous, and because of this, it's ignorant to seek out miracles. Spirituality is an internal relationship with the "spirit" that motivates us to reach our potentials, the stars, and the cosmos. The moment that his subjects reached that self-actualizing stage, they had "peak experiences" of harmony, ecstasy, and deep meaning.

Why is this purpose important? This is what will make or break you in recovery and in your life. If you're unable to connect with your "spirit," as we've defined, and embrace a purpose or find a meaning to your life, you'll walk aimlessly and lose interest in staying clean. This spirit is our driving force. Allow your inner knowing the opportunity to answer the question that has evaded you for so many years. Seek within yourself, without any outside influence, the passion you require to fall in love with yourself, take back the self you may have lost, and grab your spirit—because you'll need it.

Spirituality is nothing to fear, fight, or reject. Appreciate the differences in others as we remain compassionate and develop deep interpersonal relationships. Let us learn to be able to sit still and be OK with it. How do we do this? Let us ask the right question. You can ask God, the wind, or that internal knowing. Read the following statement and question out loud.

"I don't have the answers that I'm looking for. I'm

asking for help. What can I do today to reach my potential? Help me find that spark that will set me free. What is my purpose? What is my purpose? What is my purpose?" Continue repeating until you find an answer.

Questions to Consider

1. What miracles have happened in your life that you can't explain?
2. What is your idea of "the meaning of life?"
3. Have you ever felt that you had a purpose but lost it because of your drug use? If it's still important, maybe you can get it back.

If spirituality can define a purpose and give us meaning, why do we want to push this away?

CHAPTER 6

A Motivation That Will Destroy Failure

A single word that is cast among the common,
Sold to a peddler for a fake jewel that was foreign,
Then carried by a ship that was smuggled by a sailor,
Only to be captured and branded a failure.

Her beauty was unmistaken as an interest soon took hold.
The track was simple to maneuver as my engine was easily fueled.
Once the rubber began to spin and the sparks began to fly,
I came in second place, but I gave it one hell of a try.

It wasn't long before I got the itch to bare it once again,
To feel the rush of adrenaline as I was sure that I would win.
The lights turned green, and I floored the gas.
I reached and held first place only to end up in a crash.

History has some lessons that we must not refute,
A character we have all heard of, and I will give you a simple clue,
God gave Noah instructions and built an ark with his sons.
Instead of giving up he saved the world, and surely, he had won.

Why throw away an opportunity to someday win the race?
Do I disconnect from my desire and travel to the east?
Do you fight for first knowing there is no guarantee?
Or do you settle for second and identify another to set you free?

I want to win this race but have been told there is no chance.
Comfort is set within me as a decision has been made at last.
We will set aside this track and focus on another,
But I will never forget that joy that I felt as we raced together.

Thank you for the experience that I learned from second place.
I will take the knowledge for my future goal and quickly up my pace.
This life we have is very short, and I want to have some peace.
I will find that track for first as second will surely cease.

To lose is not an option if I keep fighting for the gold.
To fail will never exist unless I decide to fold.
My smile that you see is the same that is on the inside,
As success will be the outcome if effort is your ride.

The reasons we do the things we do (i.e., motivations) are
based on our understandings of what we'll gain or what
we'll avoid. A drug abuser's reason to stop using will always
begin with a limited insight of working to avoid pain that
has been brought about by an external conflict, such as
family, friends, or the legal system. The ability to complete
something must be motivated by something that you have
full control over, which can't be based on anything outside
of yourself. I have no control over other people, things, or
places, but I do have full control over myself unless I give
that control away with drugs.

LSD

LSD and other hallucinogens have been discussed as a path to spirituality and even a cure for addiction with the idea that they will change your brain. I have many years of experience with LSD, and I admit that I'd enjoy more times with that drug because it isn't addictive, and it would be easy to rationalize that use with one major exception, which is control. Bill W. used LSD in the sixties, making it more acceptable to some, since he claimed that it didn't change his sobriety date. My experiences with LSD, and they were all good, taught me important lessons about control and motivation. I refuse to take LSD because I'll keep control of my mind and not allow a fungus that's found on rye the ability to change my thinking and set me up for failure.

The Mind I Gave Away

I fell into that rabbit hole in 1991 and remained lost, with periodic sightings until 1995. What a weird place. I think that person lost her house. He just gave away his daughter's college education. Why did they do it? What does it mean? Why am I thinking about these questions? I feel strange but good. I can't seem to turn my thoughts into words that I can speak from my lips. I just want to laugh, giggle, and smile. Everything seems funny, but nobody else is laughing. What is wrong with these people? Who are these people? I don't really want to look anybody in the eyes. Why do we need to anyways? I can't talk to them, and even if I could, why in the eyes? What if I talked to them looking at their forehead? They would still know I was talking to them, right? What a trip. Why am I here anyways? What am I doing? Oh yeah, I came to see the Grateful Dead in Las Vegas, but I'm stuck in this casino. They won't let me go. Maybe I can leave. I'll try that door. It's hot outside! That's right, I remember: the heat is locking me in. Inside, it's nice and cool. It's heaven. Outside, it's hot and miserable. It's hell! I'm trapped between heaven and hell. Let's walk inside, avoid the outside and try to plan an escape. Nothing is coming to me. Wait, I think I have it. When the sun goes down, it must cool down enough to let me run, and run, I will.

I was lost in a dream as LSD, peyote, mushrooms, and mescaline became a norm. I "failed" in my recovery, school, and vision I had for my life. Traveling from show to show, camping at a commune in Cougar Hots Springs, Oregon, and spending time at rainbow gatherings, kept me from being responsible, productive member of society.a

Hair was impressive as the night had returned
Locking the cellophane around a curve
Look at the purple flamingo upstairs
What do you see that is light as the air?
Call the space people that fly up above
Tell them we love them and offer a dove
Don't be so distant and visit us more
Why do we care just open the door?
Lemons are ripe to pick off the tree
Mash them and squish them quickly to see
Tell me a story of life that we know
It's the meaning that's lost and dark as we grow
I don't understand as my mind is askew
Nothing is clear so let's cast out a few
Hell is this place that we all seem to hold
But I lay down my cards and give up as I fold

This poem I conceived is an example of something I could have written while on LSD, but it makes very little sense while clean and sober. LSD had been tested in the '60s to expand the mind and discussed today by users in the same fashion. It has very little value when you're unable to understand the meaning after you've come down.

Was Failure the End of My Story?

Success is not final, failure is not fatal: it is the courage to continue that counts.
—Winston Churchill

This struggle we all have about failure isn't new and has been addressed many times by various people throughout the ages. One of the greatest twentieth-century writers, Francis Scott Key Fitzgerald wrote, "Never confuse a single defeat with a final defeat," and Thomas Edison said it best, when he stated, "I have not failed. I've just found 10,000 ways that won't work."

Was I a failure in life? If I ended the story in 2001, maybe I was, but the story doesn't end there, and in fact, success came from the many failures in my life. As Thomas Edison said, "I just found 10,000 ways that won't work." Even though I saw very little future for myself, I wanted to be successful, happy, and in control. The story that I described brings some interesting ideas related to our youth because I believe that everybody has a desire at some point to succeed, so why do some go in the direction that I did? Many children realize that control is far from possible when adults are always telling them what to do. I had great parents who loved their children unconditionally, which I witnessed, as they stood by me through the poor choices I made, but everything was decided for me, which sparked an interest in taking control where I could find it.

Through my years of education and working with parents, I learned that a healthy family is a family that helps the children make choices for themselves. We educate on consequences deriving from actions, allowing them to experience the consequences that will expand their awareness. Parents usually don't want their children to fail, but success isn't necessarily time sensitive and will come if the individual can let go and learn from the experiences.

Failure Doesn't Exist

The realization I came to is that being clean was the only possible way I was ever going to find what I was truly looking for. I searched for happiness in every place imaginable except for where it was, within myself. Every mistake I've ever made isn't a failure but instead an opportunity for growth leading me to the success I was looking for. Failure doesn't exist in my dictionary if I don't give up.

When I decided that I was going to change my life and do things differently, I started working on myself. I reached a point in my recovery where I was able to say that "I'm so grateful for all of the experiences, mistakes, and errors I'd committed because even though my actions don't define me, they have helped to shape me, and I love who I am today."

Something comes up for us when we're talking about the ability for everyone to secure success in a lifetime. Is everybody capable of reaching success, or are some destined for failure? We've heard the saying that we're all products of our environments. This is a highly debated topic that I feel needs to be explored. If you grow up in an environment with a brother who's a gang member, will you become a gang member? This implies that your chances are much better in joining a gang than someone who isn't exposed to that lifestyle, but is it a requirement? I worked with a client who was a member of a white-supremacist prison gang. He'd grown up with a father who was a member of the KKK. He undoubtedly claimed that he was a product of his environment and failed each time because of that belief. His story isn't over yet, so failure may not exist for him either.

My father grew up very poor and lived in a single room in Santa Ana with my grandmother and his stepfather. He taught me, through the story of his life experience, that it's possible to bring yourself out of struggles and rise to success. Success, just like recovery, is a process filled with many tests, tribulations, and scars, but those scars allows your triumph to mean something much bigger than if it was given to you. My father fought hard to achieve his goals and worked each day to rise to his dreams.

I've heard many times from the less fortunate individuals excuse after excuse of how they'll never succeed because of the "products of their environment." I believe that no matter what your upbringing looks like, you can do anything you want if you're willing to fight for it. We've all heard of these stories so why are they different? The answer to this is commitment. Those people who grew up in poverty, beaten because of their race, raped by a family member, or caught up in criminal activities that sent them to prison were committed to the changes that they fulfilled. If you want to stay clean and sober and achieve those life goals that you're seeking, you must be 100 percent committed to fulfilling that dream.

No matter what your misfortunes were in your life, you're responsible to let them go so they don't consume and destroy you in the present time. *Forgiveness* is often a misunderstood term that many people feel requires a sense of remorse or regret on the responsible party. Once we understand that we have no control over other people, but we do have full control over ourselves, we'll begin to see the power we hold. I don't need someone to say he or she is sorry or repent to forgive someone. Forgiveness isn't what we do for other people; it is, instead, a release that I do for myself. I let go. Forgiveness is letting go of all the anger, hatred, and disgust for the words, actions, or behaviors of other people. Why would I choose to hold onto these negative feelings that are affecting my life by waiting for something that I have no control over. Would you stand in the middle of a highway expecting the car to swerve around you? I hope not. Why do you expect someone to say he or she is sorry? Expectations will surely harm you emotionally.

Let's remove failure from your dictionary. Every experience you've ever had in your life can be a lesson. I had a goal to get a doctorate in psychology, which I never fulfilled. Did I fail in that vision? No, I didn't. I can choose to return to school and receive that doctorate, or I can go in a different direction, which is what I've currently done. That goal of being a psychologist took me through school as I learned and became more intrigued in the study of human behavior. Nothing is a waste of time if we're willing and able to gain lessons through each experience.

The Power in Words

There's an enormous amount of power behind words that we use in relation to our sense of power. "Have to," "need to," and "should" are statements designed to control. You don't have to or need to do anything. Do you have to go to work? Do you need to stay sober? You should go to bed. You don't have to, need to, or should do any of those things. I choose to go to work. I choose to stay clean. I choose to go to bed. Say each of those statements aloud. I choose to go to work. I choose to stay clean. I choose to go to bed. That's empowering. Once we realize that we have choices in life, we'll now experience a sense of freedom. "Choice is the father of freedom."

Now is the time to rewrite your dictionary and remove all the words that take your power away. Have you ever heard that words hurt? Words don't hurt. I've never been able to throw, smash, cut, or shoot a word at someone to cause physical harm. It's not the words that people say that hurt someone. It's the meanings behind the words that people say that hurt us. It's time we remove the buttons we have that people can push to control us. I control me. I create my destiny.

Motivation, or the reasons that we're getting off drugs, will have the greatest impact on your success and enjoyment in being clean. To maintain your motivation to stay clean, it must be based on something that's within yourself and not through anything or anyone that's outside of your ability to control.

Why Do We Do What We Do?

Everybody does things for a reason. *Psychology* is defined as the "study of human behavior." Why do we do the things that we do? Everybody on this planet does things because they want to. There's no other reason that we do anything. The common misperception of human behavior is that we, at times, will do things that we don't want to do. I disagree. The only reason we ever do anything is because our choices are structured around a desire to either benefit from positive consequences or to avoid negative consequences. Both options revolve around that premise of human behavior in doing only what we want to do.

Everything we do, we do for a reason, and drug-and-alcohol use are no different. The reasons why drug or alcohol use began for most people is because they were told it's cool, it feels good, or maybe a doctor prescribed something for pain or anxiety. Pain will be required to motivate you into having a desire to stop. Wait a minute. Didn't we decide that pain is a factor in continuing our use? How is pain going to stop us or at least motivate us to go to rehab if that's what keeps us using? For the purposes of educating the uninformed, I'm going to reiterate this idea again and hopefully allow those who have never experienced this, the opportunity to step into the mind of an experienced individual and see the insanity and challenge behind drug and alcohol dependency.

My Motivator

The reasons why people continue the use varies across the board. Methamphetamine triggered a false sense of security, motivation, energy, concentration, and made me more outgoing. To use myself as an example and the experience of watching others use with me, I can attest that we experience positive results in the beginning, which are not bad things in and of themselves, that triggered my desire to continue using them. The problem that we all face is that by the time they stop working our bodies have become so dependent to maintain allostasis (that new norm our body has created) that it seems impossible to quit.

"Pain is our greatest motivator." First, we can all agree that when we do something that feels good, we naturally want to continue doing it. I don't think that anybody will disagree with this. Putting aside the reason we first attempt it, which is usually because it sounds fun, something happens to us that resolves some internal conflict, feels good, and eliminates pain. In my case, methamphetamine didn't relieve physical pain but instead confused my emotional pain so I didn't care about things negatively affecting my life. I was benefitting from my use, and there appeared to be no down side, so I continued with the use. As days, weeks, and months went by, my body began changing to accommodate for the substances that I was putting in my body. The more I used the less impact the drug had on me. My tolerance was going up. The reason for this was that my neurons, which are important for feeling good, were being killed off. I was numb, and pain was my greatest motivator to continue using. How could pain motivate me to get clean while pain was motivating me to continue using? The answer to this is simple yet difficult to put into practice. The pain must be more powerful to get clean than to continue using, but this is what we define as being "between a rock and a hard place." All drugs of abuse lead to this same conclusion but can look slightly different with heroin, alcohol, or sedative hypnotics as they continue using to avoid physical pain from detoxification. Why do we continue to do what we do? Avoid pain.

I Am So Impulsive

Impulse control is a struggle that many have in our culture in general. We live in a fast-paced society that requires we think on our toes or opportunities may pass us by. Many times, we must decide without having the time to think things through all the way, so we must train ourselves to be able to do this quickly. How many times have you decided something, only to look back and regret that decision you made? Life is a bowl of lessons.

When I decided in 2003 to return to school and study psychology, I was nervous and had very little confidence in my abilities. My prior attempts at college had all been failures up to that point. Due to the mistakes I'd made in school prior to this time, I was committed to doing it differently. I was going to participate, study, and ask a lot of questions. I'd always been taught by teachers that "there are no stupid questions." Dr. Alibrandi, the professor I had for my first class returning to school, stated on the first day, "Many people say that there are no stupid questions. I disagree. A good question is a question that leads to another question, while a stupid question ends there." I'm sure you can understand at that moment that my heart sunk.

Impulse control is a process of looking at your options and asking yourself questions of what could happen, will happen, and might happen. If I ask myself, "What will happen when I use drugs?" and I identify pleasure as the answer. This leads me to another question of the long-term effects, which will get me to think more long-term. The strategy of impulse control proves Dr. Alibrandi's point. Every action in our lives have a consequence. There are positive and negative consequences to everything that we do. Those of us that make good choices in our lives, think about the consequences before we do things. Is it perfect? No. But it will allow us the opportunity to make the best choice that we can make with the information that we have. The art of impulse control requires that we identify all the positive and negative consequences to every option that we have. Many clients I've worked with over the years use impulse control as an excuse for not getting better. "I just keep making bad decisions because I have poor impulse control." This gives the counselors and therapists an opportunity to teach the skills required to make better decisions.

I'm going to ask everybody reading this book to do a simple exercise. I want you to identify an upcoming decision that you're going to need to make and follow my instructions. For those who have a substance-abuse problem, I request that you use *sobriety* and *using* as your two options. The first step in decision making is to identify your possibilities. On a piece of paper, write your identified option number one at the top of the paper. Draw a line down the middle of the page and write positive on one side and negative on the other side. The exercise entails that you complete this task for each of your views. Write your list of positive and negative consequences to each of your options. Based on the information you gather, you'll then have a better chance of making the right decision. This requires that you ask good questions that will lead to other questions. I have never had a client do this exercise and decide that using was the best choice.

Motivation Inspired by Pain Will Never Last

The pain I experienced in my life that was the greatest motivator was all the contributing factors, such as being arrested, physical health declining, family refusing to support my behaviors, and my friends either dying or in custody. I was all alone on January 3, 2002, when I was taken back into custody.

The question I'm asked the most by families is "is there hope for my child in staying clean because he or she has failed so many times?" The answer is always yes. Why is the relapse rate so high for these individuals, and where do they go wrong?

They don't have a motivation that they control. Everybody is originally motivated by moving away from a painful experience. I've never had anybody come into treatment without some form of pain in their life. Getting arrested, getting a divorce, being homeless, or loss of a job can be the pain they're experiencing. Read this very carefully: a motivation from pain will never last. These are all temporary consequences that will either resolve themselves or go away. Once they disappear, using will return, and new pain will arise, sending them back into the cycle of recidivism.

The premise of human behavior we discussed earlier says that we only do what we want. Nobody wants to go into rehab, so why are they full? Why do people want to go to rehab if nobody wants to go? Nobody wants to go. Everyone wants to go. It appears we've reached a conundrum. If we only do what we want to do, then how do we do things we don't want to do, which we do all the time? The answer is simple. The reasons become "something that we want to do," or the things we didn't want to do now become things we do want to do. I don't like to do dishes or laundry, but I like to wear clean clothes and to eat off clean plates.

Pay Attention—The Motivation That Lasts

Clinicians make mistakes when they only reinforce the pain that brought them into treatment. "If you leave, you'll get arrested." For any of us to take control of our motivations, me must utilize those things that we have control over, such as our dreams, vision, passion, and goals that can drive us. Instead of "pain as our greatest motivator," let's rephrase that statement into "dreams are my greatest motivator." Look at the success stories in recovery, and we'll all find a common denominator. Success in recovery demands that we identify a path, set goals, create a vision, and find a passion of something that means more to you than the drug itself.

What is the motivation that will last, and is it something that we have control over? Motivating ourselves by moving toward good things in life is the answer to that question. Getting clean because I don't want to lose my marriage, don't want to get arrested, or don't want to be homeless are temporary reasons, while wanting a college degree, wanting to be happy, or wanting to be successful are long-term answers. People get clean because of what they don't want, while people stay clean because of what they do want.

> **You cannot escape the responsibility of tomorrow by evading it today.**
> **—Abraham Lincoln**

This is the opportunity for you to write your book. If you had a blank white canvas, what would it look like? Success requires a direction to know where we're going and why we're doing it. It doesn't require all the answers because things will change, allowing us the ability to alter our paths.

In 2009 when I opened Serenity Life Counseling, I knew what I was going to accomplish. I didn't know exactly how I was going to do it, but I knew two things that were going to make it happen. I was committed and confident. This outpatient program was directed by a strong passion I had for alternative sentencing. I wanted to work with the criminal justice system and help give people an opportunity for good treatment rather than sending them back to prison. The problem that I faced was that I knew nobody in that arena, and my record with the criminal justice system was severe. How was I going to gain access to individuals in custody to assess them, and how would I gain access to the judges to gain their confidence?

This complex scenario required creativity, problem solving, and courage to stand tall when I was rejected. That vision was a driving force that consumed me, day and night. I remember a counselor who told me, "All you need to do is to suit up and show up and put one foot in front of the other." I hated that saying, but it clicked and finally made sense. I spent hours and days going from one courtroom to another, asking the bailiff if I could speak to the judge, and getting rejected about 70 percent of the time. I got rejected 70 percent of the time. "The glass is half full?" I met with about 30 percent of the judges. I requested clearance to visit inmates at the Orange County Jail and was rejected time after time. Failure after failure. Failure couldn't exist so I eventually got it. Perseverance, consistency, and never giving up gave me success. I continued going to the court-houses and meeting with private attorneys, public defenders, district attorneys, and more judges. We began receiving an average of ten calls a day from the jails and fulfilling my goal of providing good quality care with the criminal justice system. A six-time convicted felon was meeting with the district attorneys, private attorneys, and judges in their chambers, discussing the release of inmates into my custody for treatment.

No matter where you've been or what you've done, you can do anything you want if you put your mind to it. Will you have disappointment, rejection, and frustration? Yes. Will you struggle with doubts at times and worry that your efforts will be for not? Yes. Will you want to give up at times because things are not working out the way you expected them to? Probably. I think very big and have many things I'm working on that have no solid steps in place to make them happen. I have the goal in place and the "problems" that I know I'll face. I work very hard to practice what I teach, and here's another one. I have no problems in life; I only have opportunities. Each opportunity that I have will offer me a lesson that will move me closer to achieving that goal.

I'm no longer controlled by pain in my life. I am motivated by my dreams, visions, and passions. This book that I've written has been a long-standing goal which began over seven years ago. I was very unhappy with the original version, and I restarted writing it this year, 2018. For every person reading this book who has struggled with alcohol or drug use, I may present a conflict that goes against your current lifestyle.

Goals that will truly mean something to you require effort and that you "defer immediate gratification for that goal." Every dream that you desire will rarely come quickly. The struggle with many is that you want everything right here and right now. Let's remove "I want it now" from our minds. I'll tell you that I want it when it's complete. In this new life that I live, I want everything that I work hard on to be the best that it can be. I'm not looking for mediocrity or anything that will "do."

Perfectionism is a quality that should be avoided, as this will prevent many things from being accomplished and completed. I've started many things that I pushed aside because they didn't meet my standards, which are very high. If you feel that something you're working on doesn't meet your standards, give it to someone else to evaluate, because a different perspective can give it a new light. If this book has been published and you're reading it, I've passed it over to another set of eyes for review, as I'll change it many times because I'm my worst enemy in critiquing my work.

Having confidence that you'll succeed is what will determine your success. I don't have all the answers, but what I do know is where I can go to start finding those answers. My program began as a goal, as I mentioned, but the solutions were not as clear because I had no professional experience in the alternative sentencing arena. How did I do this? My business partner and I planned a grand opening for the facility to introduce ourselves to the public. We invited representatives from the sheriff's department, the chief of police from Anaheim, parole officers, probation officers, therapists, counselors, and judges. This event was the answer that I was looking for to answer the question that I presented above. You go to the source.

Those of us who are always looking to improve and move toward better things in life will have a passion for something, and helping is that drive that I have. The substance-abuse industry, which is where my passion originates, is being torn apart by the unethical, immoral, and illegal activities of many providers. A group of us are fighting for a common goal of restoring ethics back into the industry. None of us have all the answers, but as a group, we're exploring different avenues. I'm going to discuss this in a future chapter along with ideas of how to improve this problem. We know what the goal is, but unfortunately, some of the answers are still evading many of us. We'll succeed and accomplish our goal, but we must be patient and not jump too quickly.

I'm motivated today by a strong passion to help people who have gone down similar paths to me, and I offer the lessons that I've learned, teaching clinicians an approach that's effective. I control this motivation, and it can never be taken away unless I hand it back over to the drug. The only way for me to fulfill my goals is to stay clean, stay committed, and remain excited about the possibilities.

Pain is something that we must work through, so be careful about holding on to it. Now that we're becoming honest with ourselves, have eliminated failure from the equation, and have defined a motivation that will last through our goals, dreams, and vision, it's time that we learn to love and appreciate ourselves. If I can truly love and care about myself, using drugs or alcohol will no longer be important. What will be important is a desire to reach your ultimate potential, and this is where things get fun. If pain is the motivator, healing will offer the opportunity for success.

Questions to Consider

1. What goals do you believe you've failed at? Do you still want to achieve those goals? What is keeping you from achieving them?
2. What is a goal that you want to achieve in the next thirty days? Six months? One year? How committed are you at achieving them?
3. What can you do today to move you toward your goals?
4. What negative feelings are you holding onto?
5. What has pain motivated you to do?
6. What (major) goal do you want to achieve?
7. How can your goal motivate you? Remember that people get clean because they don't want pain but stay clean because they do want to achieve their goal. Once you achieve your goal, set a new goal.

If your attempt at something fails, you can now move to the next strategy that you've identified to achieve your goal. Failure is nothing more than an attempt that didn't work. Move to the next method. I'm motivated to do what is best for me. I use to find life mundane, but now I find it exhilarating.

CHAPTER 7

Loving Ourselves Will Spark the Flame

The most famous of tragedies is a Shakespearian tale
of two feuding families, and a love that would kill.
It was the party by the Capulets, the place where they met.
Romeo and Juliet's fate was carefully set.

Love has a power to transcend as it holds,
Risking death for exile, and breaking all the rules,
A broken heart for you to bear, as love was up for grabs.
He was unsure of the goal as he saw her on the slab.

A story that is classic, that we will never set aside,
Her death was designed to live, as it wasn't passed on right.
Romeo's lack of knowledge led him to take his life.
Juliet saw what he had done and jabbed a dagger led by strife.

This mystery that drives us creates a meaning for our existence,
Nothing more important than this spark that you will get.
That tale of a double suicide has something they ignored.
There life was set on another, not a love that truly soared.

We enter this life alone, with nothing that really matters,
To leave this world, we step aside into something that's unknown.
Who is the most important person in my life today?
They're not outside but instead inside, so don't you look away.

The Post set the conflict of the hawk, with a jess around each leg.
The crisis she created favored an air strike on that day.
The dove refuted the plan of war and whispered from above.
Peace is that image of harmony, so look inside for love.

Standing on the mountain, I was lost above the clouds.
I saw an image in the distance and tried to scream and shout.
The fear that had consumed me, which was all that I could see,
The relief that finally settled in as the image was of me.

It doesn't matter what I did since an action is not you.
They have shaped my life and nothing more or have offered up a tool,
Grateful for all the lessons as today I am happy to be,
A man of integrity as I can help and show that I love me.

Fear Can Be Our Enemy

In 2016, I married my best friend, who was an inspiration
in my life. We'd been through a lot together, including a relapse, divorces from our prior spouses, and a mixed family
that included two of my children and three of her children.
Fear was one of my greatest weaknesses in life that had
kept me from doing many things that would have helped
me while continuing to do many things that harmed me.
Uncontrolled fear is the most dangerous emotion for an
individual in recovery.

About a year prior to my wedding, I decided that I
wanted to create my vows through music. We both decided
to write our own, but I wanted to play and sing a song,

with my vows read halfway through the piece. I had two dilemmas that I faced with one being that I've never played or even picked up a guitar in my life. The second revolved around my fear of singing in public. Sure, I sang in the car or in the shower but never in public. Being a Grateful Dead fan, I decided to play and sing one of the very few love songs the Grateful Dead performed, "If I Had the World to Give." I bought a guitar, hired a teacher, and started my lessons because I was determined to accomplish this. A year may sound like a long time to prepare for one song, but it was not. I had to learn the chords, rhythm, and then singing while playing at the same time. It reminded me of patting your head and rubbing your belly simultaneously? I practiced and practiced as often as I could and became more frustrated as time went on. The day was coming closer, and I'd forget the chord changes, forget the lines, and was out of rhythm most of the time. I kept thinking that when I was on stage, the time had arrived, and I was on the spot, I was going to fail. There's that *failure* word that kept creeping in my mind.

I'd learned something many years prior to this in 2003 when I'd received a phone call from the owner of the rehabilitation center that I was in, requesting that I meet with the district attorney and speak with him at an H&I (hospitals and institutions) convention. Public speaking was a terrifying experience for me, and I'd have refused that offer in the past, but I accepted the invitation because I was trying new things and listening to advice. The DA was interested in meeting with an individual who had a prior drug problem and experience with H&I while in custody. Many people may think it can be challenging to share your story with a sponsor; well, I can tell you it may be easier than sharing your story with the district attorney. I shared about my drug use, family issues, and crimes that I was arrested for as well as crimes I committed that I'd never been arrested for. It was an amazing lunch, but fear kept me uncertain of how productive that lunch would be, as I was still going to have to speak in front of hundreds of people.

Appreciation Is the Answer

The district attorney and I reconnected for the convention, and he spoke, telling much of my story as an example before introducing me. I walked on the stage and attempted to stay calm and speak clearly and insightfully. I did something that allowed me the ability to keep my fear from controlling me, and it stemmed from appreciation. For the first few minutes, I told H&I members that "I truly and genuinely appreciate you for spending your free time visiting me and bringing hope for my life that I thought was lost." Genuine appreciation removed all my fear, allowing me to continue speaking intelligently, confidently, and comfortably for another twenty minutes. Years later, I read a book by Dan Baker, PhD, and Cameron Stauth titled *What Happy People Know: How the New Science of Happiness Can Change Your Life for the Better*, which explained the phenomenon. I learned that appreciation was the strongest outbound kind of love, and it's about the idea of giving everything and requesting nothing.

Science has stated that your mind cannot be in a state of fear and a state of love or appreciation at the same time. This was the answer to eliminating fear, or at least taking control of my fear. Appreciation may be the cure to fear. Try it out yourself sometime. When you're fearful, uneasy, or anxious about something, begin to think about appreciation, love, and gratitude. What do I truly appreciate today? What am I grateful for?

On the day of the wedding, my vows and performance of the song was perfect. I didn't miss a beat or forget any of the lyrics, and I stayed perfectly in rhythm. I was in love, appreciated my new wife, and was confident in my vows. It was the perfect mix of feelings to keep that fear at bay. I can say with my life experience that fear is something I've learned to control. That's what this is all about. The more confidence, love, gratitude, goals, and responsibility I take for myself, the more control I have.

Creating What You Believe

Albert Bandura, a Canadian psychologist, came up with self-efficacy theory. Bandura (1995) explains that it "refers to beliefs in one's capabilities to organize and execute the courses of action required to manage prospective situations." This is what I believe I can accomplish using my skills under certain situations. Do I believe that I can get and hold a job? Do I believe that I can stay clean and sober? Can I structure my life in a fashion that will allow me to balance all my activities to not become overwhelmed?

To remain clean and sober, as I'm hoping that you're working toward, requires you to take proactive measures to prevent relapse. The nature of life is about changing circumstances, situations, people, places, things, and feelings. Stagnation will destroy you as the world is changing around you and leaving you unprepared. I no longer find change frightening, and I embrace the possibilities with open arms.

Within a week prior to my release from custody, an uneasy feeling created a hope that a new charge would be filed requiring that the sheriff's department not release me.

This fear that I had wasn't a sign of being institutionalized or enjoying the idea of incarceration. I wanted to be free, but I had no confidence in my abilities. I was clean, stable, and happy in custody, but I didn't trust myself under new circumstances. I trusted my instincts and decisions while I was behind bars, but I had no idea what decision I'd make when I walked out those doors.

Once the spark is lit from the love we have for ourselves, a harmony will begin to develop and a relationship with various components will exist together without destroying one another. Self-esteem is a term that's so highly misunderstood and is rarely taught in a manner that can be utilized from people because it's so vague. If I were to ask you if you believe that you can stay clean and sober under any circumstance, what would your answer be? This is a question related to confidence in your abilities, which is a component to self-esteem.

> **If I have the belief that I can do it, I shall
> surely acquire the capacity to do it even
> if I may not have it at the beginning.**
>
> **—Mahatma Gandhi**

Living proactively is to manage my life by seeking and changing according to the unexpected. What new trials and tribulations will I encounter that will need to be considered? When I see my drug of choice, how will I respond? What new triggers, feelings, and struggles will I encounter? Recovery is about learning to live in a world where drugs and alcohol exist while not having to use myself. Let us not run from drugs but instead conquer the plight of relapse.

Self-efficacy states that I believe that I can stay clean

and sober no matter what circumstances arise in my life. This belief that I have will allow me to execute my skills to manage the situation that arises. I could have saved a lot of time by explaining very simply how to stay clean and sober in the beginning. How do you stay clean? Wait for it! Don't pick up and use. Simple. The complexity lies if you're seeking much more then to just stay clean and sober such as happiness, confidence, self-esteem, and a genuine desire to be trustworthy and successful.

Believe that life is worth living and your belief will help create the fact.

—William James

As I began studying the concepts of self-esteem and learning to teach the principles, I realized that self-esteem isn't something you can wish, hope, or directly work on. Instead it's a result of action taken to promote self-efficacy, self-worth, and self-respect. If I set small tangible goals, such as waking up at 7:00 a.m. every morning instead of a normal habit of waking up at 10:00 a.m., things will change. Simple tangible goals that show that I'm progressing or changing a habit that will benefit me in a positive way will increase confidence.

Learning to love myself is a process that will require a first step of accepting myself. Carl Rogers, an American psychologist who was among the founders of the "humanistic approach" to psychology, stated, "The curious paradox is that when I accept myself just as I am, then I can change." Many people feel that acceptance requires that I approve of something or it's something that I can't change about myself. Acceptance has been defined as the precondition to change. Before I can change anything in my life, I'll first need to accept it as real. I must first realize and accept my drug problem before I can change it.

- "I can control it."
- "I can stop anytime I want."

These are statements that dispute any acceptance to having a problem, and there's no need for me to change anything.

Many things about ourselves can be changed once we accept the reality of the situation. Some things about ourselves will require we change our beliefs. The deep seeded beliefs that we carry about ourselves can either help us or harm us in our current life.

- "I'm ugly."
- "I cannot stay clean."
- "I'll never amount to anything in my life."
- "I hate myself."

How many of your beliefs that you carry were forced upon you as a child by your parents, teachers, and friends. What we're told as children may begin to define us as adults. I've worked with clients who have struggled with eating disorders that have proven the harmfulness of many beliefs that don't hold any validity to the real world. If you have a female who is five six and weighs eighty-five pounds, how can she rationalize her belief that she is fat? An ideal body weight for a female who's five three is approximately 126 pounds.

Males and females in our society are blasted with information about beauty through magazines, newspapers, commercials, billboards, movies, and social media. These airbrushed images and "perfect" models are relentlessly stamped in our minds as the way we're supposed to look and the image we're demanded to portray. Advertisers are relentless and consistent. They target your emotions to get you to stand up and buy what they're working to sell. Emotions are that neurological impulse to create some action in your life. Advertisers can be our greatest enemy when we're talking about self-image, but they can be our teachers in changing deep-seated beliefs that harm us.

Affirming the Truth

Just as the Wright brothers watched how birds fly to learn about flight, we can watch how advertisers promote their beliefs and use their tools to create change. Positive affirmations have been used for some time to change beliefs that we have but we'll refer to a similar practice that I like to call "affirming the truth."

"Affirming the truth" is any positive self-talk that we can utilize to help us reach our greatest potential. Affirming the truth is an affirmation that ends with "I'm speaking the truth." This ending will create a powerful "truth to your statement." In 2004, when I was delving into self-esteem, I started looking at and changing my belief system into something that empowered me. I held a strong belief that I was a failure and was never going to amount to anything in my life. Beliefs, just like feelings, are not facts, because they're not constant and will change based on circumstances or situations. Just because I believe that something is true doesn't make it so.

I began creating positive affirmations that were based on certain rules that were designed to make them most affective. I was taught that affirmations must be positive, written in "I" statements, and written as if they're currently happening at this moment in time. What belief do I need to have to achieve what I want? This was the question that I needed to answer. I still remember to this day the affirmation I created to destroy that negative belief I identified before.

"I'm capable of achieving anything I put my mind to and will succeed at achieving my dreams." This was the affirmation that began changing my life. Just as advertisers are relentless, consistent, and self-defeating at times, I was more relentless, consistent, and self-assured. I struggled in the beginning with fully absorbing that affirmation as true, but I realized through this experiment that just because I didn't believe it didn't make it untrue. I believe that affirmation with all my heart, and I can achieve anything I put my mind to. I was living in a sober-living facility when I started this practice and would quietly go into the bathroom and repeat this in my head, five or six times a day. After about two weeks, I started saying them out loud as I stared confidently at myself in the mirror. I eventually became so comfortable with this affirmation I added a spark to my statement. You can compare the difference between the statements, but once I started "affirming the truth," a new level of realness crept in. "I'm capable of achieving anything I put my mind to and will succeed at achieving my dreams. I speak the truth." That second statement would reaffirm the honesty of what I'm saying. "I speak the truth."

Unleashed Power of Words

We have a power that we can allow to roar through our thoughts and words. Years ago, I created a format for a group that tested this theory. I'd collect all the clients who reported that they were angry, anxious, or sad, and I sent the rest of the clients outside of the group room. I'd inform the clients that I was going to step in front of each person, shake his or her hand, and say something to them that I wanted them to confidently say back to me. I stepped in front of the first person, shook his or her hand, and stated, "I appreciate you and wish nothing, but good things come to you in life." I went from client to client and repeated that statement, with them saying it back to me. Following my involvement in the exercise, I requested that the clients verbalize this with each other. With eight clients in the group and them repeating this positive statement nine times each and hearing this positive statement reinforced to them nine times each, something happened that they couldn't possibly explain verbally, but they did feel. Every single client reported a shift in themselves that went from either angry, anxious, or sad to a sense of relief, happiness, and enjoyment in that moment.

This exercise did two things for those clients: 1) It took all their worries, stressors, and anxiety about tomorrow and spun them into the here and now; 2) It showed some validity to the idea that our brains, through positive thought and activity, can rewire and strengthen areas of the brain that stimulate positive feelings. Since the 1970s and 1980s, neuroplasticity has gained attention in the medical community that shows that networks of neurons can change their connections and behavior through new stimuli and rewire itself. This is the science that gives hope in recovery when we look at the amount of brain cells we may have killed during our use. Dead brain cells never come back, but neuroplasticity allows our brain to function as well as possible with what it has.

LOVING Yourself

What does it mean to love ourselves? We've all heard the saying that "for you to be able to love someone else, you must first be able to love yourself." Is this true or just something someone came up with as a thought terminating cliché. What is love? I'm going to leave that answer up for you to decide, but for the case of argument, I'm going to explore the answer as an action instead of a feeling. Love as a feeling isn't something I can give to anybody, but as an action, I can show you my appreciation, gratitude, and adoration. I cannot give something to someone else unless I possess the material item, quality, nature, or skill that I've developed. Any action that we've mastered requires a skill that must have been practiced for a consistent period. Love is that action that must have been mastered on a personal level to be able to share with others in your life. Let us learn what loving yourself means so we can share this with others by example.

I created an acronym to allow you to see what LOVING yourself can look like. This isn't an all-inclusive list but can get you started on that path of adoration, care, and effort we'll put into finding success. Loyalty, Open, Vigilant, Infer, Nerd, and Golden (LOVING) will spark the flame to reaching your greatest potential.

Many families and clients I've worked with over the years held strong premises that it's selfish for them to think about themselves first. Some would discharge treatment early because their wife or husband was angry, demanding they stop being selfish and return home to help the family. One problem with this argument is that if they're not stable enough to stay clean and sober outside of a structured treatment facility, a relapse will reinforce that "selfish" nature

causing them to leave home but putting them in a dangerous position of homelessness or even death. The twelve-step
program offers a paradox that says, "It's a selfish program,
but the only way you get better is by helping someone else."
Loyalty to self doesn't mean you push others away but instead taking care of our own needs first. Being loyal says
that no matter what mistakes I've made, hurtful things I've
done, or what standards I've violated, I'll not give up, give
in, or lose faith in my abilities. I stand by me, with me, and
for me each day no matter what comes down my path.

When I was new to the industry, I worked for a facility
that worked with young adults who knew "everything." I've
never figured out a good way to teach people that understand
all things especially as a human who isn't all-knowing.
Frank Zappa said it perfectly: "A mind is like a parachute;
it doesn't work if it isn't open." Knowing I know very little
has taught me the most. Being *open* to information, gaining
feedback from others, and looking within ourselves without judgment or expectations will bring many unexpected
lessons. Sadly, many of those who knew everything became
statistics in fatalities.

As we discussed earlier, having a proactive nature in
our recovery is required to succeed long-term. To truly love
myself, I must be anticipating for future problems, needs, or
changes that I can consider making to alter a path for success. Goal setting has a standard of reviewing the feedback
that we receive from our actions in determining whether
we're succeeding or failing. When I'm *vigilant* in my needs
and goals, I'll succeed by changing my course as needed.

As we move away from assumptions, expectations, and
perceptions that can all be false, I begin to *infer*, which is to
draw conclusions based on facts. Every negative belief that
you carry about yourself that harms you today is either false

or a perception that you have, and we can change this. The love that you have for yourself will change those negative beliefs because now you speak the truth. When I started as a counselor, I created an image that was based on my perception of what a counselor is supposed to be like. I acted in a way that wasn't genuine or true to me, which made it very difficult. One day, I decided to be myself, and everything instantly became easier, more efficient, and more affective.

When I was a kid, I made sure that I was never portrayed as a *nerd* because of how uncool it was. It's funny as I think back and wonder how successful many of those nerds I made fun of are today. Times have changed, and with TV shows such as *The Big Bang Theory*, a nerd is seen in a somewhat different light. Why not be a nerd today as we seek out intellectual and academic pursuits? No matter what your age, go back to school if you have that interest. Dr. Alibrandi, my professor, believed that students shouldn't start college until they're thirty because that's when people take it seriously. Her rebuttal to students fearing they wouldn't get their master's degree until they're fifty was "Well, you're going to be fifty anyways. You might as well be fifty with a master's." What's a nerd? Someone who is intelligent, smart, and has academic and dreams of a career? Let's become nerds and succeed.

Loving yourself can be seen through a radiant smile, joy, hope, and childlike demeanor. Pleasure seems to be dismissed for many in recovery. "Life is going to be so boring sober." No. Pleasure isn't something we're giving up and in fact, a main reason why I decided to get clean was because I realized that being clean and sober was the only way I was going to experience pleasure for the rest of my life. I want you to go out and have fun this week. You deserve to be happy and you deserve to enjoy life. Many people live to work, but because I love myself today, I work to live. This is *golden*. Be golden and treat yourself to something special.

What does it mean to love ourselves? It's an action in which I show, through my behaviors that I'm loyal to myself, I have an open mind to learn, am vigilant to achieve my needs and goals, I make conclusions based on facts, act and learn like a nerd, and I am golden to myself. Everything that we've talked about are ideals. Ideals are things we reach for but will miss the mark at times. When we make a mistake or catch ourselves moving backward, this is when we regroup and fix our errors. Every mistake that we make is an opportunity for growth. Once we can take one lesson from an experience, that experience has become another link we can add to the chain. Let's start looking at the world a little differently. Love yourself because you're worth it.

Questions and Exercises to Consider

1. What do you fear?
2. What negative beliefs do you carry that harm you?
3. What are you trying to achieve? Change the negative belief you identified.
4. Write a positive affirmation directed toward what you're trying to achieve. Remember to begin it with "I" statement, must be positive and must be written as if it's happening at this moment in time. Make sure you end it with "I'm speaking the truth."
5. Stand in front of the mirror and state each affirmation five times, five times a day. Do this for one month and see if it changes anything.

Loving yourself will be the most powerful way for you to stay clean because it's genuine.

CHAPTER 8

The World Can Look Different If You Choose

An author and an activist, unlike you would ever see,
She was blind to the world but saw better than me.
To listen to her speak could be hard to understand.
But she spoke beyond clear to the unfortunate first hand.

To see something today doesn't always make it real.
It often is an illusion that is twisted by how you feel.
What about the kiss that was magic on that day?
A glimpse of something more gave hope that was betrayed.

Black-and-white is limited with no shades of gray.
My way or the highway is a loss of goals today.
Let us remove the barriers and those sharp and jagged rocks.
Open up your mind, and let's look outside the box.

Hate is an expression that is told through many stories,
Like Hitler and the Nazis, who slaughtered in the forties.
The color of a person does not improve your game.
Love and hate is the difference, and then we are the same.

Choice is the power that we define as freedom.
To let go or let in can be our ultimate demon.
To open your heart and then open your eyes,
Can conflict with your nature and then be penalized.

Letting go of an illusion is the paradoxical gain.
You can't find another until you have allowed for the pain.
Poetry has metaphors that are true to the author,
A story of love yet a tragedy we foster.

The meaning we see can be different if we choose.
Don't think through my mind as you may construe,
Nothing is certain, but there is one thing I know of,
As my heart is not empty and it's full of love.

Regrets are abundant as we think what might have been.
I will never be certain but not allow this again.
Choose to be happy and don't let the world pass you by.
What can you lose if you give this a try?

Death as an Excuse

Many years ago, I lost an individual in my life, which devastated me, caused guilt that nearly killed me, and became
an excuse to increase my drug use. When I returned from
Maryland in 1998, I moved in with Granny, my father's
mother, who I was very close with. I felt that she was the
only person I could confide in about my struggles, pain,
and heartache that was primarily self-induced. I was using

methamphetamine, and even though we specifically never talked about the actual use, she encouraged me to eat and made remarks that showed me that she knew something was off. She was eighty-seven years old but had a spirit that was young and vibrant, changing the way I viewed her, specifically in relation to her age. She never appeared old to me, even though she was deteriorating physically, with severe osteoporosis causing a bone in her back to mysteriously break. In 1999, she moved into a supportive housing community that allowed her to be independent while individuals assisted with some things that became too difficult for her to do on her own.

I moved into an apartment with some friends where my drug use continued, and I received a page—if you remember pagers—to call my father. He informed me that Granny had heart pain and checked into the hospital. I went to visit her prior to going to work and told her that I'd come back to the hospital at 7:00 a.m. the following morning to visit her. At 6:30 a.m., I got off work and decided to go home to get high. I forgot that I'd told her that I was going to visit. At around 10:00 a.m., I received a 911 page from my mother. She asked me to come to the hospital immediately. When I arrived, my mother informed me that Granny was gone, having passed away at around 9:00 a.m. It took a minute to register, but I broke down in tears. I could not forgive myself for not visiting her at 7:00 a.m. even though witnessing her death wouldn't have been any easier. How can we look at this situation differently or view the world in a different light?

As I mentioned, the loss of Granny became an excuse to increase my use as I buried my emotions, and I wasn't able to see anything beyond "death" until many years later. Unlike heroin, methamphetamine doesn't have the same numbing power regarding emotions, and it can make things more difficult to manage. Many years after her death, I changed my view of her loss into a more powerful gain. I became grateful for the many years she was in my life and the knowledge she gave me of her life experience that allowed her to live on in others. The death of our friends and loved ones can be the most difficult experiences of our lives, and if we're unable to cope, manage, or deal with the loss, many of us will fail, and recovery will seem impossible.

Death isn't a unique experience to anybody and coping strategies can be passed on if we are open to learning from others.

Granny was an example of a life full of losses, and she was able to grieve in a healthy manner that never destroyed her. Her first husband, my dad's biological father, passed away in the forties, and her second husband passed away in the sixties. She experienced loss of her parents, siblings, friends, and family members throughout her life, yet she was able to cope and continue to live on.

Advocacy Can Change the Way We View the World

I recently had an opportunity to meet with Jodi Barber, an advocate against the overprescribing of prescription drugs, and learned about where her passion came from. Her son, Jarrod Barber, had broken his collarbone and was pre-scribed Vicodin that he quickly became addicted to. Like many of our youth today, Jarrod went doctor shopping, seeking out prescription medications for abuse. On January 8, 2010, at the age of nineteen, Jarrod overdosed on the family couch with a cocktail of medications that included opiates, antidepressants, antianxiety medications, and antipsychotic medications. We're seeing this similar story happening across the country with the rise of this opioid epidemic. Jodi Barber lost her son, but that story doesn't end there. The loss of her child became an advocacy that has saved the lives of many people including the creation of two documentaries: *Overtaken* and *Overtaken 2: Where Are They Now*. How do you move on after burying a child?

Jodi Barber contributed the following statement that I'd like to share for all the families suffering from the loss of a child.

"There's no other option when I have another beautiful son who was born happy and needs me. If I'm not happy, Blake won't be happy. Would that be fair to him? No way! He and my husband deserve all the happiness in the world. I don't have to work for happiness when they're around. Do I have my moments when I just want to scream out loud, wishing for my son back? Absolutely, and I think about him every minute of every day. Would Jarrod want me to be sad? Absolutely not. He loved me very much and wants me to live on and work to save lives— the reason why God took him."

Jodi Barber is an amazing lady who has given the loss of her son a purpose. Jarrod didn't die in vain while his loss has saved thousands of lives.

You begin by looking at the world a little bit differently. The greatest mistake that people make is by avoiding or numbing the feelings that naturally come from a crisis in your life. I spent years numbing my pain from my excessive drug use that delayed all the progress I may have made. It wasn't until I was clean and sober that I was able to feel the anger, sadness, guilt, hurt, pain, and sorrow that I needed to be able to stand up tall and utilize those emotions to make them useful. Anger isn't a problem and it can teach us what we truly care about. "We never get angry about things we don't care about."

Our response to our anger is what gets us in trouble and I've learned that when I'm angry, not to make any decisions at that moment in time.

Once I can resolve the anger, my decisions become much healthier and more productive. Allow yourself the opportunity to feel and talk about those feelings, and over time, you'll find that they have much less power over you. Own and embrace your feelings.

Get Outside the Box

I've worked with families over the years and the most common mistake that people make when expressing feelings is to say, "You make me feel." Nobody can make you feel anything. Counselors and therapists will tip toe around clients because they "don't want to hurt the client's feelings." It's not your responsibility to protect someone's feelings if you're being honest, respectful, and informative. When we take ownership of our feelings, we take control away from others. I choose to no longer be a victim and give anybody any say in my feelings.

The typical thinking pattern in our society is black-and-white. Black-and-white thinking will never allow you to see the world very differently because it will keep you trapped inside of the "box." Some self-help meetings, many treatment facilities, and some families are consumed with "my way or the highway." I've had conflict with many professionals in the industry who claim, without a doubt, that the twelve-step program is the only way for people to succeed.

How can that be possible if I have friends who have years clean and sober who have never stepped foot in a twelve-step meeting? When we blend the black-and-white together, our eyes begin to open as we begin to see the shades of gray.

One way that we can begin to see the world a little bit differently is when we're able to focus on the similarities rather than the differences. When I focus on the differences, I push people away and leave myself alone to ponder the answers that others may have already solved. I can't tell you how many times I've heard from clients that they can't learn anything from the individual with an alcohol problem because they're a heroin abuser or even a client working with a counselor who hasn't had a drug problem in their life. These statements are designed to create a separation and many times an excuse to avoid dealing with their problems because of this self-induced distraction.

I had a counselor when I was housed in an in-custody treatment program at Theo Lacy who was one of the best counselors I've ever had, and she never struggled with chemical abuse. She taught me the true definition of empathy. Sympathy, which is what counselors shouldn't embrace, is to feel sorry for someone, while empathy is to have an understanding. We can understand things without having ever gone through something ourselves. How was I able to work with females who had eating disorders while never having had one myself? We do it through the ability to identify similarities and having that understanding we refer to as empathy. Some factors that play into eating disorders can be psychological such as low self-esteem, lack of control, anxiety, and depression. Social factors of societal pressures and cultural norms of body image, and interpersonal factors such as being teased for body weight and inability to express emotions and feelings. These are the things that I can relate to and find the similarities that can make me an affective counselor, not the overeating, anorexia, or bulimia. Similarities are what will allow me to connect with people and through synergism, we may be able to accomplish things together that wouldn't have been fulfilled independently.

Let's Work Together for the Common Goal

Too many times, I see internet posts or hear arguments from clients stating that "addiction is a disease" or "addiction isn't a disease," but they have no informative facts to back up the statements. When we begin to look at the world differently, we decide to open our minds and start understanding the ambivalent nature of things. If you're a fan of SMART Recovery and believe that addiction is unhealthy behaviors caused by irrational beliefs, or you stand strong on addiction as a disease, stated by individuals in the twelve-step program, can you explain what those mean and why those organizations hold those beliefs?

Here is a tool for those who spend time arguing the cause of addiction, from what some may say are trivial arguments. Know what the facts are on both sides and have a clear understanding of why each of those organizations or science believes the two models. I've heard counselors who state opinions as if they're facts while never considering the possibility that they could be wrong, as opinions are usually based on your life experience, potentially putting clients in danger if they're wrong.

I identified the cause of addiction above as trivial to some, which I'm going to explain. I've taught the premise of addiction being a disease as well as the cause that's identified in SMART Recovery, which required the ability to understand the ambivalence. I realized, and spoke to numerous colleagues, some agreeing with me, that whether it's a disease or a behavior, does it really matter? The only real benefit in understanding the cause of something is that we'll have a clearer understanding of how to treat it. Dr. Kevin McCauley, creator of an award-winning DVD, *Pleasure Unwoven*, explores and argues the medical science explaining addiction as a disease. He does have the best explanation to validate the argument.

The Big Book of Alcoholics Anonymous never states that addiction is a disease unlike what most people claim, but instead an illness. The original term *illness* isn't something we can argue as fitting an alcoholic. It's defined as an "unhealthy condition of mind and body."

SMART Recovery utilizes rational emotive behavioral therapy (REBT) that was created by Albert Ellis in order to identify irrational beliefs that will naturally affect your behavior. If we change our beliefs, our behaviors will change, and we'll get better. SMART Recovery isn't a "higher-powered program," doesn't believe that you need to attend for a lifetime, and focuses on self-reliance and self-empowerment. What if these two organizations came together, identified their similarities, and were able to blend solutions to create something new, more affective and more powerful. These organizations appear to be working against each other when they're working toward the same goal.

When we look at the trivial aspects of defining the cause of addiction, many people miss the point. Whether I have a disease or not, I know what happens when I use methamphetamine, which would be no different than I identified earlier. The cause doesn't matter because my life will fall apart either way. Many of the points identified in the Big Book are valued as well as the evidence in SMART

Recovery. There are many paths that you can take that can work for some and not for others. Let us stop arguing and find what works. Your life story can be magnificent if you find the right path.

We Choose How We View the World

Life has thrown me many curve balls such as the closing of a residential detox facility I started, an arteriovenous malformation (AVM), which is a tangle of abnormal blood vessels connecting arteries and veins in my brain that has caused grand mal seizures, and losses of family and friends because of substance-abuse problems. If I lump these together as the poor-me syndrome and focus only on the deficits, depression, and anxiety, it will likely consume me and send me into a tailspin. Maybe what I'm seeing can be viewed in a different light if I choose. The initial shock of trauma or losses can be devastating and leave us in a state of confusion causing a desire to sleep, avoid life, or trigger angry feelings, pushing us to act on a whim and poor choices begin to develop. What if we were able to turn our pain into a victory? What if we were able to turn our greatest weakness into our greatest strength?

I choose today to view the world in a different light by my optimistic vision. You've heard the saying "when a door closes, a window opens." Nothing is constant, and what may seem like a failure becomes an opportunity for something new. It has taken many years for me to master the mind-set of positive thinking, yet nothing is perfect today. Our views of the world can be twisted by our perceptions, thoughts and ideas, and can change in an instant. Think of a time when someone can say something to you, and it doesn't affect you in any way, and when it's said the next day, you can fly off the handle. Nothing has changed but your perception or situations that arose that have escalated your feelings. When you're driving and someone cuts you off, it usually isn't something someone did as a vendetta against you, but you decide to take it personally. That person may have been cheated on by his wife and needs a pardon.

I've known many people who had views of a world that didn't exist and who would attempt to take you with them. I live in a world today where I no longer allow people the ability to make dishonest statements and take it personally. How many times have you been accused of something that you didn't do and fly out of control to prove the dishonest statement?

I choose to love, I choose to forgive, I choose to have freedom, I choose to control my emotions, and I choose to see the world in a positive light. You can choose a life that's in your control. I have no control over other people, but I do have control over my associations, goals, and dreams. When you say no, it drives me to find that path where you'll say yes. Happy people enjoy this moment and look forward to opportunities in the future, while angry people regret the past and hate this moment. My past is gone, but the lessons I gained are useful. Today is a blessing because I choose to enjoy the moment, and the decisions I make today will open a new door for tomorrow that's unknown and yet exciting.

Questions to Consider

1. What do you waste time focusing on by blaming when you could spend time solving?
2. Who or what do you separate from by focusing on the differences?

3. Looking at those people, organizations, or qualities, what similarities do you see?
4. Try this. Talk to someone who holds very different beliefs than you, (i.e., politics, religion, or sports) and just listen to them without judgment or persecution. We want to understand their belief. How was it? Could you do it without arguing your side?

To give or take is the two words that will define your world. Which do you pick?

CHAPTER 9

Who Am I?

The years I betrayed the standards I set,
Have confused and pushed me much closer to death.
It's sad when you reached out as I climbed up a tree.
I was defined by my actions and told this was me.

I have been numb to the world in recent times,
Looked down that road and walked a fine line.
My morals and values didn't seem to exist,
As I cared for a moment and returned with a list.

My words and my actions were not in line.
I was destined for habit and would never find.
The person I lost, and it was many years ago,
Was gone in a flash with a snort of blow.

I'm nothing but to be viewed in shame,
An image I portray as crazy or insane.
I'll steal your heart as I push and shove,
Then tell you a vision, and it was all in love.

Wait just a minute as my head clears up.
I remember the day and I had to interrupt.
When my word was important, and motives were right,
I cared so much more, and I gave a passionate fight.

Everything seemed to come together
Lifting was easy and light as a feather.
It was the journey I made that was all in line.
But start where you are, and it will all be fine.

Love was something that I gave up.
The piece of life and the purpose erupts.
Respect for myself was that thing that I missed.
It was integrity I lost with a change that would twist.

I never was shown as my teachers instruct.
It never was intentional, but I would often seem fucked
I was ready and willing to give up and die.
To be lost in a shadow and not know who am I

To define yourself is to limit yourself. Without labels you remain the infinite being.

—Deepak Chopra

You're Not Your Actions or Diagnosis

- "I'm an addict."
- "I'm bipolar."
- "I'm a schizophrenic."

How do you label yourself? As Deepak Chopra says, "To

define yourself is to limit yourself," so in other words, when you label yourself, you limit yourself. I spent many years of my life labeling myself by my actions. Labels are useful at times but when we're defining who we are, we must be careful. How do we introduce ourselves in twelve-step meetings? We do this through a label. "My name is Eric, and I'm an addict." What do addicts do? What do alcoholics do? We use, and we drink. Do these labels influence your behavior? Do these labels unconsciously reinforce the behavior you're working to avoid? I'm not discouraging the practice as it may help many people, but instead I'm offering questions to consider.

I've seen the following quote by Mahatma Gandhi in treatment facilities and twelve-step meetings that, if true, will prove my point.

> Your beliefs become your thoughts,
> Your thoughts become your words,
> Your words become your actions,
> Your actions become your habits,
> Your habits become your values,
> Your values become your destiny.
> —Mahatma Gandhi

If I believe that I'm an alcoholic and I verbalize this from my thoughts, the label becomes my actions. Those actions, which is to do what alcoholics do (i.e., drinking), become a habit. That habit is what becomes important to me. And what is important to me becomes my destiny. Your destiny is those events that are set to happen to you in the future. You may notice that I haven't used the word *addict* or *alcoholic* anywhere in this book up to now, nor will it be used in the rest of the book to define any characters. I've heard people identify themselves in twelve-step meetings with a label that has a positive twist to it. "My name is Eric, and I'm a recovering addict."

Don't label yourself because we're not our actions. We were the ones that committed those actions, but that isn't what or who I am. It may seem inconsequential to use the twelve-step program as an example, but negligible ideas may compound other labels that can become severe. In 1991, I left a traditional society and entered the counter-culture of the more modern-day hippies. It was a life of traveling, communes and rainbow gatherings in between Grateful Dead concerts. What is the picture that you create in your mind when you hear the word *dead-head*? If you were born between the 1940s and 1970s, your image would most likely revolve around the saying of "sex, drugs, and rock and roll." That image is very correct and defined me for many years. That label that I defined myself as, kept me in that world because we were opposed to "working for the man." I'd be lying to you if I said it wasn't fun and enjoyable at times, but I did learn many things throughout that experience and probably witnessed many things that others may not have had the opportunity to be a part of.

I was labeled for many years by others and accepted those labels as my own, which kept me trapped in those behaviors. I'm not those things that I've done and needed to learn how to separate myself from them for me to get better. I was taught many years ago the difference between guilt and shame and how devastating shame can be for us. Guilt is a response to feeling bad about something that we've done while shame is when we become that thing that we've done. "I feel bad about stealing from my mother" is a statement of guilt while shame says that "I'm that bad thing that I've done." Doing and being are not how we define ourselves.

The Mind Power That We Possess

Our words, thoughts, and beliefs have some of the most powerful influences on our behavior as Gandhi had identified. Many don't understand the true power we have simply by believing wholeheartedly in something. In 2002, I'd pled guilty to six felonies and numerous misdemeanor offenses. As many individuals believe, I thought my life is over. Who is going to hire a six-time convicted felon? Why would anybody ever have faith in me ever again. While I was in custody, I had plenty of time to think, read and study, which I spent most of my time doing. I had very little confidence in my ability to stay clean, let alone get a job and hold a job. I disputed every one of the doubts I had about myself after getting out of custody.

"No matter where you've been or what you've done, you can do anything you want if you're willing to fight for it." I heard that many years ago and was empowered by that statement. I worked with a gentleman who had spent seventeen years in prison for attempted murder. When he was seventeen years old, he had shot a rival gang member in the head who had survived. He was sentenced to fifteen years to life because he committed the crime for the benefit of a gang, which added enhancements and allowed them to charge him as an adult. He was one of the nicest, motivated, and patient individuals I've ever worked with and he proved that idea. He wanted that life that we all dream about and figured out a plan that he was willing to fight for. He secured a job at a fast food restaurant and enrolled in school, majoring in business. I'm unsure on how he is doing at this point, but the last I heard was that he was proving people wrong and living a life of integrity. An ex-gang member who was convicted and sentenced to life for attempted murder is a productive member of society and studying business. This is only one story of thousands who have eliminated that stigma. If any of those people can do it, so can you. The only difference between those people and others that fail, is that they gave up or weren't willing to battle their demons or societal views hard enough.

Values Hold a Key That We Must Unlock

Who am I? This is a difficult question for many individuals early in recovery to answer but can be the most important question to think about. Rarely do counselors or therapists put much emphasis on helping their clients identify who they truly are as an individual:

- "You're an addict."
- "You're depressed."
- "You're bipolar."

These are all labels that hold many serious symptoms that are reinforced and may trigger future relapses. Much of the behavior of an "addict" doesn't fit in with the true values or morals of that individual. I've facilitated many groups on the topic of values and helping them embrace those things that are very important to them at that moment in time. What do you value and what is most important to you? Family, friends, happiness, sobriety, and health are the most common answers that I've received regarding what is most important to them. If family, friends, happiness, sobriety, and health are most important than how could anybody choose to relapse and throw all of those away.

An individual who is dependent on drugs or alcohol will hold one value, which is to get high or drunk. Since that's the most important thing to them, all their behaviors, thoughts, desires, and interests will revolve around that substance. If you're a family member and feel that you're not valued by a loved one who is currently abusing substances. You aren't. Does your family member love you anymore? Probably, but we must remember that substance abuse has nothing to do with love. It has to do with an obsession to a chemical that causes a physical dependence to function, and a mental change that creates beliefs that "I can't live without it." With awareness and an understanding of what I value clean and sober, I'll not use methamphetamine if I'm able to hold onto my values. For me to relapse, I must eliminate my awareness for it to make sense to me.

How Do You Define Yourself?

Most people early in recovery define themselves by how they compare to other people or only focusing on negative attributes. We're not talking about roles, relationships, or behaviors when we define ourselves. This isn't a job that I can do for you, but I can help identify areas that you can look for. Integrity is the foundational principle that will guide you in the right direction. Integrity is living out this "who am I" question by showing the world through your words, ideas, and behaviors a person of undeniable greatness. A person rarely seen in the world we live in today and the opportunity to look at things most people don't. The more dysfunctional you become, the more visible your unhealthy traits are. An individual who is sober, relapses, gets sober again, and relapses will live in a world of hypocrisy.

Integrity entails the integration of our values, morals, standards and behavior that we choose to live by. If I feel that treating people with respect is a moral standard that

I live by, then my behavior will show this. If I believe that stealing is wrong, and I choose to steal after a relapse, I've violated my standard. This is the reason why many in recovery can't answer this question well, especially if they have been using for many years. You may have spent time violating your values and morals and living a life without integrity, creating a disconnect in understanding what is real or not. This concept we're discussing requires the ability to behave in a way that isn't reliant on other's behaviors, actions, or attitudes. If my respect is dependent on getting respect from others, then I won't have integrity because this is based on something I have no control over. This is an ideal that allows us to make mistakes, learn from these mistakes, and change them based on the lessons we've gained. Pain, failure, misery, and mistakes are the stepping stone to success. Happy are those who feel life and grow from an opportunistic suffering.

Pain and Suffering Saved My Life

In 1998, based on a police report that was reported by a witness, I was driving seventy miles an hour down the I-5 in the fast lane and had a grand mal seizure. It was 7:30 a.m. on a weekday, and I entered the 5 at Bake Parkway, and that was the last thing that I recollect. I drove approximately twenty-two miles with no memory of the event and past two major freeways during rush hour. The actual seizure happened in Anaheim as I swerved into the carpool lane hitting the center wall, crisscrossing the freeway, and hitting the right wall so hard the front right tire folded underneath itself and parked me in the shoulder. I hit nobody. Do you believe in God? Many of us have stories of miraculous events that question the existence of some power that may have guided us. I have, and that was just one of many. That accident caused financial hardship, loss of license, and enough pain to save my life.

In 1994, I had a grand mal seizure in my apartment and was diagnosed as having an AVM that was mentioned in an earlier chapter. The doctor informed me that an arteriovenous malformation (AVM), which is a tangle of abnormal blood vessels connecting arteries and veins in the brain can eventually cause an aneurism. Every year that passes, I'd have a 4 percent higher chance of having an aneurism because of the weakening of the blood vessels. The cure was brain surgery, which I was unwilling to do, and I pretended for many years that the doctor knew nothing regarding what he was talking about. If I don't believe it, it must not be real. I lost my license for four years because I refused to continue seeing the doctor. I acquired my license back, two weeks before I had that accident on the freeway. It wasn't an immediate decision to remove the AVM, but in 1999, I decided to take care of the condition because of all the pain, problems, and hardships it had caused. The accident saved my life.

It was a good decision, even though it wasn't for this reason that I waited until 1999 to have the surgery due to the improved technology compared to 1994. UCLA ran tests and identified the AVM as being too close to the area in my brain that controls speech. They informed me that if they removed the AVM with traditional brain surgery, I'd either have a difficult time talking or even speaking at all. The decision was made to perform a procedure known as stereotactic radiosurgery. This alternative surgery was more advanced than the gamma knife but would not immediately remove the AVM and could take up to three years if it even worked. I decided for this option, and in 2000, I had the surgery. An MRI confirmed in 2003 that the procedure worked, and the AVM was gone. The accident saved my life.

Who Are the Experts?

Who am I? I'm intelligent, passionate, and driven. How much research, opinions, speculation, and theories of chemical dependency are being conducted or presented by individuals who understand first hand, the power behind addiction. You can run experiments in labs or randomly pick individuals for studies and never truly understand the minds of those suffering. From personal experience, my chemical dependency reached levels that were far out of the realm of any control I could maintain. Many researchers argue that the tolerance that's developed will cause the user to increase the amount to get the "same" high. Some insurance companies are refusing to pay for methamphetamine, cocaine, and heroin detoxification because it won't kill you. The treatment industry has now put more value on therapists, psychologists, and addiction doctors because they can charge more, and some of them have no personal experience with chemical dependency.

Being an individual in the industry who has college education and personal scientific research, I've found very little benefit with book knowledge when it comes down to the nuts and bolts of working with the clients. I rarely hear things from the clients that I haven't felt or said at one point in my life.

In 2001, when I was at my worst, I wasn't using methamphetamine to get high because it wasn't possible. I was using for the sole purpose of staying awake and being able to leave my motel room to get more drugs. It wasn't pleasurable, but it was the only thing I valued to function each day.

I loved my family very much, but the value of methamphetamine superseded any ability for them to physically see me or experience the love I had for them. Without being locked down or the assistance of a detox facility, I'd be dead today, and for those who don't have experience and disagree with me and or call me weak, I ask you to test my experience and make it yours.

Who Am I?

Who am I? I'm determined. I'm determined to make a difference, and I'm speaking out against the atrocities in this industry. Who am I? I'm the person that will speak for those who have no voice anymore. I demand that we have experts working in this industry instead of degrees. Who am I? I'm a survivor, which is defined as someone who lives after going through something where many people have died. All individuals who have survived the near-death experiences of chemical abuse are survivors. This survivor quality carries many traits that we own and can utilize if we choose that can help define us. Surviving that lifestyle requires creativity and improvisation that can help you become a great leader. When I'm myself, I'm genuine, caring, loving, in control, and passionate, without any worries about what other people think about me. I'm reliable, honest, respectful, and I'll go the extra mile to help others and myself. All the qualities that I look for in people are naturally important to me; otherwise, I wouldn't seek those out in others.

I choose to only associate with individuals who respect me, are happy, and have a purpose that directs them. Why is this important to me? Respect, happiness, and purpose intertwine within each other and create characteristics that become enjoyable experiences to associate with. I respect all values, opinions, beliefs, and perspectives unless they're designed to inflict harm on someone. My values, opinions, beliefs, and perspectives will intertwine with my purpose, adding fire to the happiness that I already experience. I choose to associate with individuals who respect that. As an analytical thinker, I enjoy discussing difficult topics and listening to other ideas without judgment or condemnation, as I'll be able to remain a student. This doesn't mean I'll agree with everything I hear, and many times I don't, but I'm able to gain knowledge through my disagreements.

"Who am I?" I'm empathetic, trustworthy, and caring. I hold strong values of ethics, and I'm disgusted by agendas and personal interests that are killing people. What you see is what you get. I'm real, which says that I'll make mistakes, say nothing behind your back that I wouldn't say to your face, and speak as truthful as I can, based on the information I have.

"Who am I?" This is a trick question, and you'll never come up with a solid definable answer to. It's an exciting question to ask as it will take you on a journey of exploring, transforming, and engaging a process that's ongoing. Don't get stuck on the "who," but rather on "what."

- "What am I passionate about?"
- "What are my desires?"
- "What do I believe?"
- "What am I going to achieve?"

These are questions that we can answer and eliminate the vagueness and uncertainty of the first question.

Answer the Following Questions as These Will Help You Learn More about Yourself

1. What are your values?
2. What are your morals?
3. What short term goals do you have?
4. What long-term goals do you have?
5. What are you passionate about?
6. What are your strengths?
7. Who are you now and are you living the life that reflects who you are?
8. What does living with integrity look like to you?
9. Do you need to make changes to live this life you envision?
10. Are you afraid to be yourself?
11. In one sentence, how do you define yourself?
12. What does integrity mean to you and how important is it?

Add additional "what" questions to help you learn more about you.

I'm nothing more and nothing less than me. I'm my friend, my ally, and my helper.

CHAPTER 10

A Greater Success from a New Pain

Time is something trivial, losing as we go.
Today and not tomorrow is all we really know.
Nothing is ever certain; even change can end today.
I'll never lose a moment, as you have found your way.

A question that I ask can help to set me straight,
Is how do I proceed, or pretend it's all been fake?
I've pulled away before, but was it to pretend,
To put my lips upon you, to hold you close again.

Feelings can seem daunting, with a love that speaks through fear,
Of living without something that you really held so dear.
Sight has been a problem, as my eyes don't always see.
The intention of my mind is wrong and won't agree.

Understand my vision that I want to share with you,
Is to proudly be as one and laugh in all we do.
Complications are the reasons that we ended what I sought.
Should I let go of you and never give it another thought?

That cloud you see above will in time be gone forever.
This note I write to you started as a love letter.
How can I forget that time when my legs began to shake?
The power you had over me as I lost control, for fuck's sake.

Love can flip to anger, as rejection takes the stage,
As craving are the suffering, but our loss will disengage.
Courage is the power that allows me to say to you
It's wrong to be together, but unsure if that is true.

I'm not always correct, as right is sometimes wrong.
The south will often tell you about evil in a song.
Hallucinations are reported in a mind that's not alone.
The pain that you provoke can never be condoned.

You will always be with me, and we will never be apart.
A mind will never lose it, as a rainbow with no arch.
Told that I am evil, if you are in my life,
A choice between you two and if it's you I lose my wife.

Life was good, and I was independent, in love with a woman who loved me back. I was employed, had goals, and wanted a good future. I'd been a counselor for years, program director, executive director, and educator in the field. I spoke at colleges teaching upcoming counselors about ideas and tactics for working effectively with clients. How would somebody with eleven years clean and sober, with all that experience, relapse and throw everything away? My story continues as life experiences unfold, and poor choices return me to a place where my life spins out of control.

Life Is Full of Change

In 2005, I got married for the first time because it was
what I thought "normal" people did, and I felt it would help
keep me out of trouble. Unfortunately, I married a woman
who was insecure, had low self-esteem, and was very controlling. She always wanted to know where I was, who I
was with, and what I was doing. This didn't sit well with
me. I'd worked so hard on feeling secure, improving my
self-esteem, and living a life that I was proud of. Marriage
became a prison that I wanted no part of. I wanted a com-
panion who could bring out my best qualities, not my worst.

I met a woman in 2012 who would become my second
wife, unlike any that I'd met before who had qualities,
characteristics, and a personality that attracted me beyond
words. She is beautiful outside, but her internal beauty
set the stage for an uncomfortable situation that emotionally harmed a couple of individuals. She and I were both
married at the time and, on a few occasions, attempted to
remove each other from our lives because of our ideas of
what was right or wrong.

Mirella, the woman I met, was in a very similar scenario with her husband, and we both wanted out of those
relationships, but we struggled with the moral principle
that so many of us have grown up with. Do you remain in
a relationship that's painful, uncomfortable, and volatile
because divorce is wrong, or do you find love, security, and
comfort to be happy? Our meeting was a result of my desire to stay away from home by working late. We connected
online, with no intentions of a sexual encounter. Instead I
wanted to find friends since I was unable to associate with
people, and if I did, it led to arguments with my wife. We
communicated through email for over a month before we

met in person at a Denny's near my work. I felt a connection immediately, unlike anything I've ever felt before. Do you believe in a soulmate?

Our likes and dislikes were so similar as she was a Grateful Dead fan, loved to travel, and *Mary Poppins* was one of her favorite movies. No matter how hard I tried to "do what was right," I could not stop thinking about her and wishing that I'd met her many years earlier. Feelings are powerful, and love—or that desire to be loved—has been the driving force for most of humanity throughout all of time.

Both of our spouses accessed our emails, learning of our communication one day apart from each other, setting things in motion for the divorce with my wife and Mirella from her husband. The day my wife saw the communication, I moved out and rented an apartment for six months before moving in with Mirella. One month after renting the apartment, I left the program I'd worked so hard to establish due to a conflict of interest with my business partner. I took a job with another facility at a much-reduced pay. Life can be difficult with disappointments, discomfort, and fear that can cause you to make poor choices if things are not well thought out.

Having a drastically reduced pay at my new job, struggling with finances, and losing something that held me together for so many years, I lost track of my goals, vision, and commitment, sending me down a road that I thought I had left. That thing that I lost was my passion, which was to fight hard for the lives of the people that I worked with, leaving the program that I'd worked every day to build and had the power to create a program that was so effective as evidenced by the success we saw in our clients.

Every choice, whether it's big or small, can alter our

courses if we're not careful and aware of our influences. The common saying that "a relapse begins long before you pick up and use" is accurate, and I "scientifically" proved it through my experiment that was soon to come.

In some ways, I felt defeated by leaving a company that I worked so hard to create, develop, and succeed in the fashion that we had. I felt lost and uncertain on my next step in the right direction. Outwardly, I showed confidence, stability, and certainty, but inwardly it was a different story, and I failed to follow the one tool that may have prevented this, which is to ask for help and discuss my feelings. Instead, I hid everything, and lost that humble nature that had saved me in the past. Little by little, I made decisions that paved the way for the things that were about to come, nearly destroying and taking my life.

A Small Choice That Leads to a Huge Consequence

Mirella and I decided that we had an extra room in our apartment and wanted to rent it to someone to help with the cost of our lease. She had someone in mind, who had an unsteady childhood and periodically stayed with her when he had been growing up. I learned that he had a history of drug use, which was a major problem for me if this was continuing. He was gay and interested in renting the room with his boyfriend, so I had a long talk with him prior to me agreeing and giving him the offer.

"I understand that you've had a problem with meth in the past, and I want you to understand what I do for a living and a little about my history. I've struggled with that shit in the past, and I work for a drug-treatment program. I assess people in jail and go to court to fight for their release and give them an opportunity to get help. If I think that you or your boyfriend are getting high, I'll search your room, find your shit, and throw you out. I want to make this clear and let you know ahead of time."

"I haven't used in quite a while and have no plans on using. I have a job that I wouldn't jeopardize, so don't worry. It won't be a problem," he told me.

"All right, I'll let you move in. Don't make me throw you out of here onto the streets."

They both moved in, and his financial support helped our situation in the beginning. I'm the wrong person to use meth around and think that you're going to fool me. It wasn't long before I noticed the signs, so I searched his room and found four glass pipes loaded with meth. I was furious. I smashed three of them and kept one in my desk drawer to confront him with. My plan was set to throw both out when I saw them next. Throughout the years of working in the industry, I've found meth, heroin, pills, syringes, pipes, and other things that can be hard for some to handle, but it was never a temptation for me.

Not having seen them for four days, that pipe just sat in that drawer and began calling me. This may sound strange to some, but it started with a dream I had that felt so real that I believed I'd relapsed for a short moment after I'd woken up. It was so real that I could taste it. Renting the room to an unstable meth user was mistake number one, keeping the pipe in my drawer was mistake number two, and keeping it a secret was mistake number three. Mirella left for work at around 7:00 a.m. in September of 2013, and I had meth on my mind. I couldn't focus on anything except for the thoughts of smoking the pipe. My heart began racing, I started to sweat, and I couldn't get rid of that taste in my mouth. I thought that because I'd been clean for eleven years, was older, smarter, and more mature, I could handle one hit. I lost all my focus, direction, and insight for that one moment, and I did it. That one hit brought Mr. Hyde through the door and flipped that switch that I talked about earlier. I went from stable, secure, in control, and intuitive to erratic, no control, and lost. I knew instantly that life was about to get crazy again, and I felt that I had no power to stop it.

I smoked that entire bowl and went to court to meet with an attorney and help his client get out of custody. Not having used for so many years, the affects lasted much longer than it had in the past. I knew I was going to need more toward the end of the day, so I reconnected on Facebook with some people that I hadn't seen for over eleven years, with the hope that they had connections. It wasn't difficult, and I acquired a supplier within a few days who I was able to purchase large quantities at a decent cost. I no longer cared about work, which was witnessed by everyone I had contact with as I showed up late for appointments if I even showed up at all.

Abiding by Rules Will Prove Control

I set rules for myself to prove that I was in control by avoiding the use intravenously, and not going out at night. It wasn't long before I broke each of those rules and returned to my behaviors from 2001. I lost my job and returned to the life of motel hopping as I refused to return home, and as the judge told me in 2001, "I was a danger to society." I began purchasing meth by the quarter pound and selling to various individuals to support my habit.

With the enhancements of technology, I purchased credit card writers and embossing machines to manipulate prepaid Visa cards into usable credit cards by putting any number I chose onto the strip. I could drive around residential neighborhoods and open unlocked vehicles, finding wallets with credit cards inside. My reader/writer was hooked to a laptop in my car where I could transfer the numbers onto another card and return the wallet to the vehicle I took it from so nobody noticed allowing me the opportunity for more time to make purchases. It was easy to steal a prepaid Visa card from a store, remove the numbers with a solvent and emboss the credit card number onto the card. Once again, the adrenaline from my behaviors took over, and stopping was impossible, at least in my mind.

For six months, I was mindlessly heading for destruction, and I needed some pain that would be greater to continue using then to stop. My girlfriend decided to move to another city and get away from the apartment we shared. And because drug abuse has nothing to do with love, I didn't care while I was high. I really cared about nothing. Manipulation was the art form I mastered, and I used it in ways that harmed others and one who, while clean, was one of my best friends.

My friend had over eight years clean and sober when I hired him as my secondhand man at my program. He was an amazing employee who learned very quickly and assisted me with court hearings to get individuals out of custody. He stayed on at the program after I left and oversaw the operational aspects of the program. Not long after I relapsed, I phoned him and explained to him that I had a way that he could make money by selling meth because I knew that finances were tough for him as he had a wife and two children to support. We had joked in the past about being able to sell drugs, not use them, but reap the financial rewards by not having to use our supply with everything being profit.

"Remember when we used to joke about being able to sell dope but not have to do it? I ran into an old dealer of mine at court who told me that he could sell me a cheap quarter pound, and we could make some money. I'll split it in half with you if you would like. He was telling me that the shit was good, and it would be easy to sell because of the quality. What do you think?"

"You're fucking crazy, but I could use the money," he told me.

That conversation led to his demise in the future, and I was far from a friend, as I began selling to him. He was able to stay off the drug for a period before coming to my apartment and learning that I'd relapsed. After having ten years clean and sober, he requested a "needle" and relapsed. He wasn't able to get clean before getting arrested for a controlled buy, posted bail, and get arrested a second time for another controlled buy and felon in the possession of a firearm. He was sentenced to ten years, eight months, at 85 percent because of his priors that included a strike.

What Is Happening in My head?

Not being a medical doctor but having studied the following information along with the experiential knowledge, let us look at how this works from a real-life perspective. The physiological effects of methamphetamine create a dynamic in our brains that drastically affect our ability to think rationally, causing side effects that give us an understanding of how the brain changes. Drug abusers typically don't understand or think about the side effects that may result from their use and the devastating consequences that will or could happen with the changes in the way our brain functions. This information doesn't justify our behavior, but it does give us an understanding of why our behaviors change. Dopamine, the neurotransmitter related with all addictions, is involved with pleasure and reward, causing us to want to repeat behaviors because it feels good. The benefit of dopamine is the increased motivation, increased energy, ability to learn, and productivity. A meth abuser may experience those results in the beginning, but because of the drastically increased release and the ability for the methamphetamine to block the reuptake of dopamine, something much bigger, stronger, and more dangerous happens that isn't what we signed up for.

Increased levels of dopamine set the stage for symptoms related to paranoid schizophrenia as I saw with Mary and delusional components of psychosis where you lose contact with reality as I experienced. The pleasure center is a part of the limbic system located in the midpart of our brain and is related to survival. Methamphetamine manipulates this part of the brain and changes it to require the substance to function normally, or what appears to be a normal state. If I require that chemical to survive, or at least that's what my reality is telling me, I'll do anything to keep that supply. During that period of psychosis, I didn't believe I was hurting anybody, even though I was creating triggers for a friend, breaking into houses, committing check fraud, and living a life of crime. Can we understand the actions of a homeless man starving and stealing a candy bar from a store? Will a methamphetamine abuser die if he or she stops using? No, but the mind has a powerful influence on behavior when someone has lost contact with reality. Theoretically, methamphetamine stimulates the release of, blocks the reuptake of, and takes away the protective mechanisms that regulate the amount of dopamine in our neurons.

Methamphetamine also blocks the reuptake of another neurotransmitter involved in our physical energy called epinephrine. In 1999, while working graveyard at Kinko's, I had plans to go with my parents to an event on a morning after I finished work. I'd been awake for four days but wasn't worried, as methamphetamine kept me going. I arrived at home around 8:30 a.m. and was being picked up by my family around 10:00 a.m. I walked into my room, sat on my bed, and awoke around two thirty in the afternoon. I quickly asked my roommate if my parents had come by because I must have fallen asleep.

"Dude, you fucked up. I got a call from your mom around nine thirty, and she told me that they were on their way to get you. I knocked on your door, and you didn't answer. I opened it, and you were laying across your bed, and it looked like you were pulling pants over your other pants, and you had a glass pipe in one hand, holding a lighter with the other hand like you were about to smoke a bowl, but sound asleep. I tried to wake you, but you wouldn't wake up. I grabbed your pipe and lighter and stuck it in your closet. Your dad came in, and you got up and told them to get the fuck out of here, screaming and yelling. They left, but, dude, that was crazy."

I didn't remember anything about the event that he mentioned. Once that adrenaline is gone, the only way to replenish this is to sleep, which is what I always attempted to avoid. Unfortunately, as you've read, depleting yourself of sleep—and, therefore, adrenaline—can be dangerous, risking yours and other's lives when you're driving a car.

When I started using methamphetamine, the greatest impact it had on me besides the pleasure was the focus, concentration and ability to pay attention to something that I never cared to learn before. Attention deficit hyperactivity dsorder (ADHD) is a condition that's believed to be caused by a limited amount of norepinephrine in the prefrontal cortex, or the cognitive functions in our brain. Treatment for ADHD is usually an amphetamine such as Adderall or Ritalin, which blocks the reuptake of this neurotransmitter allowing the brain to work better. This created an environment that presented a strong desire to complete a task that was difficult and not easily accomplished by others. I was able to spend hours and days on Photoshop, creating templates for a driver's license that were so detailed and real that they could not be identified as fraudulent. The combination of the pleasure, energy, and focus was a perfect mix combined with the behaviors of committing crimes and test how far I could go without being caught.

As science continues to study the brain and understand more about the interaction between various neurotransmitters, studies have concluded that methamphetamine does affect serotonin, a neurochemical involved in your well-being, and happiness among other things. Some studies have concluded that methamphetamine increases while others have determined a decreased level of serotonin. One theory is that methamphetamine does kill serotonergic neurons changing the user's brain forever and causing the lack of interest to stop as major depression sets in. Why does a meth user sleep for numerous days after they had stopped? We've all heard the saying that "you can't catch up on sleep," so eight to ten hours should suffice. Methamphetamine has changed our brain chemistry where those neurotransmitters identified that give is energy, focus, and pleasure no longer work without the drug, depression causes an interest to sleep. The lack of dopamine, serotonin, norepinephrine, and epinephrine will kill any desire to do anything until sleep becomes impossible. It's believed that methamphetamine kills dopamine, serotonin, and possibly norepinephrine neurons that will never come back depleting the number of "feel-good neurotransmitters" changing the way you feel forever.

Neuroplasticity, as we discussed earlier, offers hope to us by a belief that our brains will rewire itself to function as well as possible with what is remaining. Methamphetamine use, as we've defined, creates an enormous amount of damage to the brain as some will be irreversible, and physical health declines as the interest to eating or drinking is gone causing malnutrition and dehydration. Intravenous drug users may develop abscesses that can develop into a staph infection. Lack of sleep can cause visual hallucinations and can manifest into psychosis, creating a world that isn't what it seems.

How About a Good Kick in the Head?

In March of 2014, I received the event that was needed to change my view of my predicament by a good kick in the head. My friends at the time, or better defined as acquaintances, had been staying with me at some rooms I'd rented at a hotel. I checked out and paid for the room early one morning and went to a guy's house where I'd spent time in the past making driver's licenses and printing checks for various purchases. I received a call from one of the females who was at the motel and she was frantically stating that she was left at the room with everybody's belongings and had no place to go and was in fear of police harassing her. The four others who were staying had left her to watch their property while they went to rent a vehicle because of the events that had occurred the night before.

Using an identification card and credit card I'd made, one of the females had rented a vehicle a couple of weeks prior to this and never returned it since nothing was in her name. Another member of the group had used the car the evening before I was called, and he was pulled over by the police, except he decided not to pull over. Going at high speeds, he attempted to get away from the police and crashed, flipping the car. He was arrested for grand theft, among numerous other charges, including reckless driving.

Things were getting bad, and I was sure that it was a matter of time before I was arrested. I picked up the one who had called me from the hotel, along with most of the items she was securing, unaware that the rest of the group was blaming her for stealing drugs and other things I'm still unclear on. I received a call from the accuser, and before I could answer, the accused frantically requested I not answer the phone as she explained the accusations made against her, which she claims were invalid. It's hard to say who was being honest, delusional, or crazy, as drugs consumed all of us, but crazy was probably the right term for everyone. As I didn't want to get involved in those disputes, I told the accuser when I spoke to her later that I hadn't seen the accused and was unsure on her whereabouts. I didn't plan on staying with her and was hoping I could drop her off and leave.

The female who was with me abused heroin instead of meth, and since I had no interest in associating with an individual who was going to kick heroin, I drove her to a friend's house where she could acquire that drug to feel better. Heroin users to me have always felt to be very needy as they always seemed to be running low and with withdrawal symptoms imminent, we would spend more time picking up drugs, causing me to push aside all the things I felt I needed to do. The amount she got from her friend was only enough to give her relief for a couple of hours, so he informed her he would bring her more. I rented another hotel room, informed her friend where we were staying, and he brought her more dope as he had promised, which led to things falling apart quickly, developing the beginning to an end. She remained with me, and the following evening, I was sitting at the table in the hotel room, working on things while she spent about an hour trying to hit a vein. I fell asleep at some point and awoke to the four individuals that had been seeking out the female with me standing in our room rambling on about how she stole their things and they wanted my property.

"Here is the deal. I'm taking your stuff, and it will be at my house," one of them informed me.

"You're not taking my shit," I told him.

"We're taking your stuff, and that's the end of the story."

"That isn't happening. I've been making stuff for all of you and in return that bitch has been giving me credit card numbers that don't work," I aggressively stated.

The "bitch" I referred to was the girlfriend of one of the four, and this is where things took a turn for the worse. The next thing I knew, I was fighting off three guys, and my memory gets foggy as I was punched, thrown on the ground, and kicked in the head numerous times. Somehow this fight began in the room and ended in the hallway of the hotel, and surprisingly, nobody heard, cared, or called the police. I don't remember much except the fact that I was lying on the floor in the hallway on the second floor watching the four walk away with some of my things. I stumbled into the room and learned that they had taken my embosser, laptop, reader/writer, wallet containing about $700 in cash, and most of my dope. I was furious, coming down, and wanted to kill them in the most horrific fashion that I could imagine. I found some meth that they hadn't taken, so I was able to get high and figure out my next steps in securing more dope and money. This kick in the head was what I needed to rethink my future.

A Last Hurrah

I spoke to Mirella about getting help, and she decided to pick me up. Like many others who want to finish their supply before checking into treatment, I was determined to finish what I had left before Mirella arrived, and looking back, I was playing Russian roulette. I had about three grams left. I loaded almost two grams in a syringe, located a vein, and that hit put me to my knees. My head was buzzing, and my heart was thumping with rage. I drove to the apartment where I'd informed Mirella to pick me up and decided to do one last hurrah by loading another rig filled with over a gram and blasted myself into oblivion. Once I put that in my body, I had a hard time breathing, went cross-eyed for a moment, and was confused by what I was doing. The last hurrah can be a defining moment in life or death, and it told me that I wasn't meant to die and may still have a purpose in this existence.

Can I do this again? Can I find that life I knew before this relapse? I wasn't sure, but my girlfriend was a rock for me to hold onto as my brain wasn't working favorably. Ugliness describes the world that I was leaving again, and there's nothing beautiful about that life of twisting a needle around your arm to hit a vein, helping your friend slam a shot in their jugular because nothing else was possible, and giving dope to a good friend with eight years clean and sober who was now heading off to prison. I had a terrifying feeling of letting go of that thing that I felt was keeping me alive, but I knew that if I continued, it was going to kill me.

Scylla and Charybdis were mythological creatures on opposite sides of the Strait of Messina between Sicily and the Italian mainland, in Greek mythology. The metaphor behind these two sea monsters is "the lesser of two evils" or "between a rock and a hard place." Scylla was described as a six-headed sea monster on the Italian side of the straight, while Charybdis was a whirlpool off the coast of Sicily. These were two sea hazards that were close enough together to pose a threat to ships that was unavoidable. If you were able to avoid one of the sea monsters, then you would be too close to the other, creating a dilemma of choosing between "the lesser of two evils." Odysseus, according to Homer, chose Scylla over Charybdis because it was better losing a few men rather than losing the entire ship in a whirlpool. Scylla and Charybdis is the metaphor describing the battle of an individual choosing between the pain, discomfort, and fear of letting go of something that has fooled us into believing that survival is dependent on the drug, or continue the use knowing that our lives will be cut short. The one thing that I had as comfort was knowing I had the ability to get clean and stay clean because I'd done this before. I was scared, had destroyed my self-esteem that I'd worked hard on, and was terrified of feeling what I knew was coming.

Can I Do It Again

When I was in custody in 2002, which was twelve years previous to now, my emotions were uncontrollable, and they were highly exaggerated from what may be defined as normal. I'd cry at Hallmark commercials and shed tears when they allowed us to watch *Pearl Harbor* or laughed uncontrollably to stupid jokes. I wasn't looking forward to having that loss of control, but it was much healthier than the control I handed over to methamphetamine. I decided after Mirella picked me up to check into a treatment center for thirty days to get my head on straight, and I figured there was no better time than now, because putting things off until tomorrow, which was the normal response, never comes.

Humiliated, beaten, shamed, and damaged, I checked in and recalled my experiences, lessons, and educational knowledge that I had and used it. I didn't want people to think that I knew a lot about treatment or recovery because I wanted to remain teachable, have an open mind, and just be a student. It was two weeks in the program before I shared about my history in the industry, which was a very humbling experience, but something dawned on me that I've been able to use to help individuals like me who have had years clean and sober and then relapsed.

I felt, when I first entered treatment, that I'd thrown everything away that I'd worked so hard on. Well, I didn't. Everything I'd learned, experienced, taught, and worked for was still there. I gained new information from the relapse that I hadn't understood before, and I was able to experience something, from firsthand experience, that taught me a new perspective for addiction. We can make assumptions about addiction going away or the ability for control to develop over time, but my experience was able to show me that loss of control doesn't go away after taking one hit even after having eleven years clean and sober. I went from happy, stable, secure, intelligent, honest, and confident, with high self-esteem, to the ugliness I described in this chapter from one hit on a meth pipe. When I'm clean and sober, I have an integrity that would find your house if you lost a wallet and offer it back or return to a store and give money back if you overpaid me on my change. It's a strange phenomenon, Dr. Jekyll and Mr. Hyde at its worst.

The treatment facility I entered was exactly what I needed and stabilized me to reenter that world of recovery I knew so well in the past. Recovery is a vague concept that many don't understand, and some feel that being clean is enough. But it's much more than that. Getting clean is easy, but staying clean and being happy requires work and effort. What is recovery, and why do so many struggle with staying clean? Relapse, in my story, was a result of poor choices that I made and how I allowed my recovery to become stagnant. Once I felt that I was moving backward, I gave up and gave my feelings and thoughts the lead in taking action without my intuition having a say.

Questions to Consider

1. What are your triggers that could send you backward?
2. What are things in your life, that you don't want to talk about that could harm you?

During a relapse, we can lose everything of material value, but the most important things that you gained in recovery can remain, which is your knowledge and experience. Let them do their job and bring you back.

PART 3

Stepping Stones to Success

Out of suffering have emerged the strongest souls;
the most massive characters are seared with scars.

—Kahlil Gibran

Part 3

51 Stepping Stones to Success

CHAPTER 11

Good Help for Success

The crimson that raged, oh, it blended with purple,
Amazed at the wonder and dodged all the hurdles.
Slaves being sold by cold heartless fools,
How dare you stand tall and then break all the rules?

Were told that you care, and it's because of your heart.
Nothing is true as you tear lives apart.
Stop with your lies and your unvalued promise.
It's ugly and vain or what's better is pompous.

Leave us alone, and don't ask us to stay.
I want real help, not the money you pay.
Weak is upon you, as a clown paints your face.
How sad is your life, it's a young boy that you chase?

Your tears will mean nothing, as your crime will await.
Bars are the future, look forward to the date.
Watch out your window; your door will gladly do.
I'm eyeing your place and will be coming for you.

You claim to be clean, to be seen as a savior.
Far from the truth, when I see your behavior,
I remember a time when love was our action.
Not anymore, when your heart has been blackened.

Don't get me wrong when I spell out these words.
Good treatment is offered but its sadly obscured.
Look for yourself and don't rely on what's heard.
Please don't give up and let frustration deter.

Referrers seem nice and will claim that they care.
Be honest and tell them that trust seems so rare.
Money is a goal and who pays them the most,
Not what is best as they seek the largest note.

I hope to share a message that treatment isn't dead.
Ask the right questions so you don't get mislead.
Don't get lured in by an unethical place.
Ask for it in writing to have proof, just in case.

Your first step to success might require a helping hand like mine as I was unable to do it on my own. Experts willing to help are out there, but unfortunately, the substance-abuse-treatment industry has turned into something ugly and dangerous for some. Being educated on what is happening in recent times and what to look for in finding the best program to meet your needs can be that start you're looking for. Times have changed and not necessarily for the better.

Let Me Take You Back to the Beginning

When I began working in the industry many years ago, many insurance companies or policies didn't provide coverage for substance-abuse treatment. For-profit treatment programs would require that you paid up-front, and if you had insurance that did have coverage, they would help you get reimbursed based on your policy. There were less treatment facilities at that time, and people who sought help weren't necessarily doing it for the right reasons, but they were doing it because they wanted to get clean or sober.

Marketing was organic, meaning the facilities were responsible and capable of bringing calls directly to the facility through internet marketing, which reduced the cost for this service, allowing more money to be spent on quality. Involvement of families in their loved one's treatment was a major focus ten years ago, and success of our clients was more important back then than what has superseded that goal. Success, quality, and genuine care has been trampled on by money. The Affordable Care Act opened a door in this industry of an ugly, despicable, and horrific nature, indirectly killing many people while owners of facilities are getting rich.

Good Idea but Bad Results

It's becoming more and more difficult to find facilities that we can identify as ethically sound, morally in good-standing, and providing quality care that appears more interested in success rates then the almighty dollar. Some may have seen news reports of FBI raids on treatment facilities being investigated for insurance fraud, sober-living facilities being closed for unsafe practices, and doctors being prosecuted for involvement in urinalysis scams. This is only a fraction of the problem, and much of the public is very ignorant about how deep this goes. I want to take you back to the beginning so we can all have the same knowledge and work together to find a solution. We're all experiencing pain, failure, and misery as we continue watching loved ones die from this affliction, and at times, it appears that nobody cares. Let's use this pain, failure, and misery to empower us to find those steps to success.

The Affordable Care Act required policies to provide coverage for substance-abuse treatment and eliminated pre-existing conditions that would have kept people from getting insurance, or at least at an affordable rate. Since it became mandatory for every American to have insurance, people now had policies that would pay for chemical-dependency treatment. Every facility that wanted to remain in business needed to learn about insurance billing quickly, because private pay became old news. This new payment method created a lot of confusion, creating an industry that wasn't new to the medical field but wasn't experienced for the substance-abuse industry. Aside from the explosion of treatment facilities, three other industries began reaping rewards and sending things into a downward spiral because of negligence and greed. This has put client's in danger. The Affordable Care Act was a good idea, offering health care to millions of people. The idea sounds good until money, lots of money, becomes available for the taking.

Money, Money, Money—Billers Will Make Us More Money

As insurance billing was new, and not understood by many operators, new companies began knocking on doors and confusing owners with statements like verification of benefits, explanation of benefits, billing codes, and procedure codes. Billing companies began marketing to facilities attempting to sell them on the amount of money they could make them and how easy they could make the process. Billing companies, on an average, would get paid anywhere from 8–10 percent of the amount that was collected. The more they billed and collected, the more profitable things became. Every year that passed, since the Affordable Care Act went into effect, the daily cost of treatment rose setting a new average and presenting an opportunity for anybody to open a facility and make a lot of money.

Business executives, drug dealers, neighbors, and greedy fellows with no knowledge of the industry opened locations because the word was out, and millions could be made. Marketing became less about the quality and more about the size of the house and the beauty of the property that you'd live in. Competition created a dilemma that amplified the problems, because the beds needed to be filled.

Selling People

When someone is looking for help and you have thousands of places to choose from, where do you go? Referral companies can now take the stage. All over the country, we began to see another industry unfold consisting of corporations and individual marketers selling their services on Facebook and other forms of social media. The amount of money that was made by these corporations allowed them the ability to financially support superior online marketing that facilities could not compete with. Commercials, radio, and internet were flooded with referral companies, drawing phone calls from potential clients and taking away organic marketing to good facilities. Referral companies have cornered the market and begun selling clients to treatment facilities, referred to as "body brokering." Many facilities have been paying as high as $10,000 per client. These corporations and individuals that are selling people are not that concerned with the quality of treatment, but instead they're concerned about who is willing to pay the fee that they desire.

Addiction Network is a referral company we've all seen on television, and many have questioned the legitimacy of the actor who is wearing a stethoscope. Their website flashes pictures of a medical team designed to create a comfortability of professionals that you would speak to when you call. This is a referral company that funnels calls to facilities for a per-call rate. It's highly unlikely that you'll speak to a psychiatrist, medical doctor, or nurse when you call, unless someone with those credentials answers phones for facilities, which is highly unlikely. This example is used to reiterate the inability or difficulty for the facilities posted on their site, to market for themselves.

Many small facilities were not able to pay the outside marketing fees, and they began setting individuals up on insurance, paying the premiums and waiving deductibles to fill their beds. Some programs recruited homeless individuals who may not have had drug problems but needed to fill their beds. Based on the calculations presented, and strictly as an estimate, a program would pay $450 for the first premium and bill $105,000 for thirty days of residential treatment. If they waived the deductible losing, as an example $10,000 and a coinsurance of 40 percent, they would receive a check for $57,000. A six-bed facility could bring in $342,000 per month, equaling $4,104,000 for a year. Did I say it was profitable? For many greedy individuals strictly out for the money, very little was put into qualified staff, and services became ineffective.

Referral companies are booming with business, and

individuals wanted in on the profit, so recruiting became door-to-door marketing. With the use of social media, catching vulnerable individuals in twelve-step meetings, and recruiting people already in a treatment program, paying the clients to enroll in facilities started to happen. The recruiters would network with programs willing to pay them, but the client must stay in the program between seven to ten days. "I'm only staying ten days." After the client stays ten days, the recruiter is paid $8,000, and the client leaves and gets paid $2,000. The higher the level of care the recruiter gets them into, the more they get paid. Recruiters have gone into twelve-step meetings, identified vulnerable clients, got them high, and sent them into a detox facility.

You Need to Drug Test Daily Just to Make Sure You Aren't Getting Loaded

The third industry that has had a lot of media attention are the urinalysis labs. The use of labs to determine whether a client is clean or has been using drugs has been utilized for a while but didn't become cost effective and very profitable until the Affordable Care Act was in place. Prior to this, facilities used on-site testing kits for the majority and used labs only to confirm a positive test. Insurance companies will pay for urine screens at a lab if it's defined as medically necessary, which is usually the case to confirm the client is clean. Laboratory facilities started popping up around the country, charging exorbitant amounts of money for drug screens. Owners of treatment facilities began opening their own labs or partnering with existing labs to make more profit. Clients became required by the treatment facilities to test more often so they could charge more regularly under the pretense that "we're just confirming that they're clean."

A residential facility run properly should be able to test once or twice a week, but because the facility can bill insurance for collecting urine, it became four to five times a week.

I had a client who was in the facility I worked at in 2016 who received $800,000 from her insurance company as reimbursement for the lab testing conducted over a ten-month period. Some insurance companies will pay the client for services, leaving it as their responsibility to reimburse the provider (i.e., lab or treatment facility). The facility she was enrolled in changed labs many times during her stay, but one of the companies charged $20,000 for a single test. After her deductible was met and every bit of out of pocket was met, her insurance paid 100 percent. It's scary, unnerving, and dangerous to pay a client early in recovery $800,000 in checks. How can anybody justify a $20,000 charge for a single drug test?

Is Good Help Out There?

Is good help out there? As I stated earlier, it's difficult to identify whether a facility is ethical, has morals, and provides quality service that you can trust. Facilities have recruiters as clients or have clients getting paid and use the industry as their profession. I've dealt with clients who have been in five programs in a thirty-day period. Treatment isn't what it used to be, since some of the clients have no intention of staying clean as they switch from facility to facility.

Everybody needs to understand that much of the following information is my opinion, which is true to me, but may not be your opinion. My opinions are not facts, but they are based on many years of experience in the industry and years of experience recovering myself. When you're looking for good quality treatment, what are you looking for? The National Institute on Drug Abuse (NIH) discusses research findings on effective treatment approaches. What you'll find for effective treatment according to their site is very vague and does define addiction as a complex disease. It goes on to state that "no single treatment is right for everyone" and "effective treatment addresses all of the patient's needs, not just his or her drug use." These are all good, but this is how every treatment facility markets their program and can be very misleading.

When I started in the industry, treatment was less of a vacation and resort and more about treatment approaches to help clients learn the tools to maintain long-term sobriety. Competition in the industry has brought many services that are not necessary and used strictly as "fluff" to bring in more people. Before people get outraged behind the statement I'm going to make, think about the purpose of the statement rather than the statement itself. Massage therapy has very little therapeutic value in teaching tools to maintain long-term sobriety and is used more as a service to bring the resort-like atmosphere and fill the beds. This resort-like atmosphere is sending the wrong message and teaching clients another lesson that's destroying their lives.

Experts in the Industry

This rehabilitation industry is selling services and the quality of the services are dependent on the staff providing them. Websites for facilities identify many of the staff providing the treatment, but does it give a clear picture, or is there an illusion of professionalism that you must be aware of? I've witnessed, over the years, the changes in staff and how medical the industry has become. With insurance companies paying for treatment, we're seeing more medical doctors, psychiatrists, psychologists, and therapists entering the picture, and is it more effective? We're hearing criticism by many that counselors, who were defined as experts in the industry ten years ago, are just recovering addicts with criminal backgrounds and are the reasons for the problems we're seeing. I don't believe that this is the problem, and in fact, if we look at it from a commonsense approach, many of the problems in the industry started when insurance companies began paying and the actors identified above became more prevalent. Having an MFT, MD, or a doctorate doesn't make you an expert in the industry.

What does it mean to be an expert in this field? I believe it's someone who can identify with your client, work with them on a level they understand, create an environment that's comfortable, and teach in a manner that's realistic and tangible. Many licensed professionals who came into the industry with no personal experience will not have the characteristics identified, and the client will feel the professional is better than them. The better-than-them feeling will push the client away, destroying any therapeutic relationship that could have been developed. Too much education in this industry, for some, will confuse many clients as a vocabulary will be used that isn't understood by many.

James Anderson, a licensed marriage and family therapist, is an example of an exception to my above statements. When I helped start a program back in 2016, he replied to an ad that I'd posted looking for a therapist to hire for the organization. Mr. Anderson has an ability to connect with clients in a manner rarely seen by others. He is an expert in this industry and fits those qualifications identified. He utilizes music as a tool to reach clients since music is universally understood and appreciated. His thinking-outside-the-box tactics helped clients who wouldn't open up and discuss their issues. He would have them write lyrics and help them record the song that they could take with them. Creativity, intuitiveness, and innovation sets him above many.

It's important to have professional staff because therapy can be dangerous, if not done correctly, in a detox and residential level of care. In the first weeks and even months for some individuals, substance abuse should be the primary focus for stabilizing someone. The greatest mistake that therapists, psychologists and other licensed professional's commit is to pull information from clients before they're ready. Many clients will sit in a fog and unclear on many things during the early stages of treatment. To target molestation, certain forms of trauma, and abuse too early can be a trigger for some to leave treatment. All professionals in this industry need to be cautious and aware that the client should be allowed to bring forth information at the time they're ready and not according to your directive.

Medical doctors and psychiatrists have become major players in the industry and bring with them many problems that I've witnessed. The more problems that a client has, the more days the facility can bill for higher levels of care. How does a psychiatrist diagnose a psychiatric disorder within the first week or two of a client entering detox or residential level of care, which they do all the time? Every person who enters treatment with a "severe substance-use disorder," will have depression, anxiety, and bipolar symptoms. Does this mean they fit the diagnosis? Not all the time. I believe that clients are misdiagnosed regularly and overmedicated to make them look sicker than they are to bill for more days. There may be doctors who disagree with this, but I've personally seen it as I've been the Program Director and Clinical Director of numerous facilities.

I left the industry in 2018 because of the things that I'd identified in this chapter. I refused to be a part of the practices and quit jobs losing lots of money because of ethics.

What to Look For

When searching for a facility or if you utilize a referral company, know the facility you're going to. Do your diligence and research the staff at their location. Look up everyone through their licensing board and understand their experience in this field. Call the facility and ask questions about the services being provided. Ask the facility how many clients reside there and the average group size you or a loved one will be subjected to. Ask for all the information you receive on the phone to be emailed to you for documented records. A common practice for the salesperson is to tell you whatever you want to hear to make sure that you come to their facility. Once you realize that you were lied to and confront the program, they will deny ever saying those things that brought you in the door. Get everything in writing.

Pay close attention to the information you receive from the insurance companies. Some facilities have been caught and prosecuted for insurance fraud. You'll receive an explanation of benefits (EOB) during or after your stay in the mail. This EOB will identify all the billing that was filed by the provider. Confirm that they billed only for dates you were there, and no services were billed that you didn't receive. Knowledge is power but unfortunately ignorance prevails. For anybody who has experienced pain, failure, or misery because of unscrupulous practices, let us stand and voice our frustrations. If we can be aware of this knowledge and catch some facilities with their pants down, we can help close the bad facilities one at a time.

There are good facilities out there so please don't misunderstand the generalization. Do your homework and study the operations of the facility. Let us work together and save lives.

Questions to Consider

1. If you're considering a rehab facility, what services would be important to you for success?
2. What qualifications are you looking for in the staff you would work with?
3. What size of facility would work the best for you?
4. Identify things that are important to you? Many looks for things within a program that will distract them. Are results the most important or your ability to have a cell-phone? Is structure important or do you want a program that doesn't care and push you to get better when your struggling?

Treatment was a necessity for me and structure along with quality was how the program showed me that they cared.

CHAPTER 12

Is Recovery Real?

Don't fool yourself, if you think you are immune,
To a puncture in your heart by a wild and accurate harpoon.
Drugs may be your demon, or the reaper came across.
Recovery is nothing more than healing from your loss.

A lifelong process that will end the day we die.
Why run from something that will only magnify?
Embrace the beautiful journey, the road we must all take.
Find that place of freedom by the choices that you make.

Last year I lost my friend, a man I was honored to know.
He would give you his last penny or a beautiful French chateau.
I was sad when that cancer consumed you and hit you like a bomb.
It was my pleasure to walk with you, and I'll forever love you, Tom.

Prepare for the inevitable, a promise that's made to you.
It's life that we must deal with, and often seems so crude.
Never will you make it and walk a perfect line.
It's strife that's right next door; let recovery heal your mind.

The job that you applied for is better than you thought,
With a pay that is more valuable than anything you've sought.
Money will bring you things that you often throw away,
While this will bring a fortune and a wealth that surely stays.

Speaking of my truth, and everything I feel,
My life is so much better, and I have to say it's real.
Dig deep within yourself and allow yourself to grow.
Everything you search for is everything you know.

A victim of abuse or a child of neglect,
Can walk through all the pain with love and self-respect.
Recovery is a process, but nothing we should fear.
It's real if you embrace it and live in a healing atmosphere.

Today, we work together through an altruistic power,
To encourage and support and divert what is encountered.
Believe in who you are, and stand tall for your beliefs.
To recover from our stories, it's time that we release.

Is There Only One Road to Recovery

Tom Wilkinson, a good friend of mine, was diagnosed with esophageal cancer in 2016 and was provided hope, that with surgery, and chemotherapy, he could recover and live a long life with it being localized at stage 1. He followed the directions of the doctor and, in early 2017, had a very invasive surgery removing a portion of his esophagus and a few lymph nodes to see if it had metastasized. The test determined that his cancer had spread, requiring that they add radiation treatment to the chemotherapy as it became stage three and time was of the essence.

For physical ailments, such as cancer, diabetes, or multiple sclerosis, treatment is typically black-and-white with very little variations for that process of recovery. Substance-abuse or mental health recovery is unlike the process of treatment for cancer, but is very vague, has many different factors, and a single approach will not work for everybody requiring professionals to remove the molds and individualize a recovery process to fit each person.

I had heard a statistic that 40 percent of individuals in recovery have never attended a treatment program or participated in a self-help group and it would be very helpful to hear the stories about their tactics to recovery because they aren't shared openly with others. Most clinicians who are in recovery themselves are sold on teaching only what has worked for them versus an open approach that leaves the door open to new and different possibilities. "Substance Abuse and Mental Health Services Administration (SAMHSA)" discuses a recovery-oriented care that identifies four areas that support a life of recovery. As compared to a surgical removal of cancer, these areas are vague, open to interpretation, and supports a process that allows the reader the opportunity to decide the path that will best work for him or her.

My renewed recovery, as I mentioned earlier, gave me a new appreciation for life and gave me the chance to rethink the efforts, foundation, and structure of the treatment approach that many facilities stand on and how we can separate from what works versus what doesn't work. What if we, as a nation of recovering individuals, empowered each other by helping those suffering from this affliction and lifted them up. "Your best thinking got you here." That statement is used so often in a condescending manner to tell a client, member of a twelve-step meeting, or anybody that they're attempting to discredit and get them to do what they want them to do because "their best thinking got them here." What if we turned this around because their "BEST thinking" got them to seek help, which is a positive thing.

All four of the dimension's identified from SAMHSA fit in with that life of recovery I've developed for myself. The first step is health so I removed the substance from my life and began making better choices by eating regularly and managing my emotional discomfort and pain. The second dimension is having a good and supportive home to reside at, which was with Mirella, who was my rock during those spouts of difficulty. The third dimension is a purpose, as I returned to the industry after I became stable, and I'm a recovery advocate fighting to help save lives in this world today. The fourth dimension is community as we need healthy relationships and a support system that we can utilize offering us hope and love. These are simple concepts and define the process for many individuals with long-term recovery.

Through my experience and training, I've discovered that one approach to dealing with drug users is to tell them that if you don't follow a certain type of program, usually the program therapist or counselor is advocating, then they will go back to using. This is untrue and unhelpful because we need to stop taking hope away from those who truly want this. A clinician's opinion and perspectives aren't facts and since people are different, we should never tell someone that it can and will work for you because it worked for me or someone else and if you don't you'll fail.

Treatment versus Recovery

There's a difference between treatment and recovery, which should be explained as treatment is designed to offer tools to develop that process of recovery. It has become unfortunate as treatment facilities are required to follow the guidelines of insurance company's removing much of the ability to "think outside the box," although we can be creative at times. Some may have heard the story of Norman Cousins, the author of *Anatomy of an Illness: As Perceived by the Patient*, who has been known as the "man who laughed himself well." Mr. Cousins was diagnosed with a rare disease of connective tissues called ankylosing spondylitis in 1964 and given a few months to live, as one in five hundred have a chance of survival. He was a journalist who decided to research his condition and concluded that both the illness and medications were depleting his body of vitamin C. He checked out of the hospital and into a hotel and hired a doctor that would work with him by giving injections of a high dose of vitamin C along with a heavy dose of laughter. He acquired a projector and began watching *Candid Camera* and Marx Brothers movies making a point to laugh until his stomach hurt. Norman Cousins died in 1990, which was sixteen years after his diagnosis at the age of seventy-five. It's unclear if his treatment cured him of his disease but science has proven health benefits behind laughter that include an increase in natural killer cells that attack viral infected cells and some types of cancer and tumor cells, an increase in activated T cells, an increase in the antibody immunoglobulin that fights upper respiratory tract infections, an increase in gamma interferon, which tells the immune system to "turn on", and a good stomach workout as well as other potential benefits. Why aren't we laughing more? Stop for a moment and start laughing as hard as you can even if you don't feel it. Force that laughter until it hurts, and you may even feel a little head rush. Try it.

Tom Wilkinson, my friend who I identified earlier, died

on October 24, 2017, and because I was clean and sober, I was able to stand by his bed, and hold his hand as he passed away. He was one of the best friends anybody could have, and was a coworker with integrity in this industry, as he has helped thousands of people learn tools and gain information about recovery. Recovery entails the ability to embrace our feelings, cry if necessary, and allow ourselves the opportunity to walk into uncomfortable situations with a confidence that doesn't allow fear to control us. Tom was loved by many people and his room was filled with friends as he passed on allowing me to see the mark that he left in all our lives. The black-and-white approach for cancer treatment didn't work for him.

Because I have known despair, I value hope.
Because I have tasted frustration, I value fulfillment.
Because I have been lonely, I value love
—Leonard Nimoy

For those of us who have suffered with the pain of addiction, had an opportunity for recovery, and came out on the other side, we have something that many don't have, and that's a life experience that has shown us a view that's ugly, painful, and deadly, therefore allowing us to truly understand and appreciate beauty, comfort, and life.

Pain is a requirement of life while failure and misery are a choice you make that will be defused if you can view the world differently. We can take pain as an empowerment to drive us to good and reframe our failures and misery into lessons that will move us one step forward to success. The pain that I've experienced in my life has empowered my passion to help others while my relapse wasn't a failure because I'm clean and sober today, which is my goal for the first step in recovery. Creativity, passion, and a new perspective on life can allow every individual in recovery the opportunity to chip away at the bricks that surround us and keep us trapped. I encourage all to think outside the box and create something that's new, mindful, realistic, and tangible that will heal the pain inside and offer hope to others.

Treatment Doesn't Have to Be Done in a Facility or by Certain Professionals

The following story is fictional and works to incorporate an example of thinking outside the box. It's a sample of an upcoming book titled *The Jester's Game*. The following is only an extract from the book to incorporate enough information to make my point. *The Jester's Game* is a story of recovery for Peter and how he learned through games and puzzles.

The Jester's Game
Part 1: Weird-Looking Man

Welcome my friends to the town that I was born and raised in. It's in the far east of the country that we all know too well. Unlike most of my friends who left this place, I'm still here and not sure if I'll ever leave.

Being homeless is tough, and I feel that there was only one thing in my life that I could trust, would take care of my needs, and be there when things got rough. Society hates me for it, but how do I let go of something that comforts me during times of emotional pain, which is every fucking day? I'm sorry to cuss, but I can get angry when I think about how my life has turned out. Everybody who walks by me will make comments and laugh when I ask for money or need help. I'm sure that you may have snickered at me once or twice. It's OK if you have because I'm a joke and feel like a child. I'm twenty-one, but I never grew up. My mom and dad used drugs, which seemed to help them get through tough times. Meth felt so good when I started but how could it be so bad when it felt so good. I don't know how I could ever live without it. I tried to get a job but was turned down when they drug tested me. I'm a good person, never steal, nor do anything that's criminal in nature. I'm tired of showering in bathrooms, begging for money to eat and living in a tent. I live in this fucking tent! Sorry again for my outburst.

You see that bathroom over there. I really need to go but there are so many people that I think I'm going to try and hold it. I hate Sunday's. It's so crowded in this park with kids. God, I wish that things weren't this way. I had such hopes when I was in school. I had good grades and was even accepted with a scholarship to a good college.

Oh my God, look over there. You see that weird-looking man in those eccentric clothes and that crazy looking hat. He is so much fun to watch, but it's weird that he never accepts money for the show that he puts on. I always wanted to talk to him, but I'm so shy and afraid that he will just laugh at me and have no interest in talking to a drug addict. I'm a loser.

I can't hold it anymore. I need to go to the bathroom. I'll be right back. Oh, by the way, my name is Peter.

After I finished in the restroom, I walked out and was stopped by that weird-looking man I mentioned.

"Good morning young man, I see you every day that I visit this park and wanted to meet you," he told me.

I didn't know what to say, but I asked him, "Why do you come here every weekend?"

"That's a good question. I'm a jester, and my name is Mirth."

"What is a Jester?" I asked.

"I'm a performer and I'm here to entertain." The Jester begins juggling and continues. "I tell jokes to make people laugh, tell stories and perform magic tricks. Can I tell you a story?"

"I guess," I responded.

"Ok, good. There was a homeless man who walks up to someone whom he has never met nor seen before and asks him, why he is here? Well, the visitor asks, why are we all here? Unsure on how to respond, the homeless man thinks for a minute with a blank stare and tears roll down his face as he is unsure on how to answer. The visitor reaches out his hand and offers the homeless man a pebble and tells him that he is there to offer him a gift, free of charge. The pebble that was handed to the homeless man from the visitor was handed to him when he was telling his story and living in pain."

I was confused on why he was telling me this, but I continued to listen.

The Jester continued his story. "A gift is something we offer and expect nothing in return," the visitor tells him. "I bestow upon you a gift that's symbolic of the pebble. The real gift for you will only be presented when you're ready. I'm only a tool to teach you how to find your gift, which will be more valuable than you could ever imagine. You'll determine the path, but I promise your efforts will be well worth it."

I couldn't understand why this crazy man was telling me a story of a visitor and homeless man. "Why are you telling me this?" I asked.

"I don't know, it sounds mysterious," he answers but

quickly becomes very serious and grabs my hand. He puts a pebble in it and closes it while telling me "I give you this pebble that is symbolic of my gift to you. Good luck and find the path to your fortune." He did a quick bow, turned, and walked away.

The pebble was purple and about three millimeters in size with veins of quartz that left an interesting impression and reminded me of my childhood as I'd seen these before when I went camping with my father. I was angry with my father as he passed away a few years ago abandoning me to the streets when I was eighteen because I couldn't afford to pay the rent. I had to give up the scholarship from the college. I wasn't sure what this creepy Jester was pulling but I was curious. He needed to learn more, so I ran to him and asked what he meant. "Was that story for me or just games that you play. Is it real?"

"What is real? I want to show you something." Mirth grabs a dollar out of his pocket and says, "I'm going to change this dollar into a quarter." He begins shaking the bill, folds it in half and then in half again. He squeezes his fingers tight and a quarter pops out. I was amazed with his skills and clapped to show my appreciation and praise. "Look over there, do you see the rainbow. Is a rainbow real?"

I looked over at the direction Mirth was pointing and could see the arch of a rainbow hovering over the only restaurant that we have in town. This town had so many memories and I wished that I was able to leave this place and start my life over, but felt it was impossible. My mother was worse with drugs than my father and I remember the last time I went to that restaurant. She took me for my birthday the day after I turned ten and we had so much fun together. She took me home after that breakfast and I never saw her again. My father told me that she was sick, loved me very much, but had to leave so she could get better. That was eleven years ago.

"I've never thought about how real a rainbow is, but it looks real," I said.

"It's a refraction of the light through water droplets, and it's all based on your location and the position of the sun. These are all illusions, but do you want to know what is real?"

"I really do. I'm so intrigued by what you're about, and I want to know more. There's something about you that I like and it's not the clothes." I told him.

"Come with me. Are you hungry?"

"Yeah, I'm starving," I told him. I was very excited about having a good meal. "I live under that tree." I pointed to my tent. "And I have another problem too." I looked away very shameful.

"I know, and I want you to bring your stuff with you to the festival, we'll do a magic trick, and then sleep until you're ready to learn."

"What is your name?" Mirth asked.

"My name is Peter and it's good to meet you." I said.

We walked through some trees, under a bridge, and into a large dirt area that I'd never seen before. There was a house and a large table that sat off to the left corner stacked with boxes and ribbons around the boxes that had the appearance of Christmas gifts. We were all alone, but I felt a sense of comfort and ease with a stranger in a place that I never knew existed even though I lived about a thousand feet through the trees.

It was getting dark and Mirth started a fire in a pit not too far from the table and asked me to grab my supplies and sit on a log next to him.

"What supplies are you talking about?" I asked him.

"You know, don't worry, I know what you do."

As we sat down, he told me to "poor the drugs onto this metal plate I'm holding, and we need to let go of the control that this substance has on your life. Drugs have the ability to change our thinking and create that illusion that we need it. Like a rainbow, it isn't real but what you see, feel, and think are results of a loss of independence and appreciation for what is genuine and real. The pleasure from methamphetamine isn't real because highness comes from you not the drug. When you smoke meth, what happens to it?"

"It melts and turns into smoke," I answered, unsure on what he was getting at.

"Yes, it changes. What is real? Real things don't change. My vision, purpose, passions, and esteem for myself doesn't change unless I relinquish it. Feelings aren't real or facts, as they change. Methamphetamine is a chemical that melts, becomes smoke, and is gone. It's time we let go of illusions and focus on reality. Take this tray, throw the drug in the fire and let go of this control."

I took the tray as I was instructed and without thinking hard, threw all the contents into the fire. "It feels good but scary at the same time as I've been doing this daily for a few years and I'm not sure how motivated I'll be tomorrow, or the next day without it." I looked at Mirth as he had a big smile on his face and told him that I was tired and wanted to sleep.

"Hang on about fifteen minutes because I think it might be important to eat something as you look like you could benefit from some food. You're thin and need to bulk up a little. Let us go into the kitchen and find something that you can nibble on."

Mirth was so nice, and there was something about him

that seemed familiar, but I couldn't put my finger on it. He reminded me of somebody that I knew from a long time ago., but who? We walked into the house that looked like the stereotypical image of normalcy as it had a white picket fence and a beautiful garden that appears to have been well kept. We walked through the front door, through the house, and into the kitchen where he had food, unlike anything I'd seen in years. The food looked freshly cooked and it was odd on how he did this since we had been together for a couple of hours.

"Peter, I have dinner for you and I want you to sit at the table and eat. I have steak, salad, mashed potatoes, and green beans. I hope you like it. Eat what you can, and I'll be right back. Once you're done, I'll show you where you can sleep."

Mirth left, and I was staring at all the food that I had in front of me. It looked good, but I knew that I wasn't going to be able to eat much of this. I had a hard time eating. I took the knife, cut into the steak and took a bite of the worst tasting beef I'd ever tasted as it was burnt on the outside, overcooked on the inside and had a bitter flavor. I wasn't going to eat this and was hoping there was nothing wrong with the rest of the food because I was starving. After looking over the salad and mashed potatoes, I became angry as he was teasing me with food that nobody would feed a dog. The salad was full of limp, soggy leaves with an unpleasant odor and no dressing to cover the nasty flavor of this terrible meal. I slid the food across the table and stood up quickly to find Mirth as he appeared in front of me.

"What is this about!" I screamed at Mirth.

"This is dinner because I knew you were going to be hungry," he stated.

"I can't eat this shit. The steak is disgusting, the salad

smells horrible, and I was afraid to even look at what was crawling in the mashed potatoes."

"The free meal isn't up to your standards," Mirth said. "I know, when I'm offered gifts, I appreciate it even though it may not be exactly what I was hoping for. You'll get everything you need, don't worry but that doesn't mean that your needs will always have the same taste as your wants. There's some cereal and bread in the cabinet and butter and milk in the refrigerator. Eat quickly."

I wasn't sure if I was going to like the games that Mirth was playing but understood his point. I ate some cereal and followed Mirth upstairs to a bedroom.

"This is where you'll sleep, you can shower before bed, and there are clothes in the closet you can change into. You'll find all your toiletries in the bathroom and I'll see you after you wake up. Sleep well and dream about an eagle seeking prey as the eagle is seeking to fill the emptiness inside."

I showered, changed clothes, and fell asleep within minutes.

Part 2: Not What Things May Seem

I awoke in the morning and felt refreshed, rejuvenated and energetic. I felt good. The sun was up so I slipped out of bed and went over to the closet to find some clothes where Mirth had mentioned that I'd find them. I opened the door and found one outfit that I wasn't comfortable wearing. I pulled it out of the closet and laughed as I realized it was exactly like the clothes Mirth had been wearing yesterday. I decided to put them on since I had nothing else to wear and he made a point last night to not be picky about things that you're offered for free. Since he was also the only person in this town who would see me, I didn't care since Mirth would be wearing the same ridiculous outfit also.

I walked downstairs and went outside into a world that I'd never seen before. "How long had I been sleeping and who were all these people? What was going on?" I tried to find Mirth but couldn't pick him out of all the other strange looking characters. I panicked and began running around yelling for Mirth and couldn't find the place that we had entered through the trees. There were people selling things, and children running around sword fighting. Something felt wrong, so I began running to the house where I had slept, and a female stopped me in my tracks.

"Hold on." She stepped in front of me. "Are you lost?"

"Yeah, I don't know what is going on, and I can't seem to find my way out of this place. Do you know Mirth?"

"Yes, I do. Why don't you ask for help? Instead of running aimlessly, you have all these people that might have the answer. If she"—she pointed to a woman—"doesn't have the answer, ask someone else. You don't have to panic. Mirth is in that red tent off to the left corner."

"Thank you," I respectfully said.

I ran to the tent that the kind lady had pointed out. I stepped inside and saw Mirth, dressed very differently than before, wearing a crown and sitting behind a desk.

"Peter, you're awake. Good to see you, your clothes look nice, and you have color back in your face. You look better, and it's time we get to work."

"What is this place? Who are these people? Why are you wearing a crown? What—"

He cut me off. "I know you have a lot of questions, and I have so many more answers to offer you, but be patient. You'll understand when the time is right," he informed me.

Mirth grabbed my hand and walked me outside the tent.

"Please listen, everybody. We have a guest, Peter, who is here to be a part of something big. You'll treat Peter as you would treat me. As the king of Bath, I declare the town a sanctuary as we give refuge to Peter as a student and a teacher," he informed the crowd. He turned to me. "Please join me at my table for a feast, and I'll inform you about our ways. My name is King Heart and welcome.

We walked into a blue tent with a giant table covered with food. I was so hungry and began eating everything I could get my hands on.

"Slow down, don't eat too much as we have work to do. It has been three days since you came into town, so we're a little behind and it's late in the afternoon," he told me.

"Three days. I thought I got here last night."

"No, you were sleeping long and hard and I kept checking on you to make sure you were OK. Bath is a festival town that brings with it knowledge, goods, and hope to those seeking a better life. Nothing is by accident and many things are easily missed if you don't have the keen eyes for the mysterious. Follow your heart and let your intuition guide you. You may not understand much of what I'm telling you, so I'll give you a clue on how to begin. Don't say or ask anything as I give you the opportunity for your life to begin today. Green is your mark to start your trail as you create a new story that begins, right now."

The king stood up and walked away as I sat confused and bewildered about the lack of information I was given. Green is your mark to start was the only clue he gave me to begin. I exited the tent the same way I came in to find all the people gone. The booths, tents, and wooden swords the children were playing with sat silent without a soul to be found. I wasn't afraid and was committed to solving this puzzle that was presented. There was nothing in this entire town that I could see, that was green. The garden in front of the house with the white picket fence was gone as I was hoping to find at least a flower with green petals. I was determined to identify green, so I meticulously wandered the property with such focus and detail only to find nothing. I wanted to give up after an hour but persisted and saw something in front of the red tent that I missed but couldn't understand how this was my clue. It was a long piece of grass but as I approached, it turned out to be a weed. I reached down and pulled the weed and found a key attached to the end of it.

A key must unlock something, but what? Frustrated but excited about this hunt, I walked around the booths, looked in the tents, and couldn't find a key hole for this type of key. It was a modern key in a medieval town. I quickly thought about the house I'd slept in as it was modern. I ran to the house and found all the doors unlocked with no need for a key. I searched the kitchen, the bedroom, the garage, and even cabinets that I knew would have locks too small for this key and found nothing. What did he say specifically, I thought? "Green is your mark to start the trail." I ran back to where I'd found the weed and noticed a small trail that ran around the side of the tent. In the back of the tent, I noticed a safe that I was able to open with the key and inside I found a letter that said:

"Happy are those who receive a gift while happier are those who give a gift."

I wasn't sure what I was supposed to do with this, but I tucked it into a pocket as the sun began to set. I was alone and worried that I was stuck in this town and nobody was coming back. I wandered back to the house and ate some food before lying in bed and staring at the letter that I'd received. I was given the gift of this place I thought, maybe? What did I have to give anybody or who would I give anything to? I was alone. The next thing I knew it was sunrise.

I decided to shower but didn't have clean clothes to put on, so I wore the same attire as the previous day. I went outside and a there were a few people scattered around the property. Things were getting a little more difficult for me as I was wanting to get high. It has been almost five days since I used and was getting squirrely and ready to leave.

A young girl walked up to me and asked me what I see when I look at the rose sitting in the garden in front of the house. That garden wasn't there the night before.

"I see a beautiful rose," I told her, but she insisted I give her more. "I don't know. I've never thought any harder on it."

"I was running through the rain one day, and I noticed the rose just sitting there patiently in the storm. I realized that we all have storms in our lives, but if we can learn from the rose as we wait patiently through hard times and not back down, the sun will eventually shine, and we'll grow. Rain is a requirement for life. Have a good day." And the girl ran off.

"That was weird," I thought. That came from, what looked like a ten-year-old girl, but it made sense and wasn't easy to argue. It didn't change the fact that I wanted to get high but maybe I can wait out the storm a little and see if things get easier. What am I supposed to do? I thought about the letter and I knew there was something about it that I was missing, but what? I remembered that I'd seen some gifts on the table the night I came in, but they were gone. I approached a man who was sitting at a booth and asked him about the letter.

"Many think that a gift is a tangible object that you offer someone for free but that may not be the only gift you can give someone. I'm busy but good luck in your endeavors," he told me.

I quickly walked off as it seemed that he didn't want me around, but I understood his answer. I thought, "What did I have to give someone?" I looked around to see what I could do, and it came to me. "What could I do for the people in this place?" I began looking at the land, the house, and any ailments that I could see. Trash needed to be picked up, the fence was missing a post, and leaves could be raked to clean up the property. At around 5:00 p.m., the area was empty again, and I began cleaning up the property. I raked the leaves, found a post in the back of the house to fix the fence, and removed all the trash that was scattered around the grounds. I spent about two hours organizing miscellaneous items, watered some plants, and fed a deer that was playing in the fields. "It feels good," I thought, "and I'm excited to see the response the next day when people arrive. I'm proud of myself and I strangely have no cravings to get high."

A Summary of The Jester's Game

The Jester's Game introduces Peter as a homeless meth user who is unsure on how to live a different life. The Jester, who is intriguing and sparks the curiosity of Peter, brings him into a world of mystery, surprise, and lessons that are acquired through normal interaction. We need to help people get people clean and sober by tempting an interest that creates curiosity and behaviors that offer an appeal that's unlike the things they know. There are many metaphors in this story and I hope they register with many of you that are reading this.

Why did I write this? As I mentioned before the story, I hope that this can spark some creativity, ingenuity, and mindfulness to offer hope to so many lost in this world through drugs. A Jester was a common character from the medieval times so am I encouraging a medieval treatment approach? Maybe. Will this work? Maybe for some because recovery is an individual journey that must be explored and identified by the person suffering. As I mentioned earlier, transforming is to take something and make it new without consideration for the norm at times. A treatment center's norm consists of individual therapy, counseling and group sessions where you're instructed by a clinician on what will work for you instead of allowing the client the opportunity to identify solutions for themselves in ways that make sense to them.

What Is Recovery?

Recovery from substance abuse entails your ability to accept a loss, feel the world around you, and develop a life that has meaning. We're recovering from a loss of self, loss of relationships, loss of purpose, loss of freedom, loss of direction, and loss of feelings. In the world of recovery, it's loss that will heal loss. I must lose that thing that has influenced those other losses to recover. Recovery to me is a life of purpose, the achieving of my goals, happiness, meaning, pleasure, freedom, network of friends, healthy relationships, financial stability, and healthy view of self. It starts within you, but people are willing to help. There's no rule on where this must be found, and recovery may mean something slightly different to you and that's OK. The only thing I ask is that you share your experience with others because something you do may help another and if you can save one life, it's worth it.

Questions to Consider

1. What can you think of that can help you or someone else?
2. What did you get from the Jester's game?

We must let go and recover from a loss to gain our life back.

CHAPTER 13

Healing Our Future

The boy was only thirteen, when he died of an overdose
Another was eighteen months, as the death toll has rose
With fentanyl mixed with heroin, and a ten-year-old that died
Our country is in crisis as our youth seeks suicide

The attempt to reduce supply has not removed it from our hand
It's time we offer hope by reducing the demand
Four children in Ohio, who awoke and found them dead
They walked into their room and found their parents in their bed

A three-year-old girl, whose parents neglected to check
Died from an overdose, of meth and Subutex.
An eleven-year-old from Pittsburgh, overdosed last year
What happened to those days when we started with a beer?

Look at how things are, as we are improving our technology
We ask to speak the truth, but we punish real honesty
The bullying of today, doesn't have to end at school
You post embarrassing videos and show that you're a fool

We teach our youth delusions, pretending it's not real
Condoms should be offered, as harm reduction is ideal
Maybe we should teach them, how to safely test your dope
Before they stick it in their arm, so they're not dangling from a rope

Kids today seem fragile, very emotionally disconnected
Nothing like we used to be as we fought when disrespected
Sensitivity has shaped our culture, and laws prevent what's right
Teach our kids the truth so we keep them in the light

Don't worry about the history, in fourth or fifth grade
It's the self-esteem and life skills, that mustn't be delayed
Parents and teachers today, must help them find a passion
Determination and empathy, it's time to have compassion

The death toll is rising, and "just say no" isn't right
We must begin the lessons, or the flames will soon ignite
Tell your kids you love them, and hold them close to you
If we don't do something know, you may lose one or even two

To stop something, we need to look at the way things are and not the way we want them to be. Our youth today, seem to be in trouble and unable to deal with or cope with the hardships of life and turning to drug use, suicide, or violence. As an adult, I remember my hate, disgust, fear, and sadness of childhood, which has very little difference than today, with one major exception. Social Media. I had bullies, fights, name-calling, and pressure like many of the kids today but it ended when I went home, and it was isolated to the people directly involved, unlike today. We've all done embarrassing things as a child but with cameras today, those shameful tasks are recorded and aired on the internet for everybody to see, laugh at, and offer ammunition to tease.

Bullying Continues with Social Media

The problems with decision making for undeveloped brains, issues with social media that can advertise murder and suicide, and the fear that runs rampant in talking about thoughts and feelings to be viewed as weak, we arrive at the place of judgment and persecution that's left open for a child to come to conclusions in a state of hopelessness. Many adults wonder why students don't come forward and tell teachers, parents, or law enforcement about bullying that they're the targets of. This isn't a hard concept to understand if you think back to when we were in school. You're a tattle tale, your weak, and you're a pussy will be added to the barrage of insults and teasing that will amplify the problems, or at least that's what the child will think.

The internet today, continues the teasing of our youth while, not at school, as they watch videos on Facebook or receive emails from students that continue the hateful messages. Sitting online with those uncomfortable feelings we mentioned earlier, the child can begin research on retribution as they formulate harm to be inflicted that may start very innocent. As research, continued bullying, and lack of control begins to take hold, the picture grows into something that's unimaginable to most of us. If this child were to come forward and tell a teacher that I plan on killing everybody in the school, what response would be received? How would this child be treated? If someone came forward with this information, it's obvious that there's uncertainty and doubt on the part of this adolescent and open discussion can develop.

What is the response that would be received? A call to the police, a trip to a mental hospital, and undeserved punishment? Our society issues negative consequences to honesty and truthfulness, which keeps some from coming forward and talking about what is in their minds. We then ask, "why didn't this person talk to anybody before committing the act?" Punishment, judgment, and rejection is the reason.

Duty to Protect and Duty to Report

This topic naturally brings up controversy with the behavioral health community as we're subjected to the "duty to report" as a condition to our license or certification. I can identify numerous individuals that I've worked with that specifically withheld information that was detrimental to their life, success, and recovery, because they understood this requirement that I had to follow. I had a client who had prior history of suicidal attempts and he failed to disclose this information during his assessment or throughout his treatment. Upon completing his outpatient treatment, he remained steady in his recovery for a period and relapsed after getting in an argument with his wife. An employee of mine received a phone call from her one day and the conversation was told to me and it went something like this.

"Hi this is Jeremy's wife," she started, "Jeremy shot himself last night and I wanted to know if he contacted you." Peggy was sobbing heavily making it a little hard to understand her.

"Did you say that he shot himself?"

"Yeah, he is dead. He said after we had gotten into a fight that he was depressed and wanted to die. We talked for a while and I asked if he had worked with your place on his depression and if he would call you," she said tearfully.

"I hadn't heard from him," he told her "and was never

informed that he had any prior suicidal thoughts, nor did he disclose any signs or symptoms of depression."

"He told me that you had incorporated it into his treatment, but it doesn't surprise me because he always feared being locked up in a hospital. He said he was going to call you and talk because you helped him work through things but doubtful he would say that he wanted to harm himself because of that possibility of being committed," she told me.

"I'm so sorry to hear about Jeremy," he told her, but it sparked in me that controversial topic of confidentiality versus "duty to report."

I learned later about the specifics behind Jeremy's suicide. After an argument with his wife, he drove to his father's house to get his gun for purposes of selling it, or at least that's what he told his father. His father notified his wife that he had his gun, so she regularly checked their shared bank account to see if he had made any purchases to try and locate him. His wife saw the purchase for bullets on their checking account and notified his father who drove to the gun shop. Jeremy was walking out of the store and gave his father a hug before getting in his truck, locking the door, and shooting himself as his father was attempting to open the door.

When a client checks into a substance-abuse-treatment program, he or she will be required to sign admission documents that explain requirements of the program to uphold confidentiality as well as exceptions to that rule. Clinicians are required to report suicidal and homicidal ideations, suspected child abuse, and elder abuse as interpreted by the expert providing the services. Harm to others has guidelines that should identify an intended target, timeframe, plan, and ability to carry out the plan that was identified.

"Duty to protect" was established by Tarasoff v. Regents

of the University of California and requires the clinician to warn the intended target. Jablonski by Pahls v. United States extended the responsibility to include the involuntary commitment to a hospital as the "duty to warn" wasn't sufficient. Another landmark case that followed was Ewing v. Goldstein that required behavioral health professionals to act upon statements made by third parties.

The following is an example of how a client might interpret what is told to them upon intake into a treatment program.

> **Thank you for coming to our facility, I'm going to be your counselor. Let me explain the process of how important confidentiality is to us and we'll never disclose anything to anybody except for a few exceptions, which I'm going to explain. As you're an adult, we'll report any disclosure you make to the police of child abuse or elder abuse. If you want to harm yourself and you tell me, I'll discharge you from this program and have you locked away in a psychiatric hospital for three days. If you claim to have any interest in harming another person, you'll be discharged from the facility and locked away in a mental hospital. Confidentiality is extremely important to us and we want you to share all your feelings, thoughts, and shame but remember that if you tell me that you want to "shoot up a school" because of rage that consumes you, or "kill your neighbor" we'll lock you up,**

**call the police, and notify everybody that
could be harmed by you. How are you
feeling now? Just remember that if you
want to do any of those things I mentioned, just don't tell me. OK?**

This may sound absurd but not too far off from how clients will interpret these disclosures creating a distance from
what is superficial and what is real. I've brought this debate
forward to evaluate the effectiveness of this topic. Sure, in
some cases, black-and-white thinking may be required but
an opportunity for open disclosure without repercussions
can be an option for some. What if I presented to the public
an open-door policy for individuals that are contemplating
a "school shooting" without judgment, consequences, or
retaliation? Would anybody come? Probably not, and much
of the reason would be the lack of trust in disclosing such
information. We want honesty but punish real honesty.

A Real Story We Can Learn From

There's a boy, and we'll refer to him as the "adolescent,"
who was attending his sophomore year in high school and
was brought into the office to meet with the principle being
accused of making statements that he was going to "shoot
up the school." His mother received a phone call and was
directed to pick him up and was suspended for three days.
She took him to a hospital to be evaluated and the following day, the police department and the school received a
fax from the hospital stating that it's their responsibility to
submit a Tarasoff report because he reported he was going
to "shoot up the school" and has "threatened the lives of
the students at the school." Because of this report, the high

school moved forward with proceedings to expel him from the school district. From face value, I'm sure that we can all agree that he should be expelled, and criminal charges of terrorist threats should be imposed upon him, which they were. This wasn't the complete story and because of the laws that we have in place this could ruin many aspects of his future and destroy some goals he has especially if he was convicted of the criminal charges. They didn't listen to him and it took money on the family's part to force them to listen.

About three months prior to being brought into the principal's office, the "adolescent" was being called a "school shooter" by a couple of students at his school. The reason that he gained this title was because he has long hair, listens to heavy metal, and periodically wears Metallica and other shirts depicting bands that he listens to with images not always presented of a happy life. As this name-calling continued for months and him repeatedly telling them to stop calling him this, one of the students asked him the following question. "When you shoot up the school, are you going to shoot me?" As his frustration had peaked and being tired of hearing this, he responded with, "I'm going to shoot you first."

Another student heard him say this and reported this to that students' mother. The school received an anonymous phone call by a mother informing them that someone, and not sure who but was in one of two classes, was planning to "shoot up the school." The principle went to investigate and received written reports from students who gave their knowledge of what they knew. A few reports identified the "adolescent" as him claiming he was going to do this. Some reported not having any idea what they were talking about and some reported the "adolescent" as being called this by others but never stating that he said he was going to do it.

When his mother arrived at the school to pick him up, the school counselor recommended that he be taken to a hospital, so they could clear him of these accusations and help resolve this matter, so he could return to school. She took him to the hospital as she was following the recommendation and sat in the interview with a nurse at the hospital getting him checked in and listening to her son explain the story I identified above. The nurse stated that "it sounds like he was being bullied and responded in anger with that statement that has caused all of these problems." It was a voluntary admission to get cleared and his mother was informed that it would most likely be just one day, so he could meet with a psychologist and psychiatrist.

His mother received a call the next day from the principle stating they were moving forward with expelling him because of the Tarasoff letter that they received from the hospital, which clearly sounded like he was continuing to make threats since he was "threatening the lives of the students at the school." She called the hospital and was informed that the Tarasoff letter was based on the information that the "adolescent" told the nurse who was also the individual who sent the letter to the school and the police department. This was also the person who said that "it sounds like he was being bullied and responded in anger with that statement that has caused all of these problems."

That boy was now being told that he should remain voluntarily in the hospital because the police might require involuntary commitment as a result of one statement he made that was a result of him being bullied that had been stated as a likelihood by the hospital and the school counselor who encouraged him to go to the hospital to get cleared so he could go back to school after his three-day suspension. A police officer arrived at the "adolescent's" apartment to search his room for weapons that he may be holding in which none were found. The district attorney's office was requesting a meeting with him as they were in the process of filing terrorist threat charges.

The family hired an attorney who analyzed the school report that they presented for the hearings that would take place for him to be expelled and found so many inconsistencies in their report. The attorney submitted a letter to the principle the day before the first hearing and his mother received a phone call within ten minutes of him receiving the letter stating that "maybe we could look at different options instead of expelling, which could be switching him to the other high school in the same district." Criminal charges were never filed after having a meeting with a district attorney and the question was asked, "why didn't you say something to the school when you were being bullied?"

I couldn't tell you what could have happened if he said that "I've been called a school shooter by other students" to the counselor or principal after experiencing the fiasco we had to go through. I was so concerned with the way the school handled this, but it did show me that common sense and really listening to what our kids are saying doesn't happen. That adolescent will probably have a difficult time saying anything to anybody especially a therapist or counselor in his future because they weren't looking out for his best interest. This process made no sense to me and the same thing could have happened if he walked into the principle and said, "I've been called a school shooter" because the words themselves instantly create accusations even if it came from someone else.

The school changed its mind about expelling him,

because the letter implied that the family would sue the district as a result of these accusations that would damage his goals for the future. All of this is based on him being bullied, which was corroborated and making one statement that was answering a question that would result in implying he would "shoot up the school" no matter how he answered—yes or no.

Harm Reduction

Our government seems to miss the mark when it comes to identifying solutions to many of our problems and seems to attempt to make changes by adding new laws that rarely have to do with helping our youth but instead, catching them once they have committed an offense. Harm reduction assumes that people are going to gain access to things that are harmful such as drugs or guns, so we find ways to reduce the harm for all involved. In some cases, we need to protect the innocent people who have nothing to do with the harmful act and are killed as a result. When laws are added that increase the penalties for that harmful thing, it becomes more valuable on the black market increasing the likelihood that they will be available.

On February 15, 2018, Nikolas Cruz was arrested for the killing of students and faculty at Marjory Stoneman Douglas High School. He has been charged with seventeen counts of premeditated murder with a semiautomatic AR-15 rifle that was purchased legally that brought to the forefront, the debate on gun laws again. The Second Amendment of the Constitution states **"a well-regulated militia, being necessary to the security of a free state, the right of the people to keep and bear arms, shall not be infringed"** but clearly has limits and doesn't prohibit the regulation of all firearms and who can purchase firearms.

Students from Marjory Stoneman Douglas High School, as well as schools across the country began rallying for tougher gun laws to make schools safer as we've seen seventeen shootings in 2018 before the massacre identified above. Violence on school property isn't a new phenomenon, with the first recorded incident happening on July 26, 1764, when four Lenape American Indian's entered a schoolhouse near present-day Greencastle, Pennsylvania and shot and killed at least nine children. According to "Every Town," there have been 291 school shootings since 2013 and what are we doing about it?

What Is Important?

The typical drug user will focus on the here and now without considering any future. Tomorrow doesn't matter, yesterday and today blend together and nothing seems to exist but getting high. The solution to the "drug war" or the "opioid epidemic" must be solved through a tactic that keeps in mind, what is important, which is to find happiness, feel good, and define a purpose, otherwise it will fail. How does a company go out of business? We've all heard that "money makes the world go around" and without money, a business will fail. If drugs enter the country and less people buy it, things will slow down. What is it that causes people to use drugs? That's what we need to focus on as we find a solution.

The best way to prevent drug addiction and overdose is to prevent people from abusing drugs in the first place. If they don't start, they won't have a problem.
—President Donald J. Trump

Donald Trump's statement sounds good, but what are the details and how do we do this? Unless we're working to help people find happiness, a purpose, passion, and the ability to feel good with confidence and high self-esteem, we'll fail. Public officials with no knowledge and experience will not find the solution unless we work to reduce demand. It's time we stop blaming and criticizing others because they feel they could have done it better. Scott Peterson, an armed officer at Marjory Stoneman Douglas High School, was criticized for failing to run into the school and take down the assailant who killed seventeen people. He was called a "coward" by President Trump and stated, "I really believe I'd run in there even if I didn't have a weapon." Officer Peterson's attorney claimed that he felt the shots were coming from outside the school, which would have created blame if he had run into the school and the assailant was outside. If the officer ran into the school and declared a "shootout" with the killer, how many more people could have been killed? Blame, criticism, and "I could have done it better" is the response to our problems. Unless you were there, nobody knows how they would respond. It's easy to sit in the White House or Congress and make statements of unbelievable courage in the face of danger "if I was there."

Prohibition and Reducing Supply Is Not the Answer

History has shown us that the federal government, through laws, utilizes prohibition as a solution to solving National problems. Prohibition, the act of forbidding something, has been the attempt to keep it from being made or entering our borders to stop the ability for people to be able to access it. Does it work? According to GovTrack, as of May 1, 2018, 128 laws have been enacted by Congress since January 2017 and 3,856 since January 6, 1999. How many of these laws are directed at taking rights away from us? How many of these laws are strictly for gaining votes or fulfilling private agendas of the lawmakers? I have yet to see how effective policy changes are for fixing the problems with gun control or the life-threatening issues we're seeing with drug abuse. Prohibition has been the solution but unfortunately has shown to be a tremendous failure. The Harrison Narcotics Act of 1914, the Volstead Act from 1920 to 1933, the Marijuana Tax Act of 1937, Boggs Act of 1951, and the Daniels Act of 1956 that would increase the penalties if you were found to be in possession of a prohibited substance have been ineffective as drug use continues. Every time that we prohibit something and make it a crime to possess, that product becomes more valuable and is guaranteed to become available because people take risks to be rich.

If we were to toughen gun laws such as requiring you to be twenty-one to purchase one, you'll still continue to have school shootings by a sixteen-, seventeen-, or 18-year-old, because changing the laws will not prevent this from happening again. A sixteen-year-old who is determined will acquire a gun, even though it may be delayed as the perpetrator develops a plan to acquire the gun illegally. If someone is committed to performing such a heinous act, the ability to gain the weapon of choice will occur and the focus should be placed on preventing the harm involved.

Even though metal detectors become a nuisance and

expensive, securing a school with barbed wire fences around the property requiring entrance in a single location, could be a partial fix. In 2016, I visited my brother in Kansas and participated in a school shooting preparedness program with the fire department, emergency personnel and law enforcement. I asked a representative from the district, "why don't you place metal detectors in your schools if this is such a concern." Her response was, "we don't want this to look like a prison." Maybe safety should be more of a concern then how it looks? Society needs to understand that events such as Marjory Stoneman Douglas High School will continue despite all law changes. Drug use will continue despite all prohibition enacted. Some prisoners in our nation's most maximum-security prisons would test positive for drugs every day in a urinalysis screen. Let us not fool ourselves with a notion that we can stop the purchase or acquisition of something and focus on harm reduction. Violence will continue no matter how much we change laws, we need to lock down the schools, put metal detectors in place, and install barbed wire fencing around the properties to protect our children. Why do we care more about what it looks like than the protection of life?

Is Evil Created by Nature or Is It Nurtured?

I have a belief that humans are not born evil. Evil is nurtured through life experiences such as trauma, parental guidance, and social interactions. Empathy doesn't justify the behaviors of people, but it does allow us the opportunity to understand the actions through the minds of someone who was unable to cope in a healthy manner. We hear stories of children who grow up in the same house, suffered the same abuse, but behaved in different ways. How does this happen? Everyone, including you and I, learn coping strategies, have different qualities, and view things in a way that may be separated by our creation of a world with an alternative understanding.

Charles Manson and to many the picture of evil, Adolf Hitler offer examples of life events that were experienced as children that may have influenced or nurtured their behaviors as adults. It was reported that Charles Manson's mother sold him to a woman who wanted children for a pitcher of beer that can be assumed to have created a tumultuous upbringing. Adolf Hitler was severely beaten by his father as a child. He began using that form of discipline to teach his sister by hitting her. Corporal punishment, sexual abuse, mental abuse, learning from fear, and societal factors open a door to massacres that, maybe, we can redirect if we can listen to our youth and allow open communication to occur.

An Unfortunate Solution

Violence, suicide, drug abuse, and murder are the solution as they see it that's forged by people to cope with their situations. This isn't to say that those solutions are justified, and our criminal justice system should punish according to our laws, but can we formulate a plan that can prevent such atrocities and empathetically, without judgment, help those who are suffering. We're not always in complete control of our thoughts as it can wander but we're responsible for what we do. Our thoughts do create, which is why we must be careful if our feelings take hold.

When I was a freshman in high school, Jim, a friend of mine, drove by in the parking lot of our school and threw an egg at me that splattered on my shirt. I couldn't understand the reason he would do this but I was angry, and I thought of nothing but revenge and hatred that raged in my body. At home that night, all I could think about was hurting him and making him pay for the disrespect and harm he caused. The world wide web hadn't been created yet, so I didn't have access to other ideas except for what I was able to create. I didn't accept sadness, hurt, and fear as feelings and would instantly convert those, which is what I felt, to anger and rage. Jim and I had science class together for second period and after learning we were being shown a video, I sat on the back counter during the movie placing me behind Jim in a vulnerable position. As I sat on the counter and the movie began to play, my mind started to imagine everything I could do to harm and embarrass him. At some point, I felt that I was unable to control my actions and kicked him in the back of the head once the teacher stepped out of the room, forcing him to make contact on the desk with his face. Revenge was my master and retribution was my game. We fought outside after class resulting in suspension for a couple of days.

Freedom of Speech—Do We Have This Right?

Adolescents have limited knowledge and experience in maintaining control of their emotions and feel that each moment that we experience will forever shape their lives. Hopelessness, as we discussed earlier, is that state of attempting all things with no solution possible. How can someone be completely hopeless and reach that state of giving up with only fifteen years of life? As I'm forty-four years old, I had thoughts of homicide, suicide, and devastation as a child but none of that matters today as I enjoy the moment and look forward to what is coming ahead. I've heard that a child's brain isn't fully developed until the age of thirty, which can give us an understanding of how difficult it can be to think rationally, realistically, and process the simple concept of common sense. If I learn from my father that physical abuse is the method of getting people to do what I want, and this is reinforced every day for ten years, my beliefs will dictate those actions.

Without justifying the actions of these violent, murderous youth, how many signs had been noticed that were left unattended? How many times had they reached out for help with little response by an adult? Murder and suicide become the coping strategy for that hopeless and helpless individual that sees no way out and usually fit together in a scheme of retribution and "nothing left to lose." More common than not, the adolescent or young adult, will plan a suicide but may feel that revenge is a necessity before it can be carried out. When someone reaches that place of having nothing left to lose, that's when horrific things happen, and prevention could have taken place. Excuses shouldn't be made for these individuals to avoid the death penalty or any justification of childhood trauma being explored for reduced sentencing. Once the act is committed, the criminal justice system should punish according to the law. We should teach our children and understand as adults a good question to ask before we follow through on our actions. Are you willing to pay the price?

The First Amendment to the Constitution states, "Congress shall make no law respecting an establishment of religion or prohibiting the free exercise thereof; or abridging the freedom of speech, or of the press; or the right of the people peaceably to assemble, and to petition the government for a redress of grievances." The first of the ten amendments that constitute the Bill of Rights was adopted in 1791. Since that time exceptions have been made that reduce this freedom, possibly causing harm in certain arenas. Some people have murderous thoughts, and it would be illegal to share those murderous thoughts. People don't share those thoughts and instead go on to murder people. It would be more useful to be able to share the thoughts and not murder people.

Learning from Our History?

In 1914, the Harrison Narcotics Tax Act was passed, which was technically the first federal law that prohibited the possession of any drug without a prescription. This act only applied to drugs derived from the coca plant such as cocaine or the opium plant such as heroin but set in motion an interest to control other substances in the future. Once this began in the United States, laws started to spiral out of control starting a "drug war" that has affected every family in this nation. Every time that President Trump presents to the public an idea as something he created, makes me realize how uninformed he is on history. He declared the solution that was presented by Singapore's policy for drug dealers, which was to execute drug dealers but failed to account for his Attorney General's fight for the death penalty many years ago. In 1996, it was reported that Jeff Sessions, Alabama's Attorney General at the time, promoted a bill that would establish a mandatory death sentence for a second drug trafficking conviction that included marijuana. President Trump stated harsher sentencing for smaller traffickers with a sentence of five years. In 1958, some states passed the Little Boggs Act and the Little Daniels Act, which increased penalties for possession of drugs to heights unimaginable. You could have received ten years for rape, fifteen years for murder, and a whopping twenty years in prison for possession of marijuana.

> **If ever a time should come, when vain and aspiring men shall possess the highest seats in Government, our country will stand in need of its experienced patriots to prevent its ruin.**
>
> **—Samuel Adams**

History should prevent us from making the same mistakes again, not repeating them. We continue to try and stop the manufacture and possession of illicit drugs, while alcohol prohibition, the Volstead Act, gave us a glimpse of the effectiveness of such laws where we saw the rise of organized crime that included corruption and violence because of how much money could be made on the black market. The Volstead Act was an amendment to the Constitution that made it illegal to manufacture, sell, import, or transport certain types of alcohol, but didn't make it illegal to possess or consume on private property. The Volstead Act was such a failure that it was repealed after thirteen years, so maybe it's time we learn from history and stop repeating mistakes.

Why Are We Promoting Violence?

It isn't surprising that our president isn't promoting policies that are designed to reduce harm because he makes comments that encourage violence repeatedly. February 23, 2016, Donald Trump made a comment after a protester was escorted out from one of his rallies and speaking to his supporters stated, "I'd like to punch him in the face." He has promoted violence with comments made against him or his candidacy, and he rejects the right of people to protest. "He should have been roughed up," he said in response to a protester who was "obnoxious and loud" and who was assaulted by his supporters. He stated, "You know, part of the problem, and part of the reason it takes so long, is nobody wants to hurt each other anymore, right? And they're being politically correct the way they take them out, so it takes a little bit longer. And honestly, protesters, they realize it. They realize that there are no consequences to protesting anymore. There used to be consequences, there are none anymore" after a protester was dragged out of his rally. Our children have a president who encourages violence and should be promoting peaceful conflict resolution.

Our Rights as Americans

It's very important for all Americans to understand, despite what you may be taught or have heard from government officials such as our president, the rights that we have. In a democracy, citizens have rights, which include the right to their beliefs, including religious beliefs, and to say and write what they think. Everyone has the right to associate with other people, and to form and join organizations of their own choice that shouldn't be coerced through fear, specifically from a trusted official. Everyone has the right to assemble and to protest government actions with an obligation to exercise these rights peacefully, with respect for the law and for the rights of others. "He should have been roughed up?" Trumps reference to dismissing negative news as fake or statements such as "the media is fake" sets some different tone then previous presidents who encouraged free press, regardless of the content. I hope that President Trump feels that all media including positive things about him are viewed as fake, since the media is fake. "The media is fake" is a great example of black-and-white.

Let's Listen and Stop Judging

This isn't a joke, it's deadly, and we can turn our eyes to the pain of others or identify a solution that works. Harm reduction can be a great place to start. If a student has a drug problem and wants to talk about it, have a conversation without judgment, persecution, and damnation.

Nothing in this chapter was designed to target President Trump in a negative view. I stand strong on our Constitution, the rights of the people, and respect for our democracy, not as a Democrat or a Republican. The political group is of no interest as the health, unity, safety, and integrity of this country is of importance. Donald Trump is president, and I expect him to consider what is best for all the people when doing his job. It's estimated that almost 10 percent of our population has a drug or alcohol problem. These people must not be forgotten. We need to find a solution that works while incarceration has rarely been that tool that's effective.

Is There a Solution?

Our youth need to be dealt with in an empathetic fashion as life is new to them. The solutions that may seem right to some people such as violence, murder, and drugs are unhealthy, irrational, and destructive with no clear rationale. Incarceration has saved lives, but without assistance or treatment of some form, the recidivism will keep them stuck in that cycle. I have a hard stance and solution to some of the issues we're facing in the industry and we must help our communities see that treatment can be effective. Referrers that bring drugs into rehabs to get people high should be turned over to the police because they're killing people. Social media can be turned into a useful source as we can show the world the faces of people that are paying clients to enter facilities or treatment programs that are exploiting and killing people for money. Solid proof can be great ammunition.

A Summary

1. Let us stop focusing on history, science, and social studies before we teach self-esteem, self-discipline, and self-responsibility. We need to teach our children how to love themselves and something that can help send them in the right direction. This should be taught at home and at school.
2. Violence will continue no matter how much we change laws, we need to lock down the schools, put metal detectors in place, and install barbed wire fencing around the properties to protect our children. Why do we care more about what it looks like than the protection of life?
3. Mandatory reporting for things that have not been committed, needs to be relooked at so we can encourage honest communication. If we question the reason why someone didn't come forward and talk to someone about bullying and commits a violent offense, then we're at fault if we don't allow honest communication to take place without condemnation. Why can't we create one office in every town that's staffed with professionals who aren't obligated to

report? Let us staff one person who can be available in every town that can be safe for people to talk to. Let us try it and see.

Questions to Consider

1. Do you recognize your own biases?
2. How would you handle a situation if someone said they wanted to harm themselves or harm others?

Let's look at things as they are and not what we want them to be.

CHAPTER **14**

Think, Think, Think

Smoke this my friend, if you want to be cool,
Or if you want to be a part of our clan.
Let us be popular at the school,
Or I will distance myself as your friend.

My failure to think for myself,
I took the pipe and hit it.
I laid it down upon my shelf,
And was hooked and couldn't quit.

His sponsor convinced a friend one day,
To avoid the treatment of hep C.
He was told to listen or if he disobeyed,
He'd quit as he knew better you see.

The sponsor told him a plan that day,
To take some herbs instead.
After some months, he would surely pay,
As cirrhosis would leave him dead.

He had a father who taught him hate,
As he was a member of the KKK.
He fed him lies as he used the bait,
To get him to alter and sway.

He just believed what was told to him,
As he was too young to think for himself.
More than half of his life everything was grim,
As prison was the life for him.

They were some very innocent males,
Who were told about this world of Islam.
When ISIS promised a virgin trail,
They felt it was nice and calm.

The training was rugged and often hard,
As death was in their sight.
It began with a job as a guard,
Turned into a bomb they would light.

Tale of Horror That We All Know

On November 17, 1957, a nightmare story emerged of a de-
ranged, insane killer. The story was retold numerous times,
through the likes of Buffalo Bill in *Silence of the Lambs*,
Leatherface in *Texas Chainsaw Massacre*, Norman Bates
from *Psycho*, and Otis from *House of a 1000 Corpses*.
Even though movies will Hollywoodize stories making them
bigger than they are, Ed Gein's tale of horror needs no
exaggeration. Since I'd clarified according to my opinion,
evil derives from a nurture not nature that's brought about
through hatred, anger, and damnation that's clearly present
in his macabre story. The following story details a man who

may have been born a "normal" child, but because of his teacher in life, he became something that's hard to fathom.

Bernice Wordon, the owner of a hardware store, in Springfield, Wisconsin, had gone missing, and the sheriff's department was notified. It was reported by a witness that Edward Gein's truck had been parked at the store on the day of her vanishing, and the store's last receipt was written to Mr. Gein. A search warrant was issued by the court, and Deputy Arthur Schley went to Edward Gein's property, according to Biography.com. Upon searching his property, the sheriffs found the decapitated body of Bernice Worden, who had been shot with a .22-caliber rifle and was hanging in a shed with ropes around her wrists. Deputy Schley also found noses, bones, masks of human skin, bowls made from skulls, ten female heads, human-skin seat covers, Bernice Warden's head, nine vulvas in a shoebox, skulls on his bedposts, organs in the refrigerator, a belt made from nipples, and a lampshade made from a human face, according to *Deviant* by Harold Schechter and Murderpedia. org. There was also the decapitated head of Mary Hogan, who had gone missing prior to Bernice Wordon, that was found on his property. He was accused of two murders but only charged with one. He was found guilty of first-degree murder, but legally insane, and spent the rest of his life in a mental hospital. Many of the body parts that were recovered were of women whom he dug up at a local cemetery. How does somebody do something like this? There's a commonality between you, myself, and Edward Gein.

I don't believe that he ever found the ability to achieve what was important, which is to feel good, because his idea of where to find it was misguided and manipulated by the one person whom he trusted the most, his mother. Augusta, Edward's mother, was a fanatically religious individual who was determined to teach her two boys that they lived in a sinful world, and women would drag them to hell because of their sexual interests and desires. They were shielded from the world except for school, where Edward was bullied and teased, as he was shy and uncomfortable around others. His interest in women created confusion, as he desired something that was sinful, evil, and wrong in the eyes of the woman he loved the most. She verbally abused her children, telling them they would amount to nothing. It's hard to say how his brother Henry would have developed, because he died during a fire on their property as they were attempting to clear away brush. The coroner declared asphyxiation as the cause, but the sheriff noticed bruise marks around his neck, causing speculation that Edward may have killed him as his body never burned, and it was reported that Henry spoke poorly of their mother, causing rage in Edward.

It has been speculated that his mother may have had an incestuous relationship with her son, been schizophrenic, and idolized her father, who was very strict and domineering. This story that I chose to use was to view something that was out of the ordinary to identify what seems to be important to all people and why so many fail to achieve it.

What Is Important?

Through all of history, it appears that our desire to "feel good" has been a dominating interest in human kind but lost to so many with misguided direction. As mental illness may detract from that ability, parents teaching bad information to children, self-exploration of drug abuse that fails, and extreme views of a God that will promise an eternity of rewards by sacrificing self or pleasant things of today, we've arrived at a world of confusion, loss of purpose, and the belief of many that they're undeserving of happiness. Having a purpose feels good, and therefore, I believe it is important, which is where many of the horrors in this world derive, including the story of Edward Gein. In families, cultures, religions, and government, many things taught are not always what things may seem, although they're presented as the way to happiness, feeling good, or having a purpose of some sort that will offer rewards of today or in the afterlife. Augusta Gein, through her understanding, may have been attempting to save her children from hell, but at what cost? She had a purpose and may have felt that happiness isn't deserved in this world but will surely be rewarded in heaven, which allowed her a brief glimpse of feeling good.

When someone is unable to achieve happiness or the ability to feel good derived from a purpose, drug use takes hold, fights begin, and suicide becomes an option once that state of hopelessness takes told. Why are we seeing this increase in violence, suicide, and drug use? I have an answer that may not be appreciated by some, but will be hopefully empowering to many. The United States of America has been called the "land of the free," which is an interesting concept but far from the truth, as freedom implies being able to think, act, or believe without restraints. I'll admit that murder and rape should be impeded because it affects another life, but finding happiness and feeling good requires an ability to judge my own actions and not be coerced by others' standards.

I believe that the ability to have a real purpose and feel genuinely good because of your passion requires the necessity to be able to think for one self and not be told what to do or how to do it. This doesn't discredit the importance of listening to other opinions, but the world in general fails to teach people what good decision-making entails and how we can formulate plans that might be different or even disagree with the norm to find happiness. When we explore the paths that others have tried to achieve a goal and only listen to another's direction, we may conclude that this road is leading to the wrong place if it's not found within our self.

If Edward Gein had learned in school, the only place he could attend, that control, judgment, happiness, decision making, and love could have been found within himself, things may have turned out differently.

Drugs Are Not the Problem

An ideal world would be a place where I could hold beliefs, thoughts, values, and a code for myself without judgment of others, and take personal responsibility. This world would be a place where control came from within and not ruled by other people, religions, and standards for personal gain, which creates torment in those controlled and those controlling. People choose to use and have that ability in this land of the free. People choose to use despite any legal consequences or harm involved because they don't know how to think for themselves. People do get arrested because the government does want to think for them, but this thinking by others fails to look at the big picture of what the problem really is. As I was arrested many times, it wasn't the consequence of incarceration that kept me clean and sober but instead my awareness that sought for what was important. Drugs are not the problem, and all laws do is create societal issues that become a blame game, sending our families and friends to an early grave.

Not Taught to Think for Ourselves

There was no interest, desire, or pursuit of getting clean and sober until I decided for myself that this was the best thing for me. Unless we teach people to think for themselves, inspire an interest in valuing themselves, encourage and develop passions that intrigue them, and empower control that's internal while rejecting demands of others that don't hold true with our interests, nothing will change. No government wants this freedom in such a clear fashion as I've defined, because control is the foundation of authority. Our educational system teaches through minimization and forced curriculums designed to control thought and maintain control. Our criminal justice system enforces laws that take away the ability of people to think for themselves as we're required to wear seatbelts, homeowner's associations that you're required to join that can control how you conduct yourself or use your property, and "just say no" are examples of a lack of encouragement to allow you to conclude what is best for you.

Since much of the recovery community doesn't teach the principles of making good decisions for oneself, we can understand the vulnerability and danger behind the power of not thinking for one self. If I'm always with someone who can make good decisions for me, never am presented with drugs or alcohol, and never have a desire to use drugs and alcohol, my sobriety will most likely be safe. Will I always have someone present when I find a bindle of methamphetamine on the ground at a gas station? Will a thought, craving, or desire to use be eradicated from my existence? Not likely. With all my personal experience, clients I've worked with, and many friends in recovery, the thought to use will periodically present itself, and for that moment, we may be alone to decide our courses of action.

Most of the racism and hate, if you think about it, is a result of ignorant people who think through the minds of others as information is passed down through generations. Why do we describe people by the color of their skin? Why do we describe people as African Americans who have never stepped foot in Africa? Why do we define gay bars as such, while I've never defined a bar as heterosexual? Why am I not referred to as a Swedish American since my mother's side of the family is from Sweden? Does it really matter if I'm white, black, or brown? The answer to this lies in a separation, and racism is found in all nationalities. Why do people blame an entire race of people for slavery who have never owned a slave? Why do people hang a Confederate flag in the South who were not alive when the Confederacy existed? This can only exist by people who are ignorant and can't think for themselves, especially when you consider that the South lost the war.

Relinquishing Power

Genuine power is the ability to hold true to our values, morals, and passions without the need for others' approval and find a happiness, freedom, and self-respect that nobody can take away. This can be used interchangeably with personal power. You can be an asset to the world, offer hope to the suffering, and share a value that seems to be lost to so many. I won't tell you what your passion is, as this isn't my responsibility, but happiness, which is what we'll find through genuine power, is derived through actions of love, altruism, and responsibility, as being a victim doesn't lend a place for freedom. Adolf Hitler held a sort of power that was only granted by his followers and would never have lasted if he couldn't sustain the numbers. Was he happy? Highly doubtful. And I apply the following concept to all authoritarian figures who strive to control others. Dictators will never understand the beauty of genuine power, as their authority, self-respect, and freedom is offered to them by fear, which is the greatest destroyer of happiness. As it has not been my intention to create a political book, Donald Trump is a great example for the point I'm trying to make.

President Trump has been attempting to transition our democracy, or at least as it appears, to an authoritarian-style regime as it's defined as "strict obedience at the expense of personal freedom." Donald Trump doesn't appear to have genuine power as he seems to need the approval or applause of others to revel in his unconstitutional belief of power. A week following his first State of the Union address, Donald Trump made remarks about a comment that was made defining Democrats as "treasonous" because they failed to stand and applaud for his speech.

> **They were like death and un-American. Un-American. Somebody said, "Treasonous." I mean, yeah, I guess. Why not? Can we call that treason? Why not? I mean, they certainly didn't seem to love our country that much.**
>
> **—Donald Trump**

Based on comments of this nature, he must be implying that all Republicans have stood and applauded all Democratic presidents in the past or they were "un-American," and vice versa, which has never happened. It also appears that he fails to understand the definition of treason and love for our country doesn't require a love, appreciation, or even respect for our president.

I've always held a strong stance on teaching people tangible, workable tools that are realistic and based on a commonsense approach of control. While using, none of this made sense to me until I got clean and realized that my enjoyment of life, happiness, security, and emotional control far superseded any importance to money, material possessions, and approval of others. What you think of me has no impact or influence on how I think of myself. Ignorance, or lack of knowledge, is prevalent in our society and is seen in all avenues of our culture. What is least important appears to be what is sought out the most, and the highest value is cast aside for something that we have no control over.

I feel sad for bullies, individuals who file for frivolous lawsuits, criminals, and those who seek revenge on people for acts committed in retaliation. This may sound strange, but let me explain how ignorant these individuals are, as I was a piece of that company, as you have read in parts of my story. If I'm genuinely happy, secure, and in control of my emotions, I'll never inflict abuse, harm, or fear on someone because this will contradict that genuine power that I control because I'd be doing it to gain something through fear that I couldn't provide for myself. Bullies attempt to seem powerful, but they're damaged people or kids that can't sustain a positive view of themselves without the approval or control of another.

In 2017, I hired an operations director for a facility. He was later fired for inappropriate behavior with females and creating a toxic environment with his staff. He would not fulfill his job requirements as he would gamble at a local casino during work hours, leaving the responsibilities to others. He became a liability to the company. About a month following his termination, he filed a lawsuit against the company for sexual harassment because of a director calling him a "pussy" and other comments that were unprofessional but reciprocated by the former employee. I'm not condoning the actions of the director calling him names, but when people fail to take responsibility for their actions, such as a termination for inappropriate behavior, genuine power is gone and anger, coupled with revenge, in pursuit of something less important. When money is more important than happiness, freedom, and control, life becomes miserable as anger takes hold.

One example of how people relinquish their personal power is when an individual in recovery decides to have a drink on an airplane because he or she is alone and "nobody else will know." "Nobody else will know" is when you give that personal power away, because you're saying that you care more about what other people think than how you think about yourself. If you ever do something shortly after that commonly used thought, then you've violated a standard that you've set for yourself. Otherwise, it wouldn't matter if people knew.

Personal power will be my greatest advocate at that moment, because then I'll hold true to my values, morals, and passions without the need for others approval, and then I've found a happiness, freedom, and self-respect that nobody can take away. I'm not clean and sober today for anybody else because I do this for me. I'm clean and sober today because of the care and love I have for myself, which I control. I use my friends, family, and co-workers for support, but I'm the one who will make the decision and do what I think is best for me.

Stop Wasting Time Changing Something You Can't Change

Chick-Fil-A, in 2012, became a newsworthy organization considering one of the country's most controversial social issues, same-sex marriage. Dan Cathy, whose father started the company in 1967, told a Christian news organization that they supported the "biblical definition of the family unit," sending protesters to picket outside the chain, fueling the argument on "gay rights." I have a son who was born a girl, and I've had many friends throughout my life who are gay who I'm very proud of for standing strong on their goal of equal rights. It's interesting to me how people spend so much time and energy fighting a cause that has nothing to do with them and will never affect them, such as same-sex marriage. If your morals state that homosexuality is wrong, then don't do it, but why spend so much time and energy keeping others from doing it? I've heard from religious fanatics that being gay is a choice. I ask all of you hetero-sexual males if you could choose today to have sex with a man? Homosexuality isn't contagious and religion, which is where the primary conflict arises, shouldn't be considered in the laws of our nation.

I contemplate with sovereign reverence that act of the whole American people which declared that their legislature should "make no law respecting an es-tablishment of religion, or prohibiting the

free exercise thereof," thus building a wall
of separation between Church & State.

—Thomas Jefferson

If you're fighting for your beliefs to be heard but preventing the right for other beliefs to be heard, you're being
a hypocrite. I believe that Chick-Fil-A has every right to
believe in their definition of marriage, and this shouldn't
be infringed upon by tactics based on emotional reactions.
Change comes when we can clearly, calmly, rationally, and
intelligently express our argument to the right source with
the right motive. Religion, throughout history, has always
been enforced through judgment, persecution, and damnation by sinful, fallible, and imperfect individuals as God is
the only perfect being according to the Bible.

**Racism gives power to those who you hate as
they will control your feelings and actions.**

If you're angry, vengeful, hateful, close minded, and
unwilling to take control of yourself, you'll never understand this concept of personal power. This power that we've
discussed can only come from within and will never be a
reality if I attempt to control another. Every decision you
make must be in line with your values, morals, and vision
that will bring happiness and self-respect, so I can achieve
my greatest need, which is to feel good.

Thinking for Yourself

Those who commit crimes have no integrity and lack a confidence and self-respect that eliminates any possibility for

genuine power. When I was involved in the criminal activity that I've discussed, I wasn't genuine, real, or authentic to myself. I lived in a world that wasn't controlled by me but instead by fear. Those involved in such activities will deny this, but ignorance, loss of respect, loss of self-love, and lack of confidence breed criminal activities. I'd not risk incarceration for stealing something if I was confident in my ability to sustain a job that would provide the income to purchase that item.

"Thinking for myself" is exactly what it says, and it doesn't include "thinking for others." I can appreciate other people's views, disagree with them, and work to change things without an emotional response that will allow me to be more productive. "Thinking for myself" entails a nonjudgmental view of the world as I lose interest in changing other beliefs and hold true to my own. You'll not change my stance on things, so I don't feel that you're required to change yours.

Religions Error in People Thinking for Themselves

The United States defines ISIS as terrorists because these extremists feel that they need to eradicate all religions and cultures that don't believe, worship, and support Allah. Young adults and even children are taught to murder nonbelievers, and are forced by fear to think through the minds of the leaders with wrong information. What I was taught by my parents and attending a Christian school was to believe in the same God as the Muslims and defined in the Quran.

> **[And mention] when the angels said, "O Mary, indeed Allah gives you good tidings of a word from Him, whose name will be the Messiah, Jesus, the son of**

Mary - distinguished in this world and the Hereafter and among those brought near [to Allah]. "He will speak to the people in the cradle and in maturity and will be of the righteous." She said, "My Lord, how will I have a child when no man has touched me?" [The angel] said, "Such is Allah; He creates what He wills. When He decrees a matter, He only says to it, 'Be,' and it is."

—Quran 3:45–47
Sahih International

Does that story sound familiar to anybody? ISIS is working to eradicate religions and cultures that do believe in the same God. There lies a problem when these extremists are carrying out a cause that's ignorant or purposefully evil with a fire-and-brimstone ending because they don't think for themselves. Suicide bombers are directed to commit suicide with the promise of a beautiful reward in heaven by killing innocent people in the name of Allah. If martyrdom was so rewarding, why wouldn't those who are leading the cause strap a bomb to themselves and reap the rewards that are given to others.

I've known many individuals who are told things and just believe them without thinking for themselves. Stop doing things just because someone told you to and decide for yourself the correct course to take. I read, researched, and studied Christianity while I was in custody, and I concluded a very different understanding from some Christians regarding homosexuality that promotes judgment, persecution, and anger with, instead, love, tolerance, and altruism.

I'm not a religious scholar, but I'd like to point out a couple of things that stand out to me regarding much of the intolerance that we see in the world of religion and how it doesn't hold true to what is written.

Do not judge, and you will not be judged. Do not condemn, and you will not be condemned. Forgive, and you will be forgiven. Give, and it will be given to you. A good measure, pressed down, shaken together and running over, will be poured into your lap. For with the measure you use, it will be measured to you.

—Luke 6:37–38
New International Version

Many will argue that this verse is only part of what is taught, which is true, but "do not judge, and you will not be judged" is perfectly clear and needs no clarification. Study, read, and decide based on your own understanding. "Think for yourself."

Stop Thinking through the Minds of Others

I'm not going to tell you what to think but instead explore the process of how you think. Since our basic desire is to feel good and be happy, we must think in terms of that personal power that we've discussed. Personal power is when I hold true to my values, morals, and passions without the need for others, so I can find a happiness, freedom, and self-respect that nobody can take away. After I've determined who I am, I'll make decisions based on the standards that I've set for myself. I set aside everything that I was taught by my parents, teachers, and friends giving me an opportunity to educate myself on my needs, desires, passions, and interests.

Early in recovery, some need to have their hand held as cravings, withdrawal, and emotional pain can be debilitating, so don't misunderstand the need for direction. Once you're stable, test yourself with knowledge of topics that are presented to you by going to the source. How many times have you been told negative information about someone and shared that story with someone else without researching the validity of the gossip and confirming the truth?

If I'd learned this concept and practiced it when I was a teenager, things may have been different but maybe not. Some will feel that it will be different for them and follow the same route I did, leading to many wasted years. The following story is an example of thinking for yourself regarding drugs as I want to show people a different way of thinking through personal power.

In high school and even junior high at times, drugs will be offered as something cool, told how good it feels, and how this substance will make you happy. From the statements just described on an outwardly view, it sounds good, and it doesn't seem to have a negative outlook. Who doesn't want to be cool, feel good, and be happy? If I were to take these statements as face value and think through the mind of the individual presenting this offer, who wouldn't try it? This is where I hope that I can show you from my life experience how dishonest and ignorant each one of those statements are. I'll explain.

If I were able to transfer my experience to you and show you how to think with personal power in mind, you would understand that it may not be what it seems. When I explore my values and morals with drug use, nothing will remain in line, and it will destroy my self-respect. Drugs will destroy your ability to experience happiness as things become less enjoyable over time and dependence doesn't feel good. If you were to research the physiological effects and how substances destroy your neurons, that feeling happy and feeling good can be lost forever. As I mentioned before, when you put something like a drug in your body, your body will change to function as well as possible with what it has. This change that occurs isn't a good thing as your body will stop producing important neurotransmitters that will take your personal power away. There's nothing cool about this, but I encourage you to think for yourself and not through my mind, so you're following the rule that we've discussed. Thinking for yourself entails a full understanding before you decide to try it. Whether you like it or not, consequences will be involved, so ask yourself the question I mentioned earlier: Am I willing to pay the price?

Questions to Consider

1. Are your beliefs conditioned from your upbringing or from your own heart?
2. Are your choices and decisions bringing you freedom and happiness?
3. What are you passionate about?
4. Do you push your beliefs onto others? Are beliefs of others pushed onto you?

Thinking for yourself doesn't request that we eliminate the feedback or knowledge we can gain from others, it just requires that we investigate the information before deciding to act.

Chapter 15

Let Our Voices Echo

Beauty cannot be viewed through a tunnel,
Nor to be justified through a fragment of time.
Love is the irrational magnet of attraction,
While pain we all keep inside.

Alone is the terror we strive to avoid,
To sit and wallow in a pity not real,
A tear sitting on a lasting void,
In a sorrow that will destroy what you feel.

Something is echoing in a mind that is hollow,
Feeling for an image that is hard to swallow.
The world doesn't seem to be a place that you knew,
Why did it change? It was a loss that redrew?

Remember the doll or toy truck you once had,
The excitement each day to play and to brag.
One day it was gone, or it had fallen apart.
Don't forget that you are losing meant once you had part.

Control is a gift yet an enemy for some,
Defining where you have it with which or which one.
The shadow you see that is cast behind you,
Will move and will change through actions you do.

Stop for a moment and let your guard down.
Open your heart and have love show you now.
Secrets and shame will give you nothing but hurt.
It's a passion to help that will heal you with thirst.

There is no end game to that feeling of grief,
The sand that spans on, that we call a beach,
An ocean of vastness that spans with cool water,
To reach for the stars and in time will get hotter.

To ask "why me" is a question not answered,
Flow through a river of rocks and debris.
"What can I do" to set the ship free,
Will set sail to calm waters and that I decree.

Note to Clinicians

With the epidemic that we're facing, death will be a reality
that you'll all continue to see. I wasn't numb to the pain that
was caused when I worked closely with a client and learned
at some point later that he or she had lost the battle. I hope
to offer solitude and comfort to the professionals working in
the industry as we'll continue to watch ex-clients lose their
lives that we may have worked so hard to offer hope, tools,
and knowledge for them to use to save their lives.

Between the years of 2005 and 2009, I worked for a
residential treatment program and recall between ten to fifteen clients who lost their lives within six months of leaving
the program. I was still in school, interning as a counselor,

and genuinely cared for the first client who was on my
caseload that died to an overdose of somas and alcohol not
long after leaving the facility. From my recollection, Paul,
enrolled in the facility for ninety days and worked very hard
on himself and improved his relationship with his family
through individual family counseling sessions with me and
had strong goals that included education and a desire for a
successful career. Paul held a secret that wasn't disclosed to
me during his ninety-day stay nor discussed by his family
that may have been a result of shame or embarrassment. It
wasn't until he had relapsed within weeks of his discharge
that I'd learned about his real discomfort in life.

I'd received a phone call from his mother, who informed
me that Paul had relapsed and was staying in a hotel and
asked if I'd be willing to go and attempt to talk with him
because "Paul felt comfortable talking" with me. I obliged
and drove to the hotel hoping I could get him to agree to
return to a facility for detox and then reenroll in our residential treatment program. After arriving at the hotel and
attempting to get him to open the door, I decided to speak
with someone at the front desk about entering the room.
I feared the worst, expecting them to open the door and
finding him dead on the floor. The hotel staff knocked on
the door, and with no response, they entered the room to
find him alive, drunk, and the room in complete disarray.
I was so relieved to find him drunk because that meant
that he was alive, and I had a chance of getting him back
to the program.

I sat down with Paul, and because he was drunk and
cared less about what people thought, he shared that he was
gay and was uncomfortable with how people would view
him if they knew. This was the moment that I made a mistake and set myself up to be hurt by the actions of someone

I had no control over. I felt sympathy for Paul as I allowed myself to feel sad and sorry for his predicament as I let my feelings become a part of my therapeutic relationship with him. Feelings will destroy us as we begin a downward spiral in that dangerous game that we call burnout.

Paul reentered our facility after completing detox and committed to another stint in treatment that he completed successfully. I'm a little uncertain on dates, but it wasn't long before his mother notified us that Paul had passed away in a motel because of the synergistic effects of combined central nervous system depressants. He was in his early twenties, and it devastated me. I cried after hearing the news. Sadly, this was the first of many to come, but I learned quickly, as I never made this same mistake again.

Sympathy can be our greatest enemy as we allow our feelings to become a part of our therapeutic relationship creating an environment of feeling sorry for our client. "Feeling" is that step we take that will destroy us in this industry and put us at danger of burnout or even something worse. I learned later that empathy, which is to understand someone's problems rather than feel for the client was a more effective method. Paul's mother made comments that I interpreted as blaming me since I was still an intern and had very little experience. This made things more uncomfortable as I started asking, "What could I have done differently?"

As I've gained many years of experience in this field, I've learned to never take credit for someone's success because I refuse to take responsibility for someone's choices to relapse. I worked at a facility where a clinician would take responsibility for her client's success and blame other clinicians for his or her client's failures. I sat in a meeting with that clinician who informed me that statistics don't lie and who appeared to blame me for their choices to relapse, which I refuse to do.

Note to Family and Friends

The sorrow that a clinician experiences will never come close to the pain that family or friends will feel, but I wanted to make note that this industry isn't always easy for those of us who truly care and want the best for our clients. Nothing about this chapter will be easy in practice, but I hope to educate and offer a sense of peace to you who are controlled by the actions of someone who's draining the life from you. There are millions of families who have lost children to an overdose and even a larger number dealing with fear every day that they'll get a call from a morgue with the news that no family ever wants to hear. It's easy to feel lost in this world with many questions and no answers. I, just like you, don't have all the answers, but what I do have is some knowledge that I hope to offer based on years of experience. I, too, have lost family and friends as nobody will be immune to this.

Using 2016 statistics, it's estimated that over twenty million Americans have a substance-abuse disorder (SUD) related to alcohol or illicit-drug use. Of that number, it's estimated that 2.1 million of those have an opioid disorder that has become the most concerning due to overdoses. The year 2016 statistics are the most current available and the number is much bigger today. Some will live, and some will die, which sadly, nobody can do anything about, as the decision is solely on the person who has no desire to change and many times doesn't care. The one who doesn't care has lost control of his or her life but appears to have full control over the lives of his or her family, which doesn't seem fair.

Unconditional love is a term that's used so often to justify those who will do anything to "save the lives" of loved ones who enter treatment numerous times only to continue using after short stints of sobriety. To save a life is an expression that applies to an immediate physical response to an emergency that has eminent danger and not something that applies to choices being made over time that are out of your control. What may seem like love has many times helped assist in the progression of a more serious nature of use that has led to the death of thousands of loved ones, so I'd like to begin with this.

Entering Treatment Doesn't Mean Sobriety Is Wanted

It may be very difficult to determine how serious someone is about getting help because the decision to enter treatment can be very skewed by lack of money, being tired, employment problems, relationship problems, or health problems that when resolved will change that decision to stay clean as they return to their previous lifestyle of getting high. Many children and young adults will learn very early on the person or persons they can use to manipulate as they use love as the tool to save them from negative consequences. Drug-and-alcohol abusers aren't stupid people. They can be great actors, in general, as they will shed tears of sadness for a tank of gas from you and leave the room with laughter as they hand their dealer the money for a bag of dope. We all must remember that when we're dealing with those who are using, they're not themselves. They're lost in a world where nothing matters but that drug. Even though you may have unconditional love for your family member, love isn't in the equation for that person whom we love and want to save. They're not requesting your love in most cases, but instead are encouraging material things to be given because of your love.

In 2016, my stepson was homeless, on the street, using heroin, and it was destroying my wife as she continuously expected the worst. After tracking him down, I helped get him into a detox program where he stayed for a short time before leaving. A few weeks later, he resurfaced, and I helped my wife enroll him in another program that he completed sixty days and then returned to his old lifestyle. Each time we heard from him, he had relationship issues, money issues and was tired as he needed a place to stay so that he could regroup and then return to using. After a third attempt and him deciding to leave, I told my wife that we would not help him anymore and that he must take the steps and enroll in a program by himself, with himself, and for himself. It was difficult for her. She would cry with worry, but a few months later, he went to Arizona and enrolled in a facility without his mother's help. He has since completed the program, lives with a girlfriend, holds a job, and is clean and sober. I give my stepson full credit, and I can probably say that it meant so much more for him to do this for himself without others doing it for him.

Many will fear that if we do nothing to help, then the person may die. I've spoken to many families over the years and have encouraged their assistance when it's their loved one's first, and even at times their second attempt, to get clean or sober. I also encourage the family member to make it very clear that this is the only time that they're going to help and, if they decide to leave or to relapse in the future, that they will be on their own, and no more help will be given. If you offer help and they refuse to take advantage of it, they may die. If you continue to help as they have less incentive to change because we can do this again later, it will increase the chances of relapse and an untimely death. Recidivism is highly dangerous—many will die as tolerance returns to normal after being clean for a while and then returning to use, as they consume the same amount that was used when their tolerance was high. Your family member needs to know and must believe that he or she will never receive help again if that person decides to delve back into their old behaviors, or else he or she will use that as an excuse, putting their lives in danger. Unconditional love doesn't mean that you need to do anything except love. Love, as I've defined, is an action as it can be doing something or maybe doing nothing for that person.

Clinicians Need to Read This Carefully

Clinicians, please consider the pillars of ethics when you're making decisions because they're the most important guide we have, and it can save lives. Beneficence, nonmaleficence, autonomy, and justice are the primary pillars of ethics and the guides we use to make decisions for clients. Many families, and for good reason in some cases, blame a treatment facility for the death of their loved one. Before we move on, I want to explore the responsibility of treatment facilities and clinicians in the guide that we have in making decisions for or with our clients. As we discussed in a previous chapter about the unethical, illegal, and dangerous practices of facilities, I want to briefly discuss our ethical duties because we don't want to be a part of killing our clients. This population is difficult to work with, as we're working with people who have very little desire to achieve what we're hoping for them to achieve.

Our primary responsibility is to look out for the best interest of our clients, and every decision is to be based on that primary responsibility. Beneficence is the ethical pillar to always do good. Nonmaleficence is to do no harm, while autonomy is to respect the clients right to self-determination, and justice is to treat people equally. These pillars are to determine our behavior and decisions for the client. We'll make decisions that will create conflict with other pillars, which is what we define as an ethical dilemma.

Every decision that we make must be considered within those pillars that can include the discharging of a client when their insurance stops paying, what to do with a client after he or she relapses, do we allow a client to go home on a pass, or keeping a client when you've determined the facility isn't the right fit. This reason when facilities are usually at fault for a death is when the owner, who is many times not a clinician, makes clinical decisions because of money or what is in the best interest of the business. Business should never get involved with clinical decisions.

How is Healthy Love Expressed?

Al-Anon teaches about detachment, which is to "let go of our obsession with another's behavior and begin to lead happier and a more manageable life." This isn't about detaching your love for this person, but it's also about loving yourself and learning to be happy with the absence of this individual. Many parents will define themselves by the roles they play as a mother or father, which makes this task even more difficult, since their very existence is based on this purpose. Dysfunctional families, as theorists of psychology have defined, are a result of needs that are not being met and a violation of boundaries that create unnatural roles to allow the family unit to function as well as possible with the dysfunction created. Parents typically parent the way that they were parented, which is why, in most cases, I don't blame parents for much of the dysfunction unless we're talking about severe boundary violations of physical abuse, sexual abuse, or substance abuse. Parents usually do the best they can with the information they have, which isn't always healthy. The cycle of violence or dysfunction does need to be broken at some point.

A healthy, functional family is created with healthy communication, allowing your child to make mistakes so he or she can learn from them, having independence and a sense of autonomy, having fun together, and not withholding love as a form of punishment. "What's good for the goose is good for the gander." According to those ideas that can help create a healthy family, it's important to separate yourself from your child and become autonomous, have fun, learn from your mistakes, and not withhold a love for yourself, as many will blame themselves for the actions of another. If you're reading this book and are a parent, I'm going to assume that you care deeply for your son or daughter and therefore did a good job and can be proud of the effort you've put forth. This is the time in your life where you define what you do have control over and focus on that. You may wonder how you can be happy and have fun while the person that you feel you love the most is suffering on the streets or may be dead. This is a difficult question to answer, but I'm going to attempt an answer.

Someone currently using and being absent from the family can be very similar to burying a child with one exception—hope. Parents will, many times, hold onto hope when they have not received news that their child died, which can make that process of detachment more difficult: "He's fine. She'll be home once she runs out of money. This is a phase." Hopefully, he or she does make it back, but during this hoping phase, this is a good time to start to learn to love yourself. It's highly recommended that you get support through a self-help program like Al-Anon, meet with a therapist, and learn to heal from your grief and loss that may be negatively affecting your day to day life. How is healthy love expressed? It starts by loving yourself.

BLAME ME

An acronym I created for BLAME ME is Because Love and Martyrdom Equals My Eternity. You're not at fault. Stop believing that you have control over another person's choices and results that derive from those choices. In a sense, this is what is known as a God complex, when an individual believes he or she has a godlike ability. You didn't decide this and therefore shouldn't suffer for the decisions made by another.

Allow yourself the opportunity to feel angry because when you forgive too quickly, identify all the things you "could have done differently," or feel sorry for your child, you'll begin to blame yourself. This isn't your fault and I'm going to switch Al-Anon's 3Cs around, that they teach, when the ill individual is casting blame on you. They state that **"you didn't cause it," "you can't cure it," and "you can't control it."** Since I'm about focusing on positive statements, then you did cause the suffering within yourself if you blame yourself, you can cure yourself, and you can control yourself.

When I was a sophomore in high school, a boy I knew had driven off an over pass and was killed instantly after he had been drinking. I'd learned many years later that this had destroyed his parents resulting in a divorce, loss of jobs, and financial ruin. This wasn't fair to them, but the outcome, such as the story above, is their fault as they allowed their loss to control them and ruin the things that they did have. Self-blame will usually cause the framework for the results that the family endured and unfortunately it could have been prevented. Parents will blame each other, blame themselves, and even blame some of their other children if they weren't an only child.

Many parents will not take responsibility for the success of their children. Many parents will be proud of their accomplishments but not credit themselves for the efforts and hard work that their children put into things. Why are you going to take responsibility for their bad choices but not take responsibility for their success?

HEALING ME

Despite what you may feel at this moment, you deserve happiness and a life that demands joy, a self-love that allows you to separate from external pain and internally appreciate what you do have at this moment, right here and right now. As I discussed earlier in the book, fear can be overthrown by an appreciation that will ground you. HEALING ME can be equated with Happiness Equals a Loving, Invigorating, Never-ending, Grateful, Multifaceted Exultation. It's the strength that comes from many facets as we come together and support each other through love and gratitude that allows us an ability to rejoice. Shame and blame is what I've seen mostly throughout the years that will hold you down and destroy your life. It's time that we stand together, as there's no need to do this alone, and LOVE together—Let Our Voices Echo.

We have millions of individuals and families that are suffering at this moment from chemical dependency, and it's time that we take a stand. I'm asking for families who have lost children to this epidemic to remove yourselves from the shadows and step forward with your stories as this will help your healing process and help others. We must stand together as a country, for our country, and with our country. With all the separations that we see in politics, religions, beliefs, and ideas, we have one thing in common, and that's this issue at hand. We've all been affected at some point, and it's time that we stand together without judgment, hatred, and disgust to address this. Why are we not discussing the truth behind this at funerals? Why are we so ashamed to discuss this problem with others? Let Our Voices Echo!

Parents sacrifice their time, energy, and existence to focus on another person and raise him or her to the best of their abilities. Unfortunately, the person that has been focused on tends to lack any appreciation and feels entitled as they nail the parents to a cross for an excruciating sacrifice.

I've been including poetry in this book for a reason, and I've found writing it to be healing. What works for me may not work for you, as we're different but the same. We have feelings, but we may process them differently. But it may be worth a try to write a poem. Read the following aloud and see if it offers an inspiration. Put the name of your loved one in the lines below so you can personalize it.

I want to tell you about my love for you,
As I hurt by the choices you've made,
Nothing will ever come between you see,
Except to heal and find joy in me.

I remember the laughter that brought us together,
As I can't think of a better time.
The joy that I had to watch you grow,
Brings a smile that I can't destroy.

You will always be with me in my heart,
As a dove reminds me of you.
You will live forever from the mark you made,
As you go upon your way.

I stand for you and tell your story,
Because you are set free.
A gift to many that are suffering,
It's the lessons you will gladly bring.

I'm happy yet sad that our time is up.
The door for us has shut.
The window has opened to a brand-new purpose,
But it's you who has cleared the dust.

I will take some time to process the loss,
An emptiness that will always remain.
I will fill the void with an untamed goal,
That is to heal through your eternal soul.

Thank you _____for that precious gift,
Of the time I spent with you.
But teachers are designed to often lead,
And then set their students free.

_____, I love you,
And rejoice in you.

Questions to Consider

1. Have you put your life aside as you were waiting for a phone call?
2. Do you BLAME yourself?
3. HEALING ME: What does that idea mean to you?

CHAPTER 16

Pain Doesn't Have to Be Miserable

You have the power to decide your fate.
Time is of the essence, so don't be late.
Pain is your lesson and is a promise to be,
While misery is a choice, so let yourself free.

Anger will get you to want to give up.
"I'll show you I swear" will sadly erupt.
Why would you do this, not sure what you gain?
You're hurting yourself and causing the pain

Nixon was the one who declared "war on drugs."
Is heroin or meth an alive violent thug?
It isn't the drug that's the enemy or abuser.
We are at war with our sick and often dying user.

Think of your thoughts—are they moving you forward,
Or are they creating a world that's backing you in a corner?
Once I decide that I can't stay clean,
I am destined to relapse and return to the scene.

Pain is your friend, although it might sound strange.
It gives us a sign when we fall out of range.
How would you know if you stepped on a nail?
Unless pain gave a warning and caused you to wail.

Emotional pain seems harder to tolerate.
Its hurt and fear that's so hard to compensate.
Why do we numb those gifts of emotions?
You will lose happiness also in the deepest oceans.

The next lines are yours, so give this a try:
Just jot down your pain in a song or a rhyme.
Give it a twist with a positive spin.
We are trying to turn your pain to a win.

Is Addiction a Disease, and if So, Why Is It Not Treated as Such?

Substance-use disorder of an illicit drug is the only clinical disorder that would require you to have committed a crime. To define something as a disease, it must be a medical condition, which insurance is now paying to be treated, then why is it not treated as such?

The "war on drugs" has nothing to do with ending the drug problem, as our country thrives financially through prohibition. According to FoxNews.com, the El Paso Police Department received $1.7 million in 2012, between local and federal forfeiture funds that included drug busts. In 1991, the DEA seized over $4 billion in drugs, close to $1 billion in cash, and seized bank accounts of all the individuals involved, making me speculate that this was a great day financially for the federal government. I'm not promoting conspiracy theories, but I've always questioned motives behind things, such as laws. Alcohol kills more people every year than all illicit drugs combined, but it isn't as problematic because it's legal. It has been estimated that cigarettes kill almost twice as many individuals as alcohol, which is also legal. I'm far from promoting prohibition on alcohol or cigarettes, but I struggle with harsh persecution for some while others are minimized or discredited because of it being socially acceptable.

Politicians identify solutions that aren't grounded in experience or having knowledge of realism within the mind of a drug user. Opinions, ideas, and truth by different people create confusion on solutions that are so unnatural to many and may harm the masses. Experts in this field with real experiential knowledge are discredited by those who have higher education with a degree. As a proponent of harm reduction, I don't understand why some counties and states don't have needle-exchange programs, but Suboxone is being offered as a solution for heroin abusers as a long-term maintenance program to reduce cravings and manage withdrawal symptoms.

We Need to Be Smart

Emotional pain can be temporary, while success can last a lifetime if we transform that thing that has been holding us back. Drugs are an illusion, or a solution to a problem that will never work and in the future will compound the problem that the substance was originally used to solve. Morphine, in moderate doses, will relieve physical pain; excessive doses will sensitize your neurons, causing exaggerated levels of pain in the future. Methamphetamine will induce a feeling of pleasure when you start, while long-term use will destroy your dopamine-releasing neurons and ability to experience real pleasure in the future.

Ignorance, failure to think for self, and low self-esteem are many predictors that will set the stage for drug problems in our society.

As I'm not going to give any drugs for medication management, tell you what to do, or identify a one-and-only solution to your problem, I'm going to give some ideas and rely on common sense as a standard as I've accomplished many goals and have acquired eleven years clean, relapsed, and another four years as of 2018. If I can do it twice, then you can do it once. We aren't very different, with maybe the exception of a few things, that I want to discuss. Pain, failure, and misery are the stepping stones to success.

Pain is a guarantee in life, whether it be physical or emotional, and I encourage people to find solutions to manage pain with a tactic that works. Having worked with many heroin abusers over the years, I know that many will identify the alleviation of emotional pain as the primary reason for them starting. Whether it be ignorance or the belief that what has happened to others won't happen to them, heroin use will alleviate emotional pain, but at the expense of physical pain that makes very little sense in my world.

Our states of mind or dispositions will determine our excitement or misery behind things that are not usually based on anything external. In April of 2002, I was happier than I'd been in years, sitting behind bars in custody. During my high school graduation and leaving behind one of the things I hated more than anything, I was miserable, with very little excitement for things. When I relapsed in 2013 and felt that rush of pleasure in a manner that I hadn't experienced in eleven years, I was miserable, with no passion for anything. Life could not have been worse when I found out on Christmas Day that I'd lost the program I'd worked so hard to make flourish, but I felt happy, content, and confident when I woke up the next morning. How do we correlate a negative experience with positive results? This is what I refer to as THE FUCK-ITS. This term is used widely by people in the recovery community as the condition where people give up and, in most cases, return to using. If you haven't learned yet, I refuse to remain in a negative world and enjoy twisting ideas, statements and circumstances into something positive and useful. The acronym that I've decided on for THE FUCK-ITS is Try Hearing Every Fallacious Unfavorable Circumstance Kindly in the Story. A mistaken belief that can be related to a situation that's unfavorable can be viewed in a positive light if you choose, which is why misery is a choice. This is the reason why people can be wealthy, have great jobs, be successful, and have great families but be miserable while the poor and unfortunate individuals in our society can be happy, joyous, and free if they choose. It isn't what you have or don't have that brings enjoyment but instead your view of the world and how you decide to take things.

Misery Is a Choice

Pain is inevitable, as this may be out of your control, but you decide on misery. During my teenage years and into my twenties, I viewed the world in hate and felt like an outcast that altered my perception that created a view of discomfort and great distress. It wasn't until years later after studying abnormal psychology that I fit the criteria outlined in *The Diagnostic and Statistical Manual of Mental Disorders* (DSM-V) for "antisocial personality disorder."

Symptoms for antisocial personality disorder:

- disregard for right and wrong
- persistent lying
- being callous and disrespectful of others
- using charm or wit to manipulate others for personal gain or personal pleasure
- arrogance
- recurring problems with the law
- repeatedly violating the rights of others through intimidation and dishonesty
- impulsiveness
- hostility, aggression, or violence
- lack of empathy for others
- unnecessary risk-taking or dangerous behavior
- poor or abusive relationships
- failure to consider the negative consequences of behavior
- being consistently irresponsible

It was an eye-opening experience to see how manipulative, deceitful, callous, and hostile I was for personal gain and direction. I lacked empathy and felt unable to develop intimate relationships with anybody. I was irresponsible, impulsive, and a risk taker. That wasn't solely a result of my substance-abuse issues; it started around the age of fourteen.

I was never diagnosed as such, but I can clearly see myself in the criteria to fit this diagnosis. In 1990, after being put on house arrest after absconding from probation, I arrived home from school and forced an argument with my mother to get angry enough that I could force myself to cut the bracelet off and evade my responsibilities. I'm uncertain on the argument that developed, but I recall grabbing a pair of scissors, telling my mother to "fuck off," and leaving the house, with my mother crying, to meet my girlfriend in Fullerton. I was seventeen during this incident, but this was far from the only time that I was impulsive, a risk taker, irresponsible, manipulative, deceitful, hostile, lacked empathy, and was set on my goal without concern of other's feelings.

I bring this information forward to make a point that relates to the ability to change a condition that has negatively affected me throughout my lifetime, and the diagnosis doesn't define me. It's difficult for me to say, without having a true diagnosis during my earlier years, that I had antisocial personality disorder, and I was able to change without psychiatric help, but I clearly carried the criteria. I do have empathy, am responsible, have integrity, and make decisions outside of being impulsive. I'm far from perfect, but I'm a very different person than I was in my twenties. I'm not a miserable person today, and I do give some credit to helping people, honesty, and responsibility, which required work, but I do feel it was well worth it.

Thoughts That Will Tear You Down

There's nothing wrong with you. I'm going to retype this sentence. There's nothing wrong with you. This doesn't mean that you're perfect, have nothing to work on, or have no issues that have caused problems in your life, but instead, this means that you've made bad choices and will require a new direction in life. But there's nothing wrong with you. You're at the driver's seat, and it's completely up to you where you want to go, what you want to do, and how you want to do it. It's time to do something, and that something can be magical. The first step that we must take is to eliminate the thoughts, statements, or ideas that keep you trapped in your nightmare. Since thoughts create, we have obligations to ourselves to eliminate untrue ideas so we can live in the real world. I want to use a few examples of statements or thoughts that people will use to restrict them in their life.

"Everything I touch seems to fall apart." Interesting idea but I doubt there's much truth behind this statement. This statement isn't literal, but please let me know if the book that you're reading at this time has crumbled or fallen apart because you've touched it as I'd be very interested in gathering statistics on that powerful ability. Every thought that we have can create or destroy, which isn't always in a literal sense, but one thought may inspire you to do something or, in the example above, to do nothing because I'll fail or break everything that I try.

"I hate when I have to do that." Many times, I'll put so much energy and dislike into a job for the future, prior to the effort it'll take to accomplish the task. Let's make life simple rather than integrating complication into so many things that we do. If you have a task that you can't avoid, how you view it will set the tone for what you'll gain from it. I don't have to do anything. It's time to choose every task that you're going to accomplish as exciting, an opportunity, and a journey, without an expectation for the outcome.

"I'm never going to be able to do this." Why not? If my goals are tangible and not based on something outside of my ability, then I can do anything that I want. I can think of many things in my life that I originally walked into with this statement that kept me from working very hard on fulfilling the task, such as getting clean, writing this book, and speaking to large groups of people. Once I was able to retrain my thinking, become aware of my thoughts inhibiting my abilities, and confidently being able to restate that above sentence to confirm that "I'll do this," then the job was halfway done. Don't give your thoughts the power to influence your behavior, especially if your emotions or feelings are involved because this is when things can get ugly.

Relationships

Relationships can be the most painful experiences that we can have as they can easily influence our behaviors and then cause us to lose focus on our rational thinking. I've never been great in relationships and for many of the same reasons that I've seen in clients that I've worked with over the years. As a young boy, I wasn't a very good son because I disliked restrictions that my parents set, and I rebelled in very unhealthy ways when I felt constricted. This independent or rebellious nature set the stage for most of my relationships in the future. These devastated some, especially women who were hoping for something long-term, as this wasn't what I wanted from a relationship at the time.

As I described earlier, I didn't allow people the opportunity to get to know me or my feelings as a protection because of my experiences as a child moving around and losing friends regularly. I had no interest in love, as this seemed to be an irrational response to something or someone I had no control over, which didn't make any sense to me. I wanted to feel good, but I knew that I'd not get this from anybody else, which is a factor in defining the reason for my excessive drug use. I held an insane belief that I'd found something that caused me to feel good and that I was in full control of this. I fell in love with methamphetamine. This was my first true love in life, which is what made it so difficult for me to give it up. It's hard to give up your first true love. Does it sound crazy? It does, but it can also give some understanding to those who have never struggled with this and how detrimental this relationship can be. It was always there, it supported me when I was down, and it felt good. All of this may sound like what you may find in a loving relationship with someone, which it was. Pain and misery were entwined together as I was forced to give this up numerous times throughout my life. It was painful, but I realized something very important that was new to me, and that was that love gives a meaning to your life and may offer another answer to that question of what is important.

It was very difficult to find this in an individual, because I spent my whole life distancing myself from people. I wanted to find someone who wouldn't hurt me, supported me emotionally, and offered hope that love can be unconditional. I didn't believe that it existed until I witnessed my parents' support and love me when I was at my most dangerous. They also taught me how important tough love can be, by not bailing me out of my situation and putting the responsibility on me for what I'd done. Emotional pain was on their faces because of their love for me, but they were able to separate from taking on misery. Good parents can teach us invaluable tools if we're observant and listen. Pain without misery requires a love, but not for others, as this is a love for yourself.

Pain Is Our Teacher

Pain can be a great teacher, especially when we're talking about emotional pain, and can offer lessons that we would never have the opportunity to learn without it. Individuals with substance-abuse problems have an opportunity to work on, learn, and identify solutions for things that others don't look at. Think about it. We're fortunate to be able to learn how to love our self, focus on healing emotional pain that isn't unique to this population, and embrace a lifestyle that requires an awareness unknown by many because of the pain that our chemical dependency has caused. Cravings, misery, and fear have been some of my greatest assets because of my desire to be happy, especially since fear is the greatest destroyer of that emotion or state of mind that we're all seeking. Unless I can acknowledge fear and accept it for what it is, I'll not be able to identify courage as its opposite.

Without pain, discomfort, hate, or misery, I'll not truly appreciate and enjoy comfort, love, real pleasure or contentment. Some of the happiest people that I know have been dragged through the depths of hell at some point in their lives because of the experience that they had, as pain and misery became the norm, only to see that other road of comfort and pleasure that they embraced and appreciated. It's unfortunate, as you'll meet many people with years of recovery who remain, angry, hateful, and stuck in misery because they refuse to appreciate and seek the tools that will bring them happiness.

If you can love yourself unconditionally, undeterred by anything that you've done as you forgive yourself, you can now let that drug go because it interferes with your life. We must seek something, and that something must be ourselves that mean more to us than that drug, so we can care about keeping only healthy things in our life. As it may be difficult, we must remove anything and everybody from our lives who isn't looking out for our best interest, surrounding ourselves with loving, caring, and supportive people. Changing our environments and our associates is the first step in loving ourselves.

Courage will be the foundation for your change, whether

this be for a family member or the individual working to get clean by letting go. Letting go will create pain, but misery doesn't have to exist in this equation. It can feel miserable to let go of the drug or let go of a family member, but that misery doesn't have to last once we can light the spark that love can bring. Loving the most important person, which is you, will turn your life around and allow you to smile and enjoy life with whatever pain you may be dealing with. Let love be your guiding force.

Questions to Consider

1. When was the last time you laughed?
2. When was the last time you felt peace?
3. When was the last time you looked in the mirror and saw the person that you used to be?

CHAPTER 17

Success Is the Final Chapter

What's last is not final as it starts a new chapter,
  Of a story you create that includes a new actor.
The location is not important, and it all may seem surreal.
Don't worry about perfection because I speak of an ideal.

Success is what we hope for, but is it something we can gauge?
It's true that it's achieved even if you're making minimum wage.
To define success for anything, we must first know what we seek.
To find an answer to this question is to achieve what is unique.

We can call a treatment facility and ask for their success.
  Its ninety percent of people that the person may profess.
  What are you defining as the answer to that number?
Is it people who are clean today or percentage of another?

  Our visions of success may be different in your sight,
  But I see a happy person, who sobriety will always invite.
    Nothing I envision, as a goal that I will gain,
Will be impossibly out of reach, as I avoid an unwanted pain.

What's easy in the story is a sight that's on the hill.
Knowledge is what I give you, but practice gives the skill.
Don't worry about what others think, nothing to do with you.
Your free to choose the path you take, because
I know that you'll pull through.

What Have You Acquired from Your Pain?

Success is often correlated with finances, but as far back as I can remember while clean and sober, money and material possessions were never important to me, or at least less important than feeling good and being happy. This chapter will be focused on more important things that will bring enjoyment and serenity not found in physical things that you possess.

You can have success in relationships, job opportunities, and college degrees, but none of this matters if you're unable to find success in your recovery, in your ability to stay clean, and in your enjoyment in life. Often, I've worked with clients who enter treatment for help and then quickly discharge because they must return to school or work. Their decision to not complete what they started, very little time clean and sober to deal with the stressors work and school bring, and the cravings that will come before some have learned tools to combat them have brought devastating consequences to some. My advice to you is to complete what you've started, so you have a solid footing in a new life that's free from chemical abuse.

Pain, failure, and misery are the stepping stones to success, which is why I've always felt that success is possible for the individuals who appear to be destined to a life of drug use. Since failure only exists if you give up, and misery is a choice, pain becomes that foundation that we're looking for. The title includes failure and misery as stepping stones to success because the term *failure* is only lessons that can define things we've done that didn't work, allowing you the opportunity for another attempt using a different tactic until you succeed. Since misery is a decision we make, it will lean us toward success when we can learn to view the world differently by integrating appreciation and optimism into our life.

When I began to change the way I viewed the world, I was able to see my drug use, my relationship disasters, and my legal issues as the greatest assets that led to my success. Every person who can walk tall through adversity and not bow to the suffering will be a greater individual because of it. Think about your life and everything that you've been through. What lessons have you gained from your pain? Every time that you've relapsed, what had you been doing that wasn't in line with a healthy recovery? Who were you associating with? What emotions had you been feeling? What happened in your story that created an environment to pick up and use?

Those questions will only be able to be answered in a productive fashion if you were interested in staying clean and motivated by a desire with goals in mind rather than being coerced to stay clean by other people. The greatest lesson that I'd learned from my relapse in 2013 was that I'll always be vulnerable and susceptible to a relapse if I don't consistently take care of myself and remain in control of my emotions. This can include my cravings to use. Cravings, after having time clean, are nothing more than a thought that can quickly dissipate by focusing on something else. You're in control of your cravings if you decide to be.

Let's Find Success

I'm not seeking anything different today than I was seeking through my drug use, but my life experience has taught me that today I'm able to find what I was looking for through being clean. I was looking for pleasure, happiness, and contentment, which I never found in drugs, but it was my life experience and pain that taught me the true definition of pleasure, happiness, and contentment. Many people would state that if they could go back in time, they would change many things. I wouldn't change anything because these things have helped shaped me as a person, and as I stated earlier, I love who I am today.

I'm not a failure today, as I believed when I was using, and misery doesn't exist as I work toward viewing the world through my optimistic glasses, with faith that I'll continue to learn and be happy and successful in all aspects of my life. Life isn't always easy, but difficulty brings enjoyment, because I have the opportunity, at times, to learn new skills and resolve new conflict. I never hold myself to perfection, but instead I hold myself to standards of progress that I can evaluate. I learned how difficult life can be when I act upon urges and desires without thinking consequences through, and it became as evident and painful as a child learning about fire and how it burns. Don't continue to make the same choices over and over only to receive the same consequences, or worse. Success is found within you, and nobody can take this away. Figure out what you really want in life and make it happen. You're in charge. You're in control. Loving yourself will show you the road while your passion will push you forward.

The path that you're about to embark on will evolve and grow as you move forward. Change, which is nothing to fear, will be the reward of your efforts, and I encourage you to embrace the possibilities. Most of the limits that you see will be limits you've put on yourself, so don't hold yourself down with judgments. Instead learn to take risks and open your eyes to new opportunities. You're worth it. You have great things to offer the world. Life is a bowl of lessons, and because you've taken the pain to acquire them, let's teach the world the things we've gained, and maybe we can help one person to not have to dredge through the suffering we did. Only when you can truly love yourself will you be able to understand how exciting it can be to reach your hands out and hold onto someone that's in pain while walking them through the path that you and I've already walked through. You'll never truly understand something until you're able to teach it. Let love be your guiding force.

The following section will guide you toward the right direction. Complete the questions, and it should start you on the right path.

It Is Your Decision: Guide to Help You Make the Choice

Mastering others is strength. Mastering yourself is true power.

—Lao Tzu

The following section are questions to help guide you to make decisions for yourself. They are questions to open an awareness to your predicament. I've decided for myself so maybe it's time you look at your situation.

How Honest Are You?

How do you know that you have a drug problem when the view of yourself can be skewed by chemical abuse, or maybe you're unaware of how the behavioral health community diagnosis someone?

Do you have a drug or alcohol problem? _____

If you're unsure, I'm going to give you the symptoms that are used by therapists and counselors to diagnose an individual as having a substance-abuse problem. The DSMV diagnoses all drugs, including alcohol, as a "substance-use disorder" that's mild, moderate or severe. The number of questions that are answered with yes determine the severity of the diagnosis. This is a summary of the symptoms identified in the DSMV.

1. Do you spend a lot of time getting, using or recovery from your use?
2. Do you try to cut down or control your use but are unable to do so?
3. Do you use more than you intended to use?
4. Does your use ever affect your job, school, or home?
5. Do you have cravings to use or use to avoid withdrawal symptoms?
6. Does your use ever cause problems in your social life?
7. Do you use, knowing that it's causing physical or psychological problems?
8. Have you developed tolerance where you require more of the substance to get the affects you're looking for?

If you were honest in those questions, can you identify yourself as two or three yes answers, which is mild substance-abuse disorder. Four to five would meet the criteria for moderate-use disorder, and six or more would meet the criteria for severe substance-use disorder. My story, as you've read, meets the "amphetamine substance-use disorder, severe" as I met every criterion possible and even more.

I encourage you to think about those questions honestly and decide for yourself.

Do you have a drug or alcohol problem? _____

The most common statement made by many is that I can control it and I can stop anytime that I choose.

Can you stop right now? _____

If you've said yes and just for the point of proving this to yourself, especially if you've said, "I can stop anytime that I choose but I just don't want to right now," I challenge you to stop for one week, so you can be sure that everything is under control. I hate to see you lying to yourself because you truly may believe this, and then you become another statistic as that lie can kill you. If you're clean, continue with the guide.

Motivation

As we're all motivated by one of two ways (the first being to avoid pain), we can use that motivation, once the pain to continue using becomes greater than the pain to stop. This is the reason why families, friends, police, and employers could help by taking away support and offering tough love to promote more pain.

What kind of pain is promoting a desire to change?

_____

_____

_____

_____

_____

Seeking help to eliminate a painful experience will never last, but congratulations on seeking help, because the reason for you wanting to change in the beginning doesn't matter. You've opened the door, but long term is what we're looking for.

Some, which I don't see that often, seek help because they desire good things or better things from their life. These are the things that will carry you that will offer a direction and hopefully light a fire of excitement.

Have you ever had dreams, a vision, or goals of what you want to do with your life? No matter where you've been or what you've done, you can do anything you want if you put your mind to it. Our thoughts will create. If you were to have a blank canvas, what would your life look like?

_____

_____

_____

_____

_____

_____

Since our feelings can get us excited, describe how your passion for that dream, vision, or goal can push you to greatness.

_____

_____

_____

_____

_____

What do you need to do to achieve that dream, vision, or goal?

_____

_____

_____

_____

_____

_____

Do you believe that you can achieve those things you're seeking? Do you believe that you can stay clean and sober?

_____

_____

_____

_____

_____

_____

If you don't believe you can stay clean and sober, say the following affirmation five times, four times a day.

"I'm confident in my ability to stay clean and sober. I'll stay clean and sober no matter what happens in my life."

Impulse Control

Impulse control, which is rarely taught in a fashion that's tangible and workable, keeps in mind that every action in our life has a consequence. Many times, the substance abuser will act on impulse and only think about one side of the coin, usually considering only this moment and not taking into account long-term consequences. Good decision making requires that we move away from "immediate gratification" for that bigger goal that you identified under your new motivation.

What were the reasons that you started using drugs and or alcohol?

_____

_____

_____

_____

_____

_____

When did alcohol and or drugs first become a problem for you? Describe four or more situations?

_____

_____

_____

_____

_____

_____

Every action in our life has a consequence, and there are positive and negative consequences to everything that we do. Impulse control requires that you identify your options and then weigh the consequences, allowing you to make the best choice you can with the information you have.

Sobriety	
Positive Consequences	Negative Consequences
1.	1.
2.	2.
3.	3.
4.	4.
5.	5.
6.	6.
7.	7.
8.	8.
9.	9.
10.	10.
11.	11.
12.	12.
13.	13.
14.	14.
15.	15.
16.	16.
17.	17.
18.	18.
19.	19.
20.	20.
21.	21.
22.	22.

Using	
Positive Consequences	Negative Consequences
1.	1.
2.	2.
3.	3.
4.	4.
5.	5.
6.	6.
7.	7.
8.	8.
9.	9.
10.	10.
11.	11.
12.	12.
13.	13.
14.	14.
15.	15.
16.	16.
17.	17.
18.	18.
19.	19.
20.	20.
21.	21.
22.	22.

Everybody eventually surrenders to something or someone. You are free to choose what you surrender to, but you are not free from the consequences of that action.
—E. Stanley Jones

Some consequences will have more of an impact than others, and it's important to keep this in mind when making your decision.

According to your list of positive and negative consequences, what would be the best decision you could make regarding sobriety versus continuing to use? Give the reasons why?

_____

_____

_____

_____

_____

_____

_____

If you decide that sobriety is your best option, you may see that your positives to using are not bad, such as pleasure, motivation, energy, and so on. Give alternative ways of achieving the positives to using, without having to pick up to get them.

_____

_____

_____

_____

_____

_____

Commitment

Many people believe that relapse is inevitable, and you'll eventually "slip" or "fall." Relapse is a choice just as much as sobriety is a choice. If I become truly committed to sobriety, I can stay sober know matter what happens.

Some people have plans to use in the future, such as, "When I turn twenty-one, I'm going to start going to bars." If you've ever said, "I'll stay clean and sober unless this happens," you're in trouble. There's no commitment in that statement, and relapse will almost be inevitable.

What things could happen that you would get loaded over?

_____

_____

_____

_____

_____

What does commitment mean to you?

_____

_____

_____

_____

_____

Relapse kills people every day, and those who have died weren't committed to a life of recovery. Many have thought,

"I can relapse because I can always get clean again in the future." **Lack of commitment kills.**

Do you believe that relapse doesn't matter because you can always come back?

_____

_____

_____

_____

_____

How committed are you, and would you stay clean no matter what happens in your life?

_____

_____

_____

_____

_____

Raise Your Beliefs

Preparation doesn't begin with what you do it begins with what you believe. If you believe that your success tomorrow depends on what you do today, then you will treat today differently.

—John Maxwell

That's the true message behind goal fulfillment. I've said it before, and I'll say it again: you can do anything you want with your life if you just believe. Our beliefs can truly make us or break us, and they can empower us or limit us.

What beliefs do you have about yourself that limits you? An example could be "I can't stay sober." A word of caution is to eliminate the word *can't* from your vocabulary.

_____

_____

_____

_____

_____

_____

What beliefs do you have about yourself that empower you?

_____

_____

_____

_____

_____

Positive affirmations, as we discussed earlier, are the greatest tools that we can use to change negative beliefs that we have that can limit us. What belief do you need to have to achieve what you want in your life?

_____

_____

_____

_____

_____

Positive affirmations follow this structure:

1. Start with "I" statement
2. Must be positive
3. Must be written as if they're currently happening

Ex. "I'm capable, willing, and determined to stay clean and sober. I speak the truth."

Write your own.

I_____

I_____

I _____

I_____

Just as you had done earlier, stand in front of the mirror, looking confidently at yourself, and state each of them five times when you wake up in the morning, five times around noon, five times at 4:00 p.m., and five times before you go to bed, which is the best time to sink it into your subconscious. Do this every day for four weeks and see how it works.

It's time that we embrace change and no longer find change frightening.

What are specific things that you may have a hard time changing or a fear of changing?

_____

_____

_____

_____

_____

_____

In times of change, learners inherit the earth, while the learned find themselves beautifully equipped, to deal with a world that no longer exists.

—Eric Hoffer

Tools for Better Living

1. Choose well. We do this by looking at all our options and weighing the consequences.
2. Believe you can do it.
3. Passion is where we'll find the MAGIC (Make **A** Greater Individual Commitment).

Where could you apply a bit of MAGIC?

_____

_____

Are there relationships or associations in your life that rob you of your passion?

_____

_____

_____

_____

_____

_____

4. Self-discipline: correction or regulation of oneself for
    the sake of improvement.

What does self-discipline mean to you and how can you
apply it to your life?

_____

_____

_____

_____

_____

_____

Crisis and adversity are deeply woven into the fabric of human existence ... Train every day to get as tough as possible ... Exercise consistence discipline in all areas of life in order to be prepared for the inevitable emotional hit.

—James Loehr

Relapse Prevention

Relapse is common, but it's preventable. Preventing relapse requires awareness of triggers and cues and willingness to do something about it. You have the information that will help you become more aware of situations and feelings that can set you up for relapse. Relapse is a choice, which means you do have options and can choose to stay sober.

Who are the people that are most likely capable of influencing you to use?

_____

_____

_____

_____

_____

For each of those people you listed, describe how you'll avoid relapse triggered by these people's actions.

_____

_____

_____

_____

_____

What are social situations that could create danger for you to stay clean and sober?

_____

_____

_____

_____

_____

_____

How could relationship difficulties place you at risk?

_____

_____

_____

_____

_____

_____

What's your plan to handle pressures and temptations to drink or use that are associated with the situations you've listed?

_____

_____

_____

_____

_____

What thoughts place you at risk to relapse? Example: "I can do it just once; it will be different next time."

_____

_____

_____

_____

_____

_____

What are the possible changes that you could see in your behavior, such as loss of self-control, that could lead you toward relapse?

_____

_____

_____

_____

_____

What are the possible feelings and moods that could be your most dangerous leading you toward relapse?

_____

_____

_____

_____

_____

If you've been in recovery before and have the experience of relapsing, what things could you identify that led to your relapse?

_____

_____

_____

_____

_____

_____

Relapse Prevention Planning

Your relapse prevention plan should include what you will do if you encounter a crisis, or a stressful situation that triggers a strong urge to use. If you encounter this, your action plan will be the following:

_____

_____

_____

_____

_____

_____

If your plan isn't enough and you use, what will you do to get back on track?

_____

_____

_____

_____

_____

Recovery Plan

Your recovery plan is a commitment that you make with yourself to ensure success, and it must be realistic. This plan is something that you create, only identifying things you're willing to do. I've always felt that balance is one of the most important things we incorporate in our lives so we don't become overwhelmed. It starts with meetings that could be SMART Recovery, twelve-step, and so on, but as I've defined them as an option, you decide your course.

The following outline may help to design your own individual plan:

Meetings: I encourage a support system that will help you, watch out for you, and be there when times get tough.

Day	Time	Location
Monday		
Tuesday		
Wednesday		
Thursday		
Friday		
Saturday		
Sunday		

Where, when, and how often will you go to meetings?

_____

_____

Support System: Identify your support system.

_____

_____

Employment: Are you employed? Where do you work and how many hours? Are you looking for work?

_____

_____

Physical Health: Do you go to the gym? Are you eating healthy?

_____

_____

Social growth: Who do you feel you trust and why? What qualities do you look for in people?

_____

_____

Fun Activities: Sobriety should be fun. What are ideas of things that you can do to have fun?

_____

_____

Legal issues: Do you have any pending legal issues? What things do you still need to do for past legal issues?

_____

_____

The emotion that places me at the greatest risk for reactive behavior is _____.

When I experience this emotion, I will

A. _____
B. _____
C. _____
D. _____
E. _____

When I have a strong desire to use, I'll do these five things:

1_____

2_____

3._____

4._____

5._____

If I relapse, I will

1._____

2._____

3._____

4._____

5._____

Write out your recovery plan and create a schedule that allows you the opportunity to fit each component into your week. Balance is key. Make sure that all the following components are in your schedule.

1. **Self-Growth:** church, support groups, therapy, counseling, and so on.
2. **Finances:** employment, financial management, improving credit, and so on.

3. **Physical Health:** physical fitness, eating healthy, and so on.
4. **Quiet time:** reading, napping, alone time, and so on.
5. **Friends and family:** family gatherings, socializing and must be with supportive, loving, caring people who are looking out for your best interest.
6. **Fun:** skydiving, comedy clubs, skiing, surfing, and so on.

All those areas can be addictive, so balance and moderation will create an enjoyable, productive, happy, and successful life.

FROM THE AUTHOR'S WIFE

I'm honored to have the opportunity to be a part of writing this book, as an individual who is in recovery, a mother who has struggled with a son who has been in and out of rehab facilities with a heroin problem, and the wife of an individual who has truly shown me the power behind addiction and, more importantly, a man who has walked away from it with pride. I began using methamphetamines at the age of fifteen and continued until the age of twenty when I became pregnant with my oldest son. It was a struggle, but I was able to step away from the drug, with my parents' help, to try and be a good mother for him.

I met Eric some years later and eventually divorced the father of my kids because happiness and love seemed to be something I was missing and found with Eric. Eric and I had some experiences together that were painful and nearly tore us apart, but in the end, it made our relationship stronger and more successful. *The Stepping Stones to Success Are Pain, Failure, and Misery* is a perfect title for our story and many other stories I've heard. I've never seen those first three words in the title blend together so powerfully as I did with him.

Early on in our relationship, there was a six-month period where we started using methamphetamine together, and it was nothing like I'd ever seen throughout all my years of life. I was able to maintain a job, take care of my home and children, pay my bills, and live a "normal" life. Eric lost total control, and this is when I understood the saying "if one is good, more is better." Eric changed instantly and fell into a whirlwind of drugs, lying, cheating, stealing, and disappearing for several nights on end, reconnecting with old drug connections all while trying to appear "normal" to the rest of the world. When I saw him, I begged him to quit, and I told him that we could quit together and resume the life that we were building on. It broke my heart as I saw this man who appeared uncaring, angry, and discontent on the outside, but in his eyes, I could see the man I'd fallen in love with. I was losing him, and no matter how much I begged him to come home and get clean, he turned things around on me, saying that I was trying to control him and that, even though he loved me, he didn't want to be tied down. I'd lost the man of my dreams, I was starting to lose my job, and I was being an awful mother because I was so focused on this man, trying to save someone who didn't seem to want to be saved.

I had to make a change, and even though it was difficult, I decided to move from Anaheim to Pomona to get away from that lifestyle. My children were important, and I had to get my priorities straight. Many things happened that I was unaware of at the time, such as Eric getting jumped by three guys. He had all his drugs and belongings stolen and was staying wherever he could, just to survive. He was losing weight fast, and it was apparent that if he continued using at the rate he was, death was going to be the next step in his adventure.

He obviously lived to write this book, but it's an amazing story of a fight for survival. Eric was clean when we met, and I saw the horrific transformation as it appeared his brain was hijacked by that drug and wasn't going to let go, and I don't think it had any intention on it. Eric fought, and it turned out that he won the battle.

Years after this ordeal, we said our vows and committed the rest of our lives to each other. Being truly in love for the first time in your life makes you feel like a teenager all over again, and all you want to do is see the house and the white picket fence. It's easy to forget the pain and heartache that drug addiction can cause, and we went into this really believing that we could do this for one weekend and be okay. No matter how many years we had clean, we'll always have this struggle, and we must be vigilant when money, relationship, or work issues arise, because we're always susceptible to relapse.

One way that Eric and I choose to live our lives is by always keeping things fun, not allowing work or money issues to overwhelm us and to tap into our own creativity. I took Eric back after that nightmare, and I received quite a bit of criticism from friends and some family. If I'd chosen to listen to them, I don't know where I'd be today. I decided to go with what I wanted and what my needs were. Making a choice to do what was best for me may not always be the popular vote, but it was about my wants, needs, and desires. This wasn't necessarily easy, but I worked hard to remain true to myself, knew what I wanted (which did change as I grew), and always remembered to tap into my fullest potential. I'm more than an addict or an enabler (Eric dislikes those words), but I'm a person who can contribute to this world if I choose.

CPSIA information can be obtained
at www.ICGtesting.com
Printed in the USA
BVHW031020050320
574205BV00001B/18